Praise for
An American Experience:
Adeline Moses Loeb (1876–1953) and Her Early American Jewish Ancestors

A model for genealogists, a gift to historians, and a treasure for anyone who loves American portraiture, this magnificently produced volume sets a new standard for family history. It reveals much not only about John L. Loeb Jr., Adeline Moses Loeb, and the ancestors who shaped them, but also about the American Jewish experience as a whole, from its early colonial beginnings.

—Jonathan Sarna
Joseph H. and Belle R. Braun Professor of American Jewish History, Brandeis University
Author, *American Judaism*; coauthor, *The History of Jewish People*

This exquisitely edited and beautifully illuminated volume is much more than a family history. The story of Adeline Moses Loeb and her early American Jewish ancestors constitutes a veritable epitome of the American Jewish experience. The contributors have successfully reconstructed the lives of an impressive array of captivating personalities—men and women whose biographical sketches genuinely enrich our understanding of Jewish life in the American world from the colonial period through the twentieth century. Readers who enjoy discovering and rediscovering why Whitman described this country as "a teaming nation of nations" will relish exploring each and every page of this book.

—Gary P. Zola
Associate Professor, American Jewish Experience, Hebrew Union College–Jewish Institute of Religion
Executive Director, Jacob Rader Marcus Center, American Jewish Archives
Coauthor, *American Jewish History: A Primary Source Reader*

How fresh and illuminating to tell history through the lens of a woman, her world and her words. Adeline Moses Loeb emerges in these pages as a determined woman. Thinking of American Jewish history from her perspective offers a unique engagement with history. The fact that this book looks backward from her times to the experiences of previous generations of American Jews, again with an eye toward women's experiences, makes this an important book.

—Hasia Diner
Paul and Sylvia Steinberg Professor of American Jewish History
Director, Goldstein-Goren Center for American Jewish History, New York University
Author, *The Jews of the United States, 1645–2000* and *The Jewish Place in America*

An American Experience: Adeline Moses Loeb and Her Early American Jewish Ancestors is an extraordinary tapestry composed of variously colored threads—of anecdote, of biography, of gossip, of memoir, of scholarly genealogy, and of rich American history—all of which come together to create an intricately lacy valentine to a great American Jewish family, such as few other families are likely to receive.

—Stephen Birmingham
Author, *Our Crowd* and *The Grandees*

Jewish immigrants, seeking religious freedom and financial opportunity, arrived in the New World more than a century before the American Revolution. Many of them prospered through trade with the British. But these pioneers, entrepreneurs, and patriots—including the ancestors of Adeline Moses Loeb—gave up their fortunes, their freedom, and often their lives for America's independence. In telling the story of his grandmother, former ambassador John Loeb shines a light on the even greater story of American Jewish history and the founding of the nation that endures as the symbol of freedom for all.

—Diana L. Bailey
Author, *American Treasure: The Enduring Spirit of the DAR*

John L. Loeb Jr. over the years has emerged as one of the outstanding benefactors of American Jewish historical study. This book, a combination of personal memoirs, genealogy, and family history helps further the message that John has preached for years—that American Jewish history is American history, and from it we can all learn.

—Melvin I. Urofsky
Author, *The American Presidents* and
The Levy Family and Monticello, 1834–1923: Saving Thomas Jefferson's House

Adeline Moses Loeb stands out as a lovable matriarch in a distinguished American Jewish family, including Revolutionary and Civil War veterans and leaders in philanthropy, diplomacy, and finance. Adeline's remarkable ancestors participated in the creation and expansion of our nation, while remaining true to a Jewish heritage. Their lineage is traced in this book from colonial Newport and New York to antebellum Charleston. Born in Montgomery, Alabama, Adeline enjoyed a life of privilege until the 1893 market crash wiped out the Moses wealth, forcing the entire family to relocate to St. Louis and a life of genteel poverty. Adeline, however, rose from that genteel poverty in the New South to become a member of the DAR and New York's "Our Crowd."

—Kenneth Libo
Professor of History, Hunter College
Coauthor, *Lots of Lehmans, All in a Lifetime* and *World of Our Fathers*

An intimate portrait of an American Jewish family at once typical and extraordinary. The impetus to recall the life of Adeline Moses Loeb has stimulated an unusual blend of genealogy, memoir, and social and cultural history that is well worth exploring.

—Deborah Dash Moore
Frederick G. L. Huetwell Professor of History
Director, Judaic Studies Program,
University of Michigan

Evoking love of family and country, Adeline Moses Loeb traces an eminent contemporary American Jewish family to its origins more than three centuries ago. It is a loving tribute to America's capacity to embrace people of all persuasions, and to provide them with the opportunity not only to succeed as individuals but, as well, to contribute to the greater good of community and nation. For genealogists and students of American Jewish history, it contributes significantly to our knowledge of the American Jewish experience, especially in the nineteenth and twentieth centuries. It is a splendid addition to the annals of the American Jewish record.

—Eli Faber
Professor and Chairperson, History Department
John Jay College of Criminal Justice
Author, *Jews, Slaves and the Slave Trade: Setting the Record Straight*

An American Experience

Adeline Moses Loeb

(1876–1953)

and Her Early American Jewish Ancestors

An American Experience
Adeline Moses Loeb
(1876–1953)
and Her Early American Jewish Ancestors

INTRODUCTION

Eli N. Evans

CONTRIBUTORS

John L. Loeb Jr.

Kathy L. Plotkin

Margaret Loeb Kempner

Judith E. Endelman

Sons of the Revolution
in the State of New York

Published by

The Sons of the Revolution in the State of New York

54 Pearl Street

New York, New York 10004

Fraunces Tavern® Museum is owned and operated by, and FRAUNCES TAVERN® is
a registered service mark of, Sons of the Revolution in the State of New York, Inc.,
a not-for-profit corporation instituted in 1876 and incorporated in 1884.

Distributed by Syracuse University Press

ISBN# 978-0-9822032-0-0

Manufacturing supervised by Active Concepts, Inc., N.Y.

Printed in Canada

Illustration credits for pages 24 and 25

Dedicated to the memory of
Patricia Walton Shelby
1928–2002

President General
1980–1983
National Society
Daughters of the American Revolution

Produced by MTM Publishing

President	Valerie Tomaselli
Designer	Annemarie Redmond Design
Editorial Coordinator	Zach Gajewski
Production Coordinator	Nura Abdul-Karim
Editorial Assistant	Ingrid Wenzler
Copyeditor	Allison Wofford
Proofreader	Peter Jaskowiak
Indexing	Katharyn Dunham
	Heritage Muse, Inc.

Additional genealogy and historical research, graphics pages,
and family tree development by Heritage Muse, Inc.

President	David M. Kleiman
Research & Editorial	Kate Myslinski
	Jessica Hodge
	Heather Wood
Graphic Arts	Scott Citron
	Amanda Jones
	Debra Schorn
Synagogue Sketches	Mark Tothill (ThinkersDesign)
Maps	Charles Syrett (Map Graphics, Inc.)

Consulting by Our Living Tree

President	Bob Breakstone

AN ACKNOWLEDGMENT

Adeline Moses Loeb was understandably proud of the part that her early American Jewish ancestors played in our country's heritage. But this remarkable lady also has descendants of whom she can be equally proud.

We would like to take this opportunity to recognize not only her late son, John L. Loeb, but also two of her grandsons, John L. Loeb Jr. and Arthur L. Loeb, who for many years have supported the work and ideals of the Sons of the Revolution in the State of New York.

John Jr. and Arthur Loeb have made it possible for the Sons to publish their grandmother's personal and ancestral history, containing stories that are synchronous with the spirit of this organization's purpose: honoring the roles and contributions of America's earliest citizens.

In the words of Edmund Burke, "People will not look forward to posterity who never look back to their ancestors." The Sons of the Revolution in the State of New York are delighted to offer this historically valuable publication about a family whose American footprints marked a path of patriotism enthusiastically followed by their descendants.

Colonel Charles Clement Lucas Jr., M.D.
PRESIDENT

Richard A. Gregory
EXECUTIVE DIRECTOR

Sons of the Revolution in the State of New York

THE CONTRIBUTORS

INTRODUCTION
Eli N. Evans

PART ONE
Kathy L. Plotkin

Margaret Loeb Kempner

PART TWO
Ambassador John L. Loeb Jr.

PART THREE
Judith E. Endelman

TABLE OF CONTENTS

PART THREE

THE ANCESTORS OF ADELINE MOSES LOEB
By Judith E. Endelman

LIST OF ILLUSTRATIONS

APPENDIX ONE

LIST OF FAMILY CHARTS AND MAPS

INTRODUCTION

PART THREE

Ancestors and Descendants of

Adeline Moses Loeb

Sampson Mears ═══ M ═══ Joy Franks
(CA.1670~CA.1711)

Moses Michaels ═ M ═ Catherine Hachar
(1677 ~ 1740)   (D. BEFORE 1740)
HIS GRANDDAUGHTER ELKALEH MARRIED MYER MYERS, COLONIAL
SILVERSMITH · OTHER DESCENDANTS INCLUDE GENERAL ALFRED
MORDECAI, SAMUEL MYERS, AND ALLEN WARDWELL

Moses Levy ═ M(2nd) ═ Grace Mears   Judah Mears ═ M ═ Jochabed Michaels   Rebecca Michaels
(1665 ~ 1728) 1718 (1694 ~ 1740)   (D. 1762)   (D. 1801)
═ M (1st) ═   ═ M ═
1695   1734/35
Richea Asher   Judah Hays
(D. 1716)   (1703 ~ 1764)

Among her descendants are:
MRS. WILLIAM A M BURDEN, JR.
SUPREME COURT JUSTICE BENJAMIN
N. CARDOZO · BARNABY CONRAD, JR.
JOSEPH F CULLMAN, III · THE POETESS,

Abraham Isaacks
(D. 1743)
═ M ═

Reyna Hays
(1743 ~ 1787)
═ M ═
1773

Abigail Levy
(1696 ~ 1756)
═ M ═
1712
Jacob Franks
(1687 ~ 1769)

EMMA LAZARUS · JUDGE MOSES LEVY
EDGAR J. NATHAN, III · LLOYD PEIXOTTO
PHILLIPS · GERSHOM MENDES SEIXAS
MRS. R. PETER STRAUS · ARTHUR OCHS
SULZBERGER ·

Hannah Mears
(D. 1745)

Isaac Touro
(1738 ~ 1783)

Phila Franks
(1722 ~ 1811)
═ M ═
1742
BRIGADIER GENERAL
Oliver DeLancey
(1718 ~ 1785)

Rebecca Mears ═══ M ═══ Jacob Isaacks
1760   (1718 ~ 1798)

Hannah Isaacks ═ M ═ Jacob Phillips
(D. 1798)   1785 (CA. 1750 ~ CA. 1820)
REVOLUTIONARY · WAR · ANCESTOR

Judah Touro
(1775 ~ 1854)
FIRST GREAT AMERICAN
PHILANTHROPIST

DURING THE MID 18TH CENTURY
THE DELANCEY FAMILY OWNED
THE HOUSE AT PEARL AND BROAD
STREETS, WHICH IS NOW KNOWN
AS FRAUNCES TAVERN

Rebecca Phillips ═ M ═ Isaiah Moses
(1792 ~ 1872)   1807 (1772 ~ 1857)
OWNER OF THE OAKS PLANTATION
GOOSE CREEK, SOUTH CAROLINA

Historic Touro Synagogue
at Newport, Rhode Island,
designed by Peter Harrison,
was named for Judah Touro.
The Temple burial ground
inspired Henry Wadsworth
Longfellow's Poem
"A Jewish Cemetary at
Newport."

Other Descendants of
Moses Levy and Richea
Asher are:
RICHARD THOMAS ORLANDO
BRIDGEMAN, VISCOUNT NEWPORT
WINSTON LEONARD SPENCER
CHURCHILL, MP · MRS. W. AVERELL
HARRIMAN · LAVINIA MARY~
DOWAGER DUCHESS OF NORFOLK
HONORABLE MICHAEL PEARSON,
FUTURE LORD COWDRAY · NEIL
ARCHIBALD PRIMROSE, 7TH
EARL OF ROSEBERY ·

Levy Moses ═══ M ═══ Adeline Moses
(1808 ~ 1876)   1832   (1809 ~ 1873)

Alfred Huger Moses ═ M ═ Jeannette Nathans
(1840 ~ 1918)   1871 (1849 ~ 1919)
FOUNDER, SHEFFIELD, ALABAMA~
HIS BROTHER, MORDECAI MOSES, SERVED AS MAYOR OF MONTGOMERY,
ALABAMA, WHERE HIS HOME IS KNOWN AS "THE HOUSE OF THE MAYORS"

"FOR IN THE BACKGROUND
FIGURES VAGUE AND VAST
OF PATRIARCHS AND OF PROPHETS
ROSE SUBLIME,
AND ALL THE GREAT TRADITIONS
OF THE PAST
THEY SAW REFLECTED IN THE
COMING TIME."

Adeline Moses ═ M ═ Carl M. Loeb
(1877 ~ 1953)   1896 (1875 ~ 1955)
HER PORTRAIT HANGS IN FRAUNCES   LOEB BOAT HOUSE IN CENTRAL
TAVERN MUSEUM IN PERPETUITY   PARK & LOEB STUDENT CENTER
                                 AT N·Y·U NAMED IN HIS HONOR

Margaret Loeb   John L Loeb   Carl M. Loeb, Jr.   Henry A. Loeb
(B. 1899)   (B. 1902)   (B. 1904)   (B. 1907)

Clara Melcher Ward 1980

FOREWORD

WITHOUT A SCINTILLA OF DOUBT, it was my paternal grandmother, Adeline Moses Loeb, who sparked my lifelong passion for genealogy—especially Jewish genealogy. That passion was the genesis of this three-part book.

The stories Granny told the Loeb grandchildren about her family's glory days in Alabama were absorbed while we sipped cinnamon tea or hot cocoa along with chicken-sandwiches-with-no-crusts in the heyday of the Plaza Hotel in New York City circa 1939. Granny Adeline would treat her young "beaux and belles," as she called us, to lunch at the Plaza's posh Persian Room in tranches of one or two at a time, and then shepherd us into her shiny black chauffeured limousine for the final treat of the day, a Broadway matinee.

During the Plaza luncheons, in mellifluous Southern cadences, she regaled us with tales of the 1880s when she and her four siblings lived with their parents, Alfred and Jeannette Moses, in a luxurious federal-style mansion on Perry Street, the Fifth Avenue of Montgomery, Alabama. We heard about the financial rise and fall of her father, "Captain" Alfred Huger Moses, and the horrors of the Civil War that he and his relatives lived through. We learned that after the war, along with his brother Mordecai, he became a major figure in Alabama banking and real estate and the acknowledged *pater familias* of the Moses clan. With true entrepreneurial spirit he was soon the primary founder of Sheffield, but it proved to be a boomtown disaster in 1890–1891. Sheffield's downfall, coupled with the worldwide bank panic of 1893, brought financial ruin for the whole Moses family.

Between bites of Plaza sweets, we heard that as a young girl, Granny gave piano lessons, but that there wasn't enough money to pay for trolleys to the homes of her students, so she walked there and back, never mind how long the trek. We listened attentively as she mesmerized us with tales of how she learned to type and worked in an office to help the family fortunes limp along in St. Louis,

Missouri, where the entire Moses family had been forced to move because of their straitened circumstances. This move included *all* of the family—her sister, brothers, paternal grandparents, aunts, and uncles—except for her mother's successful brother, Judge Joseph H. Nathan,[1] who stayed in Alabama. Two of her maiden aunts even took in boarders. Granny's young audience looked dutifully solemn when hearing about these terrible events, but we were a little unsure how much of it was true. Only later we learned that all of it was. Or most of it, anyway.

Many times we heard the happy ending to her story. And how we loved this part! Where but St. Louis should the handsome young German immigrant Carl M. Loeb be sent by his employer, American Metal Company? And where should the young man find living quarters but at the very proper rooming house of Granny's maiden aunts? There the charming, dimpled, brown-eyed Adeline met and soon married the handsome, ambitious Carl M. Loeb, who became very successful with the American Metal Company, and they came to live happily ever after in New York City. The postscript to her story is that Carl moved on from American Metal to found Carl M. Loeb and Co. in 1931 with my father, John L. Loeb. It soon became the even more successful firm renamed Loeb, Rhoades & Co., when it merged with Rhoades and Co. in 1937.[2] In less than a generation, a new family fortune was realized and Granny Adeline was once again living in grand style.

But what of her parents? And grandparents? And their grandparents? And *their* grandparents? I wondered about them even as a boy, hearing Granny's stories. What was it in their Jewish genes that made them entrepreneurs, alternately successful, then penniless, then successful again? As the years rolled along, that question

1. Judge Joseph Nathan had married Minnie Burns Lindsay of Tuscumbie, Alabama, the daughter of a very prominent Christian family. Her father, Robert Burns Lindsay (1824–1902), a native of Scotland, was the governor of Alabama from 1870 to 1872. After his marriage, Judge Nathan converted to Episcopalianism and became an active participant in the Sheffield gentile community, and a very respected local judge.

2. Loeb, Rhoades & Co. merged with Hornblower, Weeks, Noyes & Trask in 1978. The firm was then merged with Shearson Hayden Stone to form Shearson Loeb Rhoades in 1979, making it the second largest firm on Wall Street. In 1981 the firm was bought by American Express.

kept recurring to me, and in my late twenties I became an amateur genealogist and self-appointed family historian, delving deeply into the Moses ancestry.

In 1976 I put the Moses heritage in the hands of a professional genealogist and American historian, Judith E. Endelman. Her greater experience and her in-depth research uncovered much material new to me. She has contributed both the extensive research and vivid narration in Part Three of this book.

In 1980 I commissioned genealogist Clare McVicker Ward to assemble the first of Granny's family trees (reproduced at the beginning of this foreword) which she based on a pioneer Jewish genealogical book by Malcolm Stern, first published in 1960 with the title *Americans of Jewish Descent.* It was republished in 1971, under the title of *First American Jewish Families, 600 Genealogies, 1654–1988,* and again in 1978 and 1990. My first Moses family tree has been greatly updated and supplanted by genealogist David M. Kleiman for this book.[3]

Studying that first Moses family tree, I was fascinated to see that Granny had enormously interesting historical connections, such as the prolific colonial letter writer Abigaill Levy Franks (1696–1756), mother of Phila Franks (1722–1811), who married a gentile, Brigadier General Oliver DeLancey (1718–1785), against her family's wishes. Her anguished mother proved to be right. Alas, Oliver DeLancey has been discovered through historical research to have been a real bounder.

In the 1700s the DeLancey family owned a house located at the corner of Pearl and Broad Streets in New York City. It was bought in 1762 by Samuel Fraunces who turned it into a tavern he first called "Queen's Head Tavern" and later the "Fraunces Tavern," the name we know today. In its "Long Room," nine days after the British evacuation of New York on November 25, George Washington bade farewell to his officers on December 4, 1783, bringing an emotional finality to the end of the Revolutionary War. A portrait of Granny Adeline—an ardent member of the Daughters of the American Revolution

3. Kleiman's ongoing additions to Rabbi Stern's research can be found on the Web site www.heritagemuse.com.

(DAR)—hangs in perpetuity on the third floor of the Fraunces Tavern Museum as a result of my family's strong connection to the Sons of the Revolution in the State of New York (which owns and is housed in the Fraunces Tavern building) and the DAR.

One-third of this book is about Granny's earliest American ancestors, such as those I've just mentioned. Some of the most historically prominent are highlighted in both Eli Evans's introduction and in the chapters by genealogist Judith Endelman. But I have been almost equally intrigued by discovering some of Granny's more recent connections, both blood relatives and lateral connections. I think especially (not in chronological order) of Mrs. William A. M. Burden Jr., one of the grandest of New York City's twentieth-century grandes dames; Joseph F. Cullman III (1912–2004), powerful former CEO of Philip Morris; Dr. Henry Clay Moses (1941–2008), who until his death served as headmaster of Trinity School, one of the most prestigious of New York City's private schools; J. Fife Symington Jr., a leading figure in Baltimore and a former ambassador to Trinidad and Tobago; Benjamin Griswold IV, a former CEO of Alex Brown & Co. (now merged with Deutsche Bank); Jack "Jay" Griswold, longtime chairman of the Maryland Historical Society; Helen Clay Chace, former chairman of the Frick Museum board; and Arthur Ochs Sulzberger, famed publisher of the *New York Times*.

Being a dyed-in-the-wool Anglophile, I was also delighted to find several distinguished English connections among the more current notables in Adeline's lineage, such as Richard Thomas Orlando Bridgeman, Seventh Earl of Bradford; Winston Leonard Spencer Churchill, a former member of Parliament; his mother, the late Pamela Harriman, widow of W. Averell Harriman, and an ambassador to France; the late Lavinia Mary Strutt, Dowager Duchess of Norfolk; the Honorable Michael Pearson (now Lord Cowdray); and Neil Archibald Primrose, Seventh Earl of Rosebery.

I had intended the results of all this genealogical research to be a private gift to my own family, but when editor Kathy Plotkin discovered the original Endelman manuscript in my archives and suggested that it should be made public,

I agreed, because I could see that the struggles of Adeline Moses Loeb's ancestors echo those of the ancestors of many Jews in America today—a story that very few, Americans (besides academics and historians) know well, if at all. Also seeing the historical value of the manuscript, the Sons of the Revolution in the State of New York (SRNY) agreed to publish this three-part book.

The Three Parts

Part One includes a brief biography of Adeline and Carl Loeb, touching only lightly on Carl's business successes. Written by the book's editor, it is punctuated and enlivened by family photographs provided by my cousin, Thomas L. Kempner. Part One is really Adeline's personal story more than that of her very successful and much publicized husband. This abbreviated history is followed by a portion of the unpublished memoir *Recollection,* by Adeline and Carl's only daughter, Margaret Loeb Kempner, which contains heretofore unpublished family photographs. This section gives the reader a sense of what it was like to grow up in the "Our Crowd" world of the German Jewish community of New York City in the first half of the twentieth century. My Aunt Margaret Loeb Kempner—who lived to the age of 101 (1899–2002)—gives a candid peek into the private lives of her parents, making the text as appealing as a family scrapbook. Her warm and sometimes funny reminiscences and memories reveal her mother as vibrant, caring, multitalented, and forceful enough to hold her own with the high-powered Carl.

Part Two provides descriptions and background of the many exhibitions and projects in American Jewish history that the Loeb family has produced and supported over the last thirty years. More recently, one of my own projects involves the Internet. The emergence of the Internet in the 1990s inspired me to preserve and make available to scholars and the general public a database of early American Jewish portraits on the American Jewish Historical Society Web site. My idea was to assemble biographies and portraits of every known American Jew painted before 1865. (The database is an enormously useful resource not only for scholars but the general public, and it can be found on the Internet at www.loebjewishportraits.com, as well as on the Web site of the American Jewish

Historical Society—www.AJHS.org.) There are currently 200 portraits in this database, with 200 more to be added by 2010.

In Part Three, Judith Endelman narrates the stories of eight generations of the Moses family from the seventeenth century onward—the ancestors of Adeline Moses Loeb. At the end of each chapter, a user-friendly family chart positions a specific ancestral family in time and sequence.

The book is accompanied by a large family tree outlining some of Adeline Moses Loeb's genealogy. This poster—enclosed in a pocket in the back of the book— is a graphic guide to the relationships between Adeline, her direct ancestors, her children and grandchildren, and other selected American and British connections of Jewish descent.

—⟳—

The lives of many Americans are reflected in Adeline's story and that of her ancestors. Perhaps this narrative and genealogical portrait of one Jewish family, and the example of one specific Jewish daughter of the South, will bring meaning to all whose families have lived, and are living, the American dream.

—⟳—

INTRODUCTION

Eli N. Evans

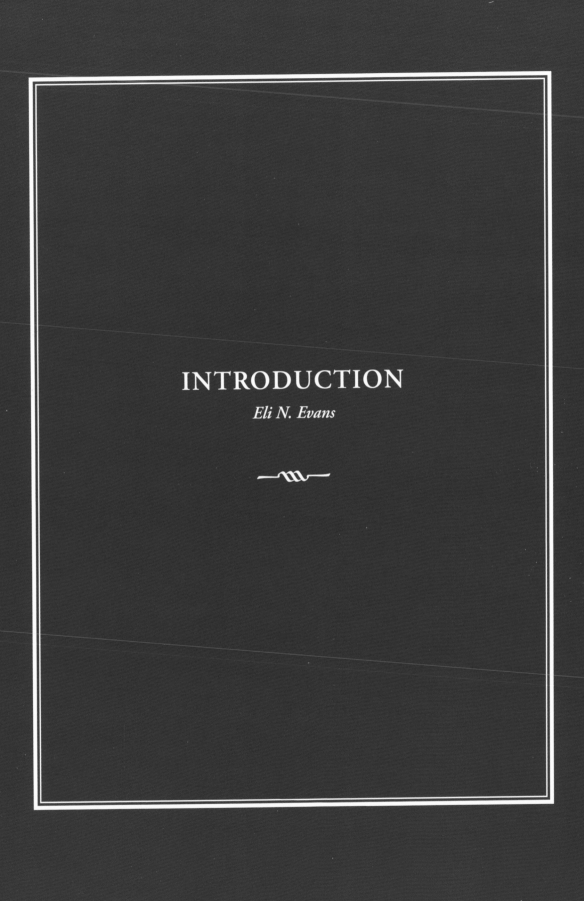

Eli N. Evans

INTRODUCTION

In a country as young as the United States, it is unusual to find a family whose ancestors have been in America for over three hundred years. When the family is a Jewish family, it is even more unusual. There cannot be more than a handful of families who can make such a claim. . . . Of this handful of families, many died out, migrated, intermarried, or were otherwise lost to history. The family of Adeline Moses Loeb has not been lost to history, even though they were probably in America for a century before the first census was taken.

—Judith Endelman
From Part Three, Chapter One, of this book

For having brought his early American Jewish family back to life, our gratitude for this beautiful and informative book goes to the determination of John L. Loeb Jr., in his own words an "amateur genealogist and self-appointed Loeb family historian." The book represents the latest chapter in John's lifetime of engagement with his family's history, which winds through three hundred years of the American experience. He has led the expedition in search of his family's roots and, once having traced the threads of elusive evidence to the beginnings of America, he sought to reweave the tapestry and share it with readers, who will discover new insights into American Jewish history. The publication of *An American Experience: Adeline Moses Loeb and Her Early American Jewish Ancestors* by the Sons of the Revolution in the State of New York (SRNY) is a reflection of John's vision and generosity in partnership with his brother, Arthur Lehman Loeb.

Coming to Know John L. Loeb Jr. and His Grandmother's History

I was already well aware of the historic importance of Adeline Moses Loeb in American history and the deep colonial roots of her forebears when I was asked by the Southern Jewish Historical Society to introduce John at an annual meeting on October 31, 1992, at the House of the Mayors in Montgomery, Alabama, the city where his grandmother had been born in 1876. It would prove to be an unusual and very memorable occasion.

I first became acquainted with John in 1979 at an exhibition he and his family sponsored called "The Jewish Community in Early New York, 1654–1800." It was held in lower Manhattan at the Fraunces Tavern Museum, an institution that celebrates a moment in history when New York was America's first capital city. The Fraunces Tavern housed the Departments of Foreign Affairs, Treasury, and War from 1785 to 1787. The site, now owned by the Sons of the Revolution in the State of New York (SRNY), to which John and his father belonged, had been preserved because it also served as the historic meeting place where General George Washington bade farewell to his officers after the British left the city. A portrait of Adeline Moses Loeb now hangs in perpetuity on the third floor of the museum in a gallery named for her.[1]

An exhibition on the theme of the Jewish role in colonial times was just one example of John's long and ongoing commitment to bringing public attention to the largely unrecognized contributions of early American Jews to this country. Paintings and artifacts were gathered from all over the country for the unique exhibition, which drew crowds from far and wide.

I was deeply stirred when I saw the exhibition, having researched and written about many of the people depicted in the portraits. I had previously seen only

---

1. Adeline's family history in the United States dates back to 1697. Through the lineage of an ancestor who served on active duty in the American Revolution, his grandmother was able to become a member of the Daughters of the American Revolution (DAR), and John to be a member of the Sons of the American Revolution (SAR) and the Sons of the Revolution in the State of New York (SRNY).

The Fraunces Tavern Museum is housed in the upper rooms of the tavern, which still functions as a restaurant at 54 Pearl Street, close to Wall Street in New York City. The historic eighteenth-century tavern, a convivial colonial gathering place, is now owned by the Sons of the Revolution in the State of New York (SRNY). It was in this tavern that General George Washington bade an emotional farewell to his officers in December 1783.

This photo was taken sometime shortly after the building's restoration in 1976, a repair necessitated by an explosion next door instigated by the FALN, a Puerto Rican terrorist group, in 1975. A portrait of Adeline Moses Loeb hangs in the museum gallery named for her.

—Sons of the Revolution in the State of New York

black-and-white photographs; now at the exhibition, when I peered into the faces in the oil portraits, noted the background furnishings suggesting the grand estates and homes they must have lived in, and observed the opulence of the clothes and the poses they adopted, I could imagine Jewish Americans living in a very young America. In the colonial period, portraits served the traditional purpose of proclaiming the subject's social status. John Mendelsohn, a New York artist who occasionally also writes about art, has suggested, "All portraits are bargains struck between artist and patron. Both the image of the sitter and the conventions of portraiture are subject to complex, if often unspoken negotiations. Together they serve as a sliding scale whose ultimate reckoning establishes the status of a public face."

For the Jews, the exhibition portraits not only affirmed their American identity; they showed that early American Jews enjoyed prosperity and elevated station. For me it was startling to look for the first time into the eyes of Jews of such wealth and status. They represented an earlier era, a time preceding the peddler past of my grandfather's generation that is so deeply ingrained in the imagination of those of us connected to the two million immigrants from Eastern Europe in the late nineteenth century. After viewing the 1979 exhibition[2] at the Fraunces Tavern Museum, a number of John's friends and I encouraged him to establish a traveling exhibition that could be seen in other parts of the country. Having spoken in cities and towns all across the South, I knew not only that the Moses family story would be of great interest to those in the region where most of the family's previous generations had lived, but that the Jewish images from early American history would also be fascinating to communities across the country.

The exhibition and its subsequent travels culminated in the first major exhibition ever held at the museum in the DAR headquarters in Washington, D.C. Renamed "The Jewish Community in Early America, 1654–1830," the exhibi-

2. The 1979 exhibition, originally planned to honor the bicentennial of the American Revolution in 1976, was delayed due to the reconstruction of the Fraunces Tavern Museum after the Puerto Rican liberation organization Fuerzas Armadas de Liberación Nacional (FALN) had blown a hole in the museum and the nearby Anglers Club.

tion opened on the night of December 10, 1980, when more than three thousand people packed the hall to hear a dedicatory speech by former president Gerald Ford. Part Two of this book describes the evening in detail.

The House of the Mayors and John's Surprising Dedication Speech

In the late 1980s John—along with his parents, John and Frances Loeb—provided funds for the restoration of Montgomery's magnificent House of the Mayors, so

The House of the Mayors on South Perry Street in Montgomery, Alabama, was home to Mordecai Moses (Alfred's younger brother) from 1885 to 1893. The first Democrat to be elected after Reconstruction, Mordecai served that city as mayor for three terms. The house is now the home of the Montgomery Area United Way.

—Ambassador John L. Loeb Jr. collection

named because a number of the city's mayors had lived there after it was built in the 1850s. Adeline's uncle, Mordecai Moses, was one of those later mayors. Elected in 1871, Mordecai Moses was the first Democrat to be elected mayor after the Reconstruction era, serving three successive terms. He retired from politics after six years as mayor, much lauded for the fiscal health and promise he brought to the city.

The House of the Mayors was worthy of restoration. It was one of seven grand homes located on Perry Street. These homes earned the street its reputation as "the Fifth Avenue of the South." The mayors' house had languished for thirty years in various states of deterioration and neglect. The Montgomery *Advertiser* on April 23, 2005, reported that "groups of homeless people had camped there . . . using the mantels and balustrades as firewood."

Fortunately, the renovation that the Loeb family had helped to underwrite restored its former ornate beauty: the elegant wood floors, elaborate mantels, coved ceilings, stained-glass windows, detailed moldings, and grand staircase. The renovation was so impressive that the *Advertiser* published a long article with photographs of the interior and exterior under the headline, "A Neighborhood Reborn." In some ways it was appropriate that the House of the Mayors would now house the offices of the United Way of Montgomery. It would also contain the Captain Alfred Huger Moses Conference Room, named after John's great-grandfather, and would be open to the public at the 1992 dedication at which I was to introduce John.

There is a videotape of the proceedings that enables one to quote with accuracy all that was said that day; the remarks of greeting before John's speech are all the more remarkable in retrospect seventeen years later because everyone there had been innocent of what was to follow. Gathered for the dedication were the mayor of Montgomery, Emory Folmar, and other members of the city's business, elected, and social elite. They were joined by representatives of the local Jewish community as well as members of the Southern Jewish Historical Society, which had selected Montgomery for their annual meeting. Perhaps one hundred people or more gathered in the Captain Alfred Huger Moses Conference Room in front of an imposing portrait of Captain Moses, portraying him against a backdrop of early Montgomery (prominently showing the "Moses Brothers Bank," the first skyscraper built in Montgomery, which at that time housed the offices of the family enterprises). Earlier, John had taken me aside to reveal his intent to talk about the exclusion of Jews from the Montgomery Country Club, noted as a bastion of many of the "best families" in Montgomery, some of whom were attending the dedication. Just that previous evening, during a tour of the city, he had discovered that Jews were excluded from the club. And it both shocked him and filled him with a measure of righteous indignation, given his family's contribution to the history of the city.

He asked me a provocative but perceptive question: If he spoke of anti-Semitism in Montgomery in front of the mayor and other officials, he knew it would be controversial. That did not bother him. He was, however, concerned about how the members of the Montgomery Jewish community in attendance would feel about it. Would they think him ungracious and insensitive to their position in the community by raising the issue at a dedication in front of the city fathers? My wife had been born and raised in the Jewish community of Montgomery. So I asked the opinion of my in-laws and their friends as well as a number of leaders from the Southern Jewish Historical Society, and they said what I expected them to say: John was a very distinguished son of a great family, a former United States ambassador to Denmark, and would be speaking in the house an ancestor had once lived in, in a city where his grandmother was born, and at the dedication of a house his family had helped restore. He could say whatever was on his mind, and this was an appropriate moment to do so.

The dedication ceremony began. There was a fulsome round of official speeches, along with a proclamation presented by a representative of the governor of Alabama, pronouncing October 31, 1992, "Loeb Family Day in recognition of the contributions of the Loeb family to the whole state of Alabama," and the reading of a plaque saluting Alfred Huger Moses as "a Son of the American Revolution and a Confederate Patriot." The mayor also presented a key to the city to John. I then introduced him, especially emphasizing the awards John had received from Jewish organizations and his membership on the boards of similar organizations,

On a day in late October 1992, Adeline Moses Loeb's father, Captain Alfred Huger Moses, was honored with a handsome portrait and a conference room dedicated to him in the newly restored "House of the Mayors" in Montgomery, Alabama. Pictured here below the Moses portrait are his grandson John L. Loeb Jr., a former ambassador to Denmark, Montgomery native Judith Evans, and her husband, Southern historian, Eli Evans, who introduced the ambassador as the main speaker at the dedication.

—John L. Loeb Jr. photo collection

and concluded by saying "Mr. Mayor, all of us in this room have roots that are entwined with the Jewish South. We welcome John Loeb to this extraordinary event in Montgomery, which illustrates his personal connection to this city and this place, and shows the kind of heart and soul that his family has." I paused and closed with, "They don't forget who they are and where they came from."

My introduction was intended to suggest how deeply felt John's remarks would be, but it gave no clue about the bombshell he would drop.

John's Remarks at the Dedication Ceremony

One has to imagine the scene in Montgomery that fall day in 1992 to appreciate fully the impact of what was to unfold when John decided to criticize, deftly, Montgomery's social discrimination of the Jews. It was after all, at least by implication, a criticism of the ruling fathers of the city, both political and social, many of whom were in the room. He began by thanking all those who contributed to the restoration, including his father, and paid tribute with a bit of humor to his grandmother, saying, "My real interest in family history and Jewish history was due to Captain Moses' daughter, my grandmother, who was born right here in Montgomery. I used to think of her as my own Grandma Moses."

John began the conclusion of his remarks to the audience (which had probably expected, if indeed they had thought about it, only a number of platitudes and bland reminiscences about his family) with carefully chosen words: "I don't want to spoil the evening but I do have a serious note about something that I heard last night which frankly saddened me. As I was driven by a glorious Tara-like building, I inquired who lived there. 'Oh,' I was told, 'that is the Montgomery Country Club.' I promptly asked, 'Are there any Jewish members?' The answer was no.

"Well, here we are at the *United* Way"—he emphasized the word "united"—"honoring a pre–Civil War Southern Jewish family, which had several members who served actively in the War Between the States and a family member who served Montgomery as mayor. And I suddenly realized that I, a great-grandson of Captain Moses, could not be a member of that club, solely because of my faith." John closed by saying, "Social exclusion such as this is collapsing all over the world, all over this country and the South. It is my hope and strong desire that a greater knowledge of the history of Montgomery, particularly, will help to open doors for all."

I was watching Mayor Folmar as he listened in disbelief, and the city fathers and wives who looked at each other as if an unwelcome relative had uttered a profanity during a toast at a family wedding. I glanced quickly at the members of the Montgomery Jewish community, and they, too, were looking at the mayor and the officials. The video of the event shows that the mayor walked quickly into the camera image, which was focused on John, reached out with his right hand, and with his left pulled him forward to whisper in his ear.

John told me later that Mayor Folmar whispered to him, "You are absolutely right. We've got to do something about it. Our families have been close since the Civil War."

Someone must have "done something about it," because in 1995 the first four Jews were accepted into the Montgomery Country Club. Among them were three members of the Weil family, the oldest and most well-known Jewish family in the city, who had founded Weil Brothers cotton brokerage in 1878. The brokerage had grown into an international company with branches in London and Australia and offices in China and Paris, run by the fourth generation of the founders, from Montgomery, where its headquarters had always been located. Their membership in the club was—let me put this delicately—well overdue. Today there are twenty-six Jewish families on the club roster.

John Loeb Jr. that day was not just a proud descendant of a great Southern Jewish family recalling their achievements at a dedication of a historic house they once lived in. Standing in front of a portrait of his great-grandfather—who had helped build the city with his great-uncle, Mordecai Moses, who had been its mayor over a century ago—John spoke more out of disbelief than rancor, portraying social discrimination as a relic of the past and pointing out that the forces of modernity seemed to be passing the city by. He put aside the temptation to lecture the audience or to express his honest anger. He chose to seize the moment and summon the military history and public service of his family to declare his solidarity with the present-day

Jewish community that made Montgomery home. It was a teaching moment for the city, when a great-grandson would return to embrace publicly the values that brought his family to America. No one who heard John's speech that day would ever forget it.

Social Validation

In the years following the dedication of the mayors' house, I have learned much more about Adeline Moses Loeb's ancestors. Along with her family's early American fellow Jews, they have provided important threads in the social tapestry of the country's pre-Revolutionary days. Adeline's family tree includes early American Jewish ancestors of both her blood relatives and her lateral connections. Not in chronological order, her extended family includes luminaries such as these mentioned below.

- *Supreme Court Justice Benjamin Nathan Cardozo*, who was appointed to the U.S. Supreme Court in 1932 to succeed Oliver Wendell Holmes and was the second Jew on the Court after Louis D. Brandeis.

- *Rebecca Gratz*, the best-known Jewish woman of the nineteenth century, was the daughter of a prominent Philadelphia family, a philanthropist renowned for her great beauty, her dedication to Judaism, and her care for the poor. She is thought to be the inspiration for Rebecca in Sir Walter Scott's novel *Ivanhoe*.

- *Judah Touro* was born in Newport, Rhode Island, grew up in Boston, but made his fortune in New Orleans in the early 1800s; his famous will leaving $483,000 to worthy causes around the world was published on the front page of the *New York Times* when he died in 1854, heralding him as America's first great philanthropist. The relative value of his philanthropy, measured in today's dollars, would be well over $161,000,000 according to economic historians.

    In my book *The Provincials* I wrote, "Among those benefiting were Jewish congregations, religious schools, benevolent societies and hospitals in nineteen American cities; Catholic, Protestant and other charities in New England; numerous churches, hospitals, an orphan home and an alms house in New Orleans. He even left $60,000 for various causes in Palestine and $15,000 to help save the Jews of China. . . . On his tombstone in the cemetery

Rebecca Gratz
(1781–1869)

Although she was so beautiful that the illustrious artist Thomas Sully painted her portrait at least three times, Philadelphia's Rebecca Gratz never married. Legend has it that as a girl she had fallen in love with a gentile, but because of her devotion to Judaism, their marriage was out of the question. Instead, she devoted her life to the education of Jewish children, establishing the first Jewish Sunday school in the United States and helping to bring up the nine children of her beloved younger sister, who died in 1823. It is also believed that she was the inspiration for Sir Walter Scott's Jewish heroine Rebecca in the historical novel *Ivanhoe.* Adeline Moses Loeb always thought that her ancestors were related to Rebecca Gratz, but she wasn't sure exactly how. Current genealogical research has found that she was not related by blood but she was indeed distantly connected through marriage.

—Thomas Sully (1783–1872)
Oil on board (1831)
Rosenbach Museum and Library, Philadelphia, Pennsylvania

12

at Touro Synagogue in Newport is inscribed, 'the Book of Philanthropy, to be remembered forever.'"[3]

- *Major Alfred Mordecai*, a West Point graduate, West Point professor, and the author of several military books, including his 1841 landmark, *Ordnance Manual for the Use of Officers in the U.S. Army*. Congress ordered twenty thousand copies to be printed because the book documented the changing nature of weaponry and munitions and their impact on battlefield tactics and military strategy. The book provided the rationale to reshape the American military in the years before the Civil War.

- *Emma Lazarus*, who penned "The New Colossus," America's beloved poem engraved on a plaque at the Statue of Liberty, which expressed the memorable anthem of our immigrant heritage, "Give me your tired, your poor / Your huddled masses yearning to breathe free."

- *Haym Salomon*, the major figure in the financing of the American Revolution, whose fiscal skill saved the new nation from collapse.

- *Gershom Mendes Seixas*, considered by many to be America's first rabbi, who walked with other religious leaders at President George Washington's first inauguration.

- *Myer Myers*, the country's most famous silversmith and one of the most accomplished craftsmen working in preindustrial America. A peer of Paul Revere (also a silversmith), though not nearly as well known, Myers is counted among a select group of highly respected merchant-artisans of the time. His work is found today in major museum collections, including the Metropolitan Museum of Art, the Philadelphia Museum of Art, the Boston Museum of Fine Arts, and Harvard University Art Galleries.

3. What makes the Judah Touro will remarkable is that in 1854 the laws of the time made it difficult to leave money to any recipients except family members. (Touro died without direct legal descendants.) The Touro will included many Christian institutions and international Jewish communities, even though there were no tax advantages for charitable giving at the time. He also left a large share of his estate to his best friend and executor, Raisin Shepherd, who had saved his life at the Battle of New Orleans in the War of 1812. Shepherd lived for a time in Massachusetts and was the great-great-grandfather of Massachusetts Senator Leverett Saltonstall, who once told John Loeb Jr., when John was an undergraduate at Harvard College, that the wealth of the Saltonstall family was based on the Touro legacy to Shepherd.

Judah Touro
(1775–1854)

Judah Touro's biographer, Leon Huhner, writes of one of America's earliest philanthropists, "His will reads like a directory of Jewish life in the United States in the middle of the nineteenth century." A broken love affair from which he is said to have never recovered may account for the fact that there are no extant pictures of him where he looks less dour, but he was known to be a warm and gentle man.

—Artist unknown
Oil on photograph, c. 1853
The Redwood Library and Athenaeum, Newport, Rhode Island

Abraham Touro
(1777–1822)

The wealthy older brother of Judah Touro, Abraham owned seagoing vessels that plied the West Indian ports. He preceded Judah as an early American philanthropist but unlike his solemn and reclusive brother, he owned a well-fitted townhouse in Boston and a mansion at Medford, where he entertained lavishly. He died at the early age of forty-five as a result of an accident involving his horse and carriage, leaving portions of his estate to such institutions as the Massachusetts General Hospital and Touro Synagogue, as well as to a trust for the State of Rhode Island.

—Gilbert Stuart (1755–1828)
Oil on canvas, c. 1817
Touro Synagogue, Newport, Rhode Island

Moses Michael Hays
(1739–1805)

The "father of modern Masonry in Massachusetts," Moses Michael Hays is perhaps more universally remembered for his role as a leading founder of the first permanent, successful bank in Boston. Before the American Revolution he was among the well-to-do Jews of Newport, Rhode Island, who helped to finance the oldest existing synagogue in the United States, now known as the Touro Synagogue. He and his family lived in a fashionable Boston home that "welcomed rich and poor," and moved in the "first circles of society," facts reported in a memoir by Samuel Joseph May, a Christian Bostonian who knew them well. When Hays's sister's husband died, her children, including her young sons Abraham and Judah Touro (who would later become philanthropists themselves), were warmly welcomed into the Hays home, already filled with their own children.

—Miss E. M. Carpenter from Gilbert Stuart
Oil on canvas, 1883
Masonic Lodge of Massachusetts

- *Colonel David Salisbury Franks*, a Jewish military officer during the Revolutionary War. According to Michael Feldberg, former director of the American Jewish Historical Society, "General George Washington had [Franks] assigned to his command . . . Franks was entrusted to carry highly secret documents to diplomats Benjamin Franklin in Paris and John Jay in Madrid, [including] the official copy of the peace treaty that ended the [Revolutionary] War and granted American independence."
- *Moses Raphael Levy*, one of the earliest major shipowners and leading merchants in America.
- *Moses Michael Hays*, an influential Boston banker who has been called "the father of Masonry in Massachusetts."

It was largely because of Adeline's venerable ancestors and connections that together with her husband, the formidable founder of Wall Street's Carl M. Loeb and Co.,[4] the couple was able to attain what might be described as "social heights" in the early twentieth century, especially in the world of the German Jews of "Our Crowd." But that success did not come immediately, as commented on by social observer Stephen Birmingham.

In his classic book *Our Crowd,* about New York's upper-class German Jews, Birmingham points out that when young Carl and Adeline first arrived in New York City from St. Louis, Carl was a minor official (rising rapidly thereafter) in the American Metal Company. They were not considered the "real Loebs" and were even sometimes referred to as the "*not* real Loebs"—the *real* Loebs being of the Kuhn-Loeb financial family. Birmingham also notes in *Our Crowd* that Adeline's "connections," as they say in the South, were "helpful" in dispelling that initial upper-crust disdain.

A later Birmingham book, *The Grandees,* a story of the Sephardic Jews in America, makes it clear that Adeline's ancestors arrived in America in the 1600s,

---

4. Carl M. Loeb and Co. became Loeb, Rhoades & Co., and still later, became Shearson Loeb Rhoades, making it the second largest firm on Wall Street. The company was eventually bought by the American Express Company.

long before those of what had been considered the *real* Loebs. He based this on information gleaned from scholar Malcolm Stern's 1960 groundbreaking genealogical study, *Americans of Jewish Descent,* a scholarly tome that became, Birmingham wrote, a combination "Jewish *Who's Who* and the *Social Register.*"

Malcolm Stern was my mentor when I first began to write Southern Jewish history. He was a gracious scholar who loved young people and helping young writers. He was encyclopedic in his knowledge of family interconnections in the South and his book was a monumental life work detailing twenty-five thousand individuals in more than two hundred family dynasties, consisting of mind-numbing numbers of charts. I saw it in its earliest form when it was an expanse of genealogical charts that covered an entire room. The book chronicled every Jew who came to America from 1654 to 1840. Malcolm chose the latter date so as to preclude the large German Jewish migration in 1848. He chose the former date so as to include the September 1654 arrival in New Amsterdam (now New York) of the first Jews in America—twenty-three immigrants from Recife, Brazil, who arrived on a ship some refer to as the "Jewish Mayflower." Because Malcolm showed the evolution of each family and their progeny, "The Book," as it began to be called in Jewish circles in New York, was filled with surprises—for example, it revealed all kinds of intermarriages to non-Jews of wealth and fame, such as the Rockefellers, the Vanderbilts, the Tiffanys, and the Lodges, thereby connecting Jews to the very top rungs of American wealth and station. According to Birmingham in *The Grandees,* "The Book created an immediate and profound stir among a small group of American Jews who had long considered themselves an elite, the nobility of Jewry . . . [and] was soon gracing the coffee tables and book shelves of some of the most elegant and prestigious houses around the country."

The Stern book was revelatory and consequential for the Adeline Moses Loeb family because it reversed their Jewish social position and proved the *new* Loebs were actually older than the *old* Loebs by virtue of Adeline's Sephardic ancestors. Birmingham notes that Adeline's son, John L. Loeb Sr. "promptly bought a number of copies of 'The Book' and sent them to friends—including quite a few Christians . . . discovered to be of Jewish descent . . . [which] must have come as something of a shock." In point of fact it was John Jr. who circulated "The Book," not his father.

It seems ironic in retrospect that it was the poor girl of struggling circumstances whom Carl Loeb had married in St. Louis, who turned out to be the key to his social status in America. Even with Adeline's antecedents it took Carl Loeb literally years to gain admission to the prestigious Jewish Century Country Club in Westchester County, New York, where membership represented full acceptance by the "Our Crowd" German Jews in New York City.

—⁂—

Adeline and the Moses Family of Montgomery, Alabama

> Our knowledge of the family's past is most certainly not due to its having been sedentary and unadventurous. The generations prior to Adeline Moses Loeb lived in Germany, England, several West Indian islands, various cities in America—New York, Newport, Charleston, Savannah, Montgomery, Sheffield, and St. Louis—as well in as smaller towns in the South and the East. Adeline Moses Loeb's ancestors changed their place of residence with almost every successive generation. . . .
>
> —Judith Endelman
> From Part Three, Chapter One, of this book

Born in 1876, Adeline Moses was the middle and reportedly favorite child of one of Montgomery's most prominent citizens, Alfred Huger Moses, and the niece of the city's popular longtime mayor, Mordecai Moses. Sporting a huge walrus moustache, Alfred Huger Moses was known as "Captain" Moses because of his Confederate service during the Civil War. A swashbuckling, eminently successful real estate and banking mogul in Montgomery, in the late 1800s he was the leading founder and first mayor of the boomtown Sheffield, Alabama.

In the 1800s, at the time of Adeline Moses Loeb's birth, members of the Jewish population were not only accepted in Alabama, but so well accepted they were able to establish prosperous businesses, be elected to public office, and live as respected citizens in the community.

However, in 1891 the Moses family lost almost all their money. The calamity of the loss of her family's fortune, and their precipitous fall into poverty caused by the Sheffield boomtown bust of 1890–1891 and an international financial banking panic in 1893 altered her whole life. The vagaries of the world economy had swept away the Moses family fortune and, after a hundred years in the South, they moved from Montgomery to St. Louis to become part of a growing Jewish community on the Mississippi River. Why they chose St. Louis has not been recorded.

Having learned to play the piano at an early age gave Adeline the dexterity to master sewing so she could make her own clothes, enabled her to master typing and stenographic skills, and allowed her to give piano lessons—all to earn extra money for a family catapulted into an economic struggle.

It was in the St. Louis boarding house run by her two maiden aunts (also looking to contribute to the family income) that she was to meet a youthful new German immigrant, Carl Loeb, who would fall in love with her dimples and dark eyes, her beautiful manners, and of course her Alabama-bred Southern belle charms and accent (which she kept all her life, even after decades in New York City).

Though Carl was only a junior official in the American Metal Company at the time, he must have reminded her in many ways of her father—in his ambition, his self-confidence, his ability to dream big, and his determination to be a success in America. And she would have been right.

In a few short years, mentored well by Jacob Langeloth, the savvy New York City president of American Metal Company (and the man in whose honor John Langeloth Loeb Jr. and his father were named), Carl Loeb, through a series of happenstances, emerged in New York City as a very wealthy international metals baron. Adeline's life changed again; she gained a position even surpassing that of her Alabama girlhood. Because of a father and then a husband, both imaginative businessmen, her life had been a roller coaster of struggle from riches to poverty and back to riches again, imbuing her life with an unshakable optimism and faith in America, which both her husband and father had shared.

Judith Endelman, in Part Three, Chapter One, of this book sums up the importance of Adeline's history and that of her family:

> The history of the Moses family is more than a mere listing of names and dates. Beyond the historical record and the fact that the Moses family can be traced to the late seventeenth century, there is another remarkable characteristic about this family history. Each generation is uncannily representative of the American Jewish experience of its period. Not only is each family representative of the American Jewish history, the family seemed always among the vanguard. They were the risk takers who struck out, moved on, and ventured where others dared not to tread.

> To read the history of the Moses family is to gain a remarkable insight into American Jewish history and American Jewry's many accomplishments. . . . The generations of Adeline Moses Loeb give us American history at its most intimate level.

Focused on the roots of the Moses family and its long journey through three hundred years of American history, *An American Experience: Adeline Moses Loeb and Her Early American Jewish Ancestors* reveals a paradigm—a model of the path taken by many other American Jewish families in this country, with varying levels of success. Readers will discover new insights into American Jewish history by traveling through time with the stories of the generations and families in this book.

The Origins of the Genealogical History

In the mid-1970s John commissioned Judith Endelman, a Jewish historian who specializes in tracing early American Jewry, to look into the long history of his family. A thorough scholar, she was a happy choice, who more than thirty years ago produced the first manuscript of the Moses family chronicles—the genesis of Part Three of this family history. When the editor of this book discovered the original Endelman manuscript in John's archives, she suggested to John that it should be made public. He agreed and asked Judith to update her original work.

Judith returned to her research. The passage of thirty years' time brought her greater access to relevant historical documents, and a subsequent career working for museums and writing for the public changed the gyroscope of her writing style. She has imbued this book with a sense of clarity and spirit that is not often experienced in the genealogical genre.

To an impatient reader, the descriptions may, on the surface, appear to be in the dry language of data and records that are the artifacts of analysis gathered by any historian. But Endelman's interpretation of material gathered from newspaper articles, business announcements, diaries, wills, *ketubot* (marriage contracts), property records, congregational minutes, accounting books, family portraits and daguerreotypes, lawsuits, and legal records has revealed the humanity of these families, seen in the historical sweep of American and Jewish history—and in this case, because so many of these Jewish families immigrated into the American South, we see lives buffeted and devastated by the stormy and often cruel cross-currents of the complex forces of Southern history as well. And life itself would hurl a thunderstorm of psychological and economic complexities that would challenge the stressful interactions of any marriage or family.

In 1718 Grace Mears, Adeline's four-times great-grandmother, at twenty-four years of age married a fifty-two-year-old widower, Moses Levy, one of New York's wealthiest merchants. He already had five children, including the oldest, Abigaill, who was just two years younger than Grace, making for tensions in every way between the two women. We know a great deal about Grace and the family squabbles and the details of daily life because the family left an important trove of significant documents and letters, now invaluable to historians. Over the next ten years, Grace had seven children of her own and also parented five stepchildren, but she was unable to manage the jealousies and outright enmity of the latter.

When Moses Levy died at age sixty-three, letters indicate all five stepchildren were gripped with even more hostility toward their stepmother. Out of spite or need of money, or from just being mean-spirited, Grace refused to pay the cost of her husband's coffin, claiming it was her stepson's responsibility as co-executor. Even after she remarried, Grace pressed for a larger share of the estate, claiming in a lawsuit that the stepsons had mismanaged the funds and left her and her new husband in debt. She continued to press for more of the Levy estate money, which unleashed a wildfire of bitter resentment. Abigaill, a prolific letter writer, in one piece of correspondence describes Grace acerbically as "a base vile woman" and speaks further of her as "the plague my father has Intailed [*sic*] upon us here in New York by that woman." Of Grace's new marriage, Abigaill declares, "nothing but a madman would Marry a Woman with Seven children."[5] Poor Grace—a widow beset with financial woes and too many children (seven) and angry stepchildren (five)—and poor Abigaill, eventually the mother of nine children herself, left with a stepmother she couldn't abide. A written record of their verbal warfare would ricochet off the walls of history for over two hundred and seventy years.

One can palpably feel the fear, anxiety, and most likely pain that must have been the experience of Adeline's great-great-grandmother Hannah, as well the great concern of Hannah's husband, Jacob Phillips, when we read that their daughter Rebecca was born at sea. Hannah gave birth without benefit of even a midwife. The sea-born child would ultimately grow up to wed the thirty-five-year-old widower Isaiah Moses when she was fifteen years old, live in Charleston, raise a family of fifteen children (four young sons were stepchildren), and become mistress of the famed Charleston plantation on Goose Creek named "The Oaks." Unfortunately, the home on the plantation burned down in 1840. Rebecca remained in Charleston until after her husband died in 1857 and the Civil War had begun.

In 1861 the widow fled Charleston to live in Savannah with her daughter and son-in-law, Cecilia and Abraham Solomons. When General Sherman's army took the city without a shot (which is the reason Savannah is such a beautiful old

5. Abigaill's papers can be found at the American Jewish Historical Society in New York City.

A Few Historically Noteworthy
Family Connections of Adeline Moses Loeb

In addition to the family members discussed in the text, the following individuals stand out in American history. They are all associated with Adeline Moses Loeb through blood, marriage, or other family relationships.

MATHIAS BUSH
(1722–1790)

Philadelphia merchant; signer of the Philadelphia Merchant's Non-Importation Resolution of 1765.

SOLOMON BUSH
(1753–1795)

As a lieutenant colonel, the highest-ranking Jewish officer in the Continental Army of the U. S.

BENJAMIN NATHAN CARDOZO
(1870–1938)

Judge of the New York State Court of Appeals, 1917–1932; associate justice of the United States Supreme Court, 1932–1938.

DAVID SALISBURY FRANKS
(1747–1793)

Lieutenant colonel, U.S. Army; aide-de-camp to Benedict Arnold; vice-consul to France.

ISAAC FRANKS
(1759–1822)

Colonel, U.S. Army; aide-de-camp to General George Washington.

MICHAEL GRATZ
(1740–1811)

Philadelphia trader and merchant; signer of the Non-Imporation Agreements of 1765; served in the War of 1812.

REBECCA GRATZ
(1781–1869)

Humanitarian and philanthropist; founder of the Female Hebrew Benevolent Society and the Hebrew Sunday School Society. Believed to be the model for Sir Walter Scott's *Ivanhoe* character, Rebecca.

MOSES MICHAEL HAYS
(1739–1805)

Patriot; a founder of the Massachusetts (Fleet) Bank; parnas of Congregation Shearith Israel in New York; grand master of Masons in Massachusetts.

LIVINGSTON HUNT
(1859–1943)

Paymaster of the U.S. Navy with the rank of rear admiral; served in the Spanish American War and was at sea from 1883–1907.

WILLIAM HENRY HUNT
(1823–1884)

U. S. secretary of the Navy under Presidents James Garfield and Chester A. Arthur; minister to Russia from 1882–1884.

EMMA LAZARUS
(1849–1887)

Poet, author of "Give me your tired, your poor..." from her poem "The New Colossus."

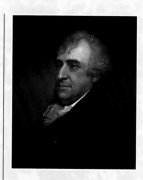

MOSES LEVY
(1756–1826)

Presiding judge of the Mayor's Court (Philadelphia); member of the Pennsylvania legislature; and a trustee of the University of Pennsylvania for twenty-four years.

SAMSON LEVY
(1722–1781)

Prominent Jewish merchant in Philadelphia; one of the 1748 founders of the City Dancing Assembly, a renowned social organization; signer of the Non-Importation Resolution of 1765.

JACOB MORDECAI
(1762–1838)

With his second wife, Rebecca, founder of the Warrenton Female Academy in North Carolina, a progressive school for young women, both Jewish and gentile.

ALFRED MORDECAI
(1804–1887)

Major, U.S. Army; West Point graduate and professor; engineer; author; Mexican American War veteran.

ALFRED MORDECAI JR.
(1840–1920)

Brigadier general, U.S. Army; West Point graduate; engineer; Civil War veteran.

JOSEPH WINTHROP MOSES
(c. 1837–1876)

Attorney admitted to the South Carolina Bar in 1858; head of the Montgomery, Alabama public school system.

MORDECAI LYON MOSES
(1842–1918)

Alderman and three-term mayor of Montgomery, Alabama. He was the city's first Jewish mayor and the first Democrat elected after the Civil War.

GUSTAVUS ADOLPHUS MYERS
(1801–1869)

Attorney; Virginia State legislator; the Confederate government's consul to Great Britain.

MYER MYERS
(1723–1795)

Dominant figure among silver- and goldsmiths in the late colonial period; patriot and leader of the New York Jewish community.

WILLIAM BARKSDALE MYERS
(1839–1873)

Major in the Virginia armies of the Confederate States of America; noted Richmond, Virginia artist.

JOSEPH H. NATHAN
(1856–1955)

Prominent citizen of Sheffield, Alabama; delegate to the Democratic National Conventions of 1912 and 1916; judge in the State of Alabama Circuit Court.

NAPHTALI PHILLIPS
(1773–1870)

Owner and publisher of *The National Advocate*, among the first Jewish newspaper publishers in the United States.

HAYM SALOMON
(1740–1785)

Financier. broker, and supervisor of finance during the Revolution; negotiated bills of exchange that largely financed Revolutionary activities of the government.

DAVID G. SEIXAS
(1788–1864)

War of 1812 veteran; founder of the Pennsylvania Institution for the Deaf and Dumb.

GERSHOM MENDES SEIXAS
(1746–1816)

First native-born Jewish clergyman in the United States; participant in George Washington's first inaugural; known as "The Patriot Preacher."

ARTHUR HAYS SULZBERGER
(1891–1968)

Publisher of the *New York Times*, 1935–1961. Under his aegis the paper's Sunday circulation grew from 745,000 to 1.4 million.

ABRAHAM TOURO
(1774–1822)

Merchant and philanthropist; a prominent Bostonian, he led the fund-raising effort in 1816 for the Massachusetts General Hospital and was an early proprietor of the Boston Athenaeum.

JUDAH TOURO
(1775–1854)

Merchant and philanthropist; he served in the War of 1812 under Andrew Jackson and was seriously wounded at the Battle of New Orleans; throughout his life he was a significant contributor to both gentile and Jewish institutions in an era when philanthropy was not the norm.

city today), Yankee officers were billeted inside the Solomons residence. It was a major humiliation, according to family legend, because like most Southern women, Rebecca was a Confederate patriot. She reportedly suffered a stroke when a newsboy outside her window announced the news of Lee's surrender in April 1865. Rebecca died in her daughter's home in Savannah in 1872 at the age of eighty years and ten months and was buried in Charleston next to her husband Isaiah. It took eight years to settle her modest estate, probably because of lawsuits among her ten children still living, who fought over the proceeds.

We take note that it was the service of Jacob Phillips (Adeline's great-great-grandfather) in the Revolutionary War that provided the lineage for Adeline and her descendants to become members of the DAR, and for their male counterparts to join the SAR and the SRNY.

One can sense the understandable pride of Levy Moses, Adeline's grandfather, when in 1866 he wrote to his mother (that sea-born baby girl referenced earlier) about receiving a silver pitcher and testament of gratitude from the Hebrew Orphan Society of Charleston "written upon parchment bound with ribbon and which I shall have framed."

Levy, a bookkeeper who never achieved the great wealth or stature of his father, had been secretary and treasurer of the Hebrew Orphan Society for eighteen years, and he had somehow managed to save the assets of that organization from the troops of the feared General William Tecumseh Sherman. The recognition of his service was perhaps the most significant event of his life. Of some note, this is the same Hebrew Orphan Society in Charleston that was so crucial to the early education of the famed Confederate attorney general and secretary of state, Judah P. Benjamin.

One must read these stories with imagination and empathy, actually filling in spaces between the lines of these generational profiles. The reader must add flesh and bone to the sometimes stark data that can only sketch major turning points in the lives of this family.

There is an element of grand opera in these Moses family stories, recovered from scant records and family archives but brought alive by Endelman's skill. It would take an American Shakespeare, committed to multigenerational stories, not of kings but of the common man, to give these stories their deserved drama. Endelman has dug deeply into the history of America to search out the nuggets of ore in the public and private records of one family. Others will have to create the culture, the art, and the literature that will derive from her work.

The Unfolding Future of John's Dream to Honor His Family History

It is clear that Adeline not only gave her young grandson the love and memories he treasures, she was also the family storyteller who inspired John with a legacy of tales about his family that made them come alive and have intrigued and stimulated his interests all his life. One pathway led him to Montgomery, Alabama, where Adeline was born and her father and her uncle helped build the city that was the capital of the state; another pathway led back in time to the American Revolution and Fraunces Tavern Museum in downtown New York, the place where General George Washington bade his officers an emotional farewell. The latest pathway has led to Newport, Rhode Island, where John became intrigued with the deeper meaning and possibilities of the Touro Synagogue as a symbol of the roots of religious freedom and the origins of separation of church and state that enabled his family and millions of Americans of all faiths to flourish in their new homeland.

The publication of *An American Experience: Adeline Moses Loeb and Her Early American Jewish Ancestors* is the latest tangible evidence of John's lifelong fascination and love for Jewish history. He holds a vision of a twenty-first century visitors center, which will function as a high-tech learning facility geared for all ages. It will make its home on the campus of the Touro Synagogue.

A work in progress as I write this introduction, the Loeb Visitors Center at Touro will focus on the history of the First Amendment and this country's initial steps towards the separation of church and state, as well as the life and times of America's earliest Jews. Visitors will leave the center with a phrase ringing in their ears, a phrase from a letter President George Washington wrote to that little Newport Hebrew congregation in 1790, in which he declared, *To bigotry no sanction; to persecution no assistance.*

It is clear that Adeline Moses Loeb not only gave John his inspiration, the stories that he absorbed as part of his life narrative, and the love that anchors his search for meaning in the past, but also his Jewish identity. Flowing from these gifts has emerged a plan for his great personal and family legacy that will create a teaching center to bear his family name at the site of the oldest synagogue in America, itself named for one of his ancestors. The center dramatizes not only the journey of his family over seven generations but his personal journey as well. John Loeb is returning home with this Newport project, and in so doing he completes the circle of his life and of the many lives of the Moses family that have been recounted in this book. That the center will serve to deepen the understanding and commitments of tens of thousands of visitors to Touro every year makes it an even more fitting tribute to one Jewish family. After all, religious freedom is America's gift to the world, an example to inspire all humankind with a uniting vision of freedom of religion and respect for other faiths that is the basis of the struggle against the fanaticism that casts a dark cloud over the future of human history.

Rarely do history, architecture, and the ideals of religious freedom and tolerance converge in a place of such exquisite beauty and design as Touro Synagogue. It is not only still a place of worship; it stands as a symbol for the American values of religious tolerance and civil liberties engraved in the American Constitution and the Bill of Rights. The center will also honor the contribution of the Touro family and by so doing, the long line of the Moses/Loeb history described in this book. They belong together because, in a way, both the Moses/Loeb family and the Touro Synagogue have experienced almost all of American Jewish history.

The mission, as John Loeb Jr. envisions it, is to integrate history into the visitor's experience, with "a world class center that innovates, attracts, and teaches . . . to educate future generations and preserve our history." For the more than thirty thousand visitors a year, and the many more who will be attracted to learning about religious liberty and the history of separation of church and state in America, John hopes to make the synagogue and the visitors center "a model and a living landmark to religious freedom."

How better to honor Adeline Moses Loeb and the long Moses-Loeb line that began in the seventeenth century at about the same time as the Touro Synagogue than by blending the two stories together on sanctified ground. They were, after all, Jews cast by history into a search for a haven from religious persecution who found a home in a future nation based on the freedom they yearned for. What they could not foresee was that they had come to a young country for whose destiny they would have to fight. It would be known a century later as the United States of America.

ADELINE MOSES LOEB AND CARL M. LOEB

Kathy L. Plotkin

and

MOTHER'S LIFE WITH FATHER

Margaret Loeb Kempner

Adeline Moses Loeb (1876–1953)   Carl M. Loeb (1875–1955)

By 1920–1925, the years between which these two complementary portraits are thought to have been painted, Carl was well along in his career, though by no means as financially successful as he would eventually become. In the tradition of Adeline's forebears, sitting for a prominent artist denoted having "arrived." Given Carl's taste for elegance, it is not too surprising that British painter Gerald Brockhurst (regarded as a young Botticelli from the age of twelve, and profoundly influenced by da Vinci as well) was chosen to memorialize the couple. Portraying them in a painterly style evocative of earlier eras, Brockhurst clearly saw both Loebs as handsome, strong-willed, and important, with Adeline the more approachable.

—Both portraits by Gerald L. Brockhurst, 1890–1978
Adeline Moses Loeb; Sons of the Revolution in the State of New York
Carl M. Loeb; Ambassador John L. Loeb Jr. collection

ADELINE MOSES LOEB
(February 11, 1876–November 28, 1953)

and

CARL M. LOEB
(September 28, 1875–January 3, 1955)

THE CINDERELLA STORY OF Adeline Moses Loeb and her future husband, Carl M. Loeb, really began when seventeen-year-old Carl left a comfortable middle-class home in Frankfurt, Germany, in 1892 to seek his fortune in what he would forever after speak of as "these United States of America." He was the middle child of three—Julius, Carl, and Elfriede, better known as Ella—born to Minna and Adolph Loeb, a successful dry-goods merchant. Carl had finished two years at a gymnasium, the German equivalent of two years of college, where his studies included the classics, history, mathematics, and modern languages.

Carl had been promised a job with the American Metal Company, a U.S. branch of the German company Metallgesellschaft—probably on the strength of the firm's respect for his brilliant brother Julius. Julius was already working in New York, having won the company's annual prize of employment for making the top grades upon graduation from the gymnasium. (Metallgesellschaft, incidentally, still flourishes today in Frankfurt.)

The youthful Carl arrived with $250 advanced by the firm, a small wardrobe, and "lots of nerve," according to his daughter, Margaret Loeb Kempner. He would begin his American career as a runner—or a gofer in today's business parlance. Though he started at the "bottom of the heap," as he later put it, just a few weeks after arriving in Manhattan, company president Jacob Langeloth—who would figure large in the young immigrant's future—offered him a post as assistant manager in the St. Louis branch of the American Metal Company.

33

Minna Cohn Loeb (1849–1921)   Adolph Loeb (1842–1918)

Photographs of Carl Loeb's parents were shot around 1896, the year that Carl Loeb and Adeline Moses were married. Adolph was a successful dry-goods merchant in Frankfurt, Germany, and Minna saw to home, hearth, and their three children: Julius, Carl and Ella.
—Thomas L. Kempner collection

Carl immediately wrote a long letter home in which he told his family he had "cheerfully answered affirmatively" when accepting the invitation.

At their Manhattan rooming house called "The Silvers," his brother Julius gave him a surprise farewell-to-New York champagne luncheon—the bubbly libation costing an exorbitant three dollars, which Carl described in the same letter dated July 17, 1893. He went on to tell of his Pullman train trip to St. Louis with stops at Niagara Falls, for which he described his amazement by writing, "I could not open my mouth," and at smoky, sooty Chicago, the host city of the world's fair, he noted that "American girls are terribly thin. . . . Buffalo Bill had his place just outside the Exposition and we spent a very pleasant evening

34

there"—the "we" being a Mr. Badmann, a fellow employee on his way to an American Metal post in Mexico.

Young Carl did very well at American Metal in St. Louis, quickly making himself indispensable in his new position. Only two years had passed when in 1895 something happened at the company that Carl correctly saw as an open door for himself—or at least a door he planned to push open. Company president Jacob Langeloth had discovered that the St. Louis branch manager was involved in something Langeloth deemed not quite ethical, though exactly what this dark deed might have been has not been recorded. He forthwith removed the manager from his post, and for some time Carl ran the branch by himself.

Never one to underestimate his own abilities, Carl wrote Jacob Langeloth suggesting that he be made the permanent manager in place of the banished employee. Jacob demurred in a strong letter. Though talented, he said, Carl was too young and inexperienced for the top job in St. Louis.

With some heat Carl wrote back that he had essentially been running the branch for quite a while, and that if someone else was to be given the job, he would find it "utterly impossible and too mortifying to stay here after being

John Jacob Langeloth
(1852–1914)
The president of American Metal Company Langeloth died at the early age of 62, which catapulted his protégé, Carl M. Loeb, to the helm of the firm in 1914. Adeline and Carl Loeb felt very close to the philanthropist from early in their relationship and named their first-born son for him in 1902. Their grandson, John Langeloth Loeb Jr., and his daughter, Alexandra Loeb Driscoll, serve on the board of the Langeloth Foundation, which makes grants to institutions for programs focused on health and well being.
—E. W. Greene, oil on canvas
The Langeloth Foundation, New York City

Carl Loeb and Adeline Moses posed in a St. Louis, Missouri, studio on April 21, 1896, for what was probably the couple's engagement photograph. They would be married on November 12 later that year. The photo is a forecast of Carl Loeb's lifelong taste for sartorial elegance and Adeline's taste for large and commanding hats.

—Thomas L. Kempner collection

deposed." That response brought Jacob hustling down from New York to St. Louis to discuss the matter. Carl got the job.

Within three years after arriving in St. Louis, Carl had met, wooed, and married spunky Adeline Moses, the reportedly favorite child of Alfred Huger Moses. At the time, Adeline's maiden aunts, Grace and Rose Moses, ran a genteel rooming house in St. Louis. (In those days, rooming houses were frequently a source of income for decorous but impecunious women, offering respectable short-term homes for young singles.) It was at the home of Grace and Rose that Carl had serendipitously chosen to board, and where Adeline serendipitously visited frequently.

The couple was married on November 12, 1896, the bride attired in a suit with leg-of-mutton sleeves, which she had made herself for $2.95. For their honeymoon Carl was rewarded by American Metal with railroad tickets to New York City. As far as can be determined, he did not find it necessary to spend any of the one thousand gold pieces he had so far salted away and hidden in a cigar box under his bed. Carl did not trust the banks to keep his savings, and he especially did not trust presidential hopeful William Jennings Bryan after his "Cross of Gold" speech, in which he argued for the devaluation of gold.

A year later, on October 18, 1897, at the age of twenty-two, Carl received his American citizenship. Margaret, the couple's first child and only daughter, was born in 1899, followed in 1902 by John Langeloth Loeb, named for Jacob Langeloth, who had by now become both a friend and a mentor. Carl M. Loeb Jr. arrived in 1904. By 1907 "C. M."—as he was called by almost everyone—had become vice president of American Metal. That same year the family moved to New York, where their youngest child, Henry, was born. American Metal continued to thrive, but at the outbreak of World War I in 1914, Jacob Langeloth died unexpectedly at the age of sixty-two, and Carl Loeb was made president of the company. He was not quite forty years old.

Because of the war, American Metal's German parent company, Metallgesellschaft, gave its proxy to Carl, who for all intents and purposes was then in control of the whole company. When the United States entered the war,

Sometime around 1909 Adeline and Carl lined up their offspring for a family photo. In stair-step order are Margaret (born 1899); John Langeloth (born 1902); Carl M. Jr. (born 1904); and Henry (born 1907).

—Ambassador John L. Loeb Jr. collection

The three sons of Adeline and Carl Loeb faced a studio photographer with aplomb in about 1912. Left to right, Henry, the youngest; John Langeloth, the oldest; and Carl M. Jr., the middle son.

—Thomas L. Kempner collection

The Loebs once again lined up for a family photo op around 1945, standing in the same order as they did in 1909, but the offspring are no longer stair-steps. Baby Henry grew to be the tallest of them all.

—Thomas L. Kempner collection

Metallgesellschaft's shares were confiscated as enemy property and put under the control of the Alien Property Custodian, although Carl continued to run the company. After the war, the U.S. government divested itself of its shares, offering them to the officers of the company. Carl bought a significant amount of stock and then expanded the operations of American Metal with the purchase of mining, smelting, and refining facilities. Although his salary never topped $30,000 a year, in 1917 he received a bonus of $1 million—tax free.

In 1916 before World I ended, American Metal bought a molybdenum mine in Climax, Colorado. Molybdenum was a relatively unknown ore at the time, but could be used as an alloy of steel in place of vanadium. However, there was more than enough vanadium available worldwide and no one wanted to buy the company's molybdenum. The mineral industry seemed of one mind: "Moly" was an unneeded commodity. But Carl steadfastly believed that it would someday be valuable. He and some of the other executives of the company—including members of the Hochschild family who were majority shareholders of the company—bought out the American Metal shares in the mine. Not until 1934 did it prove to be a good investment. Margaret Loeb Kempner comments in her memoir *Recollection*, it was ultimately *so* good that C. M. split his shares four ways to form a big chunk of the Loeb children's considerable inheritance.

Carl Loeb and American Metal sailed along together profitably until 1929. Under his leadership, the company had become a multimillion-dollar concern, and, among other holdings, the firm owned the largest Rhodesian copper mines. But that year a simmering managerial dispute came to a boil between C. M. and majority shareholders Harold and Walter Hochschild. C. M. became restive over too much board interference, despite his obviously successful management. Never one to have his authority challenged, C. M. submitted his resignation as president, and it was accepted with unflattering alacrity. He was suddenly a reluctant retiree at the age of fifty-four. But a rich one.

Margaret Kempner Loeb says in her memoir that C. M. had been "forced out" of American Metal, but she also notes that he had a bad habit of calling his partners "stupid." As fate would have it, his exodus from the company that he had

Adeline and Carl Loeb surrounded by their family around 1934

First row, left to right: John L. Loeb Jr. stands beside his mother, Frances Lehman Loeb (Mrs. John L. Loeb), who holds Arthur, one of her twins; Lucille Loeb (Mrs. Carl Loeb Jr.) holds her baby son Carl Morris Loeb III; Adeline dandles granddaughter Ann Loeb, the other twin of John and Frances Loeb; Carl Loeb holds granddaughters Judith Loeb, oldest child of John and Frances Loeb, on one knee, and Constance, daughter of Lucille and Carl M. Loeb Jr., on the other knee; Margaret Loeb Kempner, with her youngest son, Tommy Kempner, beside her. *Second row, left to right*: Alan Kempner, John Loeb with his nephew Alan Kempner Jr. standing in front of him; Henry A. Loeb, with his nephew Carl Kempner standing in front of him; Carl M. Loeb Jr.

—Nicholas M. Loeb collection

made so successful couldn't have been timed better from C. M.'s standpoint. Only three years after C. M.'s departure, the American Metal stock for which he had received $85 per share (realized from a "put" option to his former fellow directors of the American Metal Company) was selling for only $1 a share, owing to the Depression, but perhaps also a result of not having C. M.'s uncanny business sense at the helm.

Carl and Adeline loved to travel, and during his short retirement they took a lengthy trip around the world. But according to his oldest son, John, "C. M. had too much energy and too much wisdom to stay on the sideline for long." Within a year, Adeline, who had taken Carl for better or worse but not for lunch, was frantic about what to do with her restless mate. John quoted her in the John and Frances Loeb memoir *All in a Lifetime*: "John, you have to do something to get your father out of the house. He is like a caged lion and he's driving me absolutely mad!"

So John began to think. After graduation from Harvard in 1924, he had had a brief sojourn at the American Metal Company, but recognized early on that it wasn't the field for him. He had then joined Wertheim and Company, a Wall Street firm, and found the financial world more to his liking. The idea he proposed to his father was rather daring, it then being 1931 in the depths of the Depression: Together they should form an investment banking firm to be called Carl M. Loeb and Company. After a few preliminary hiccups, the father-and-son venture began to flourish. A bit later one other Loeb son, Henry, joined the firm. Eventually morphing into Loeb, Rhoades & Co., the firm continued to expand, and in its heyday was a major New York City financial entity. From Adeline's "caged lion" to a financial lion king, C. M. reigned in the Wall Street jungle until he died in 1955, less than two years after his beloved Adeline.

Though the couple enjoyed spirited shouting matches, according to Margaret Kempner, there were no serious disputes—at least none the inside world of "Our Crowd" ever knew about—and the marriage of Adeline Moses Loeb and Carl M. Loeb can be described as a successful partnership on all fronts. Adeline managed family, household, and civic obligations with authority and panache, while C. M. steered the family fortunes into mega-millions and, by example, preached philanthropy to his heirs. This Jewish family, though members of Temple Emanu-El, were for the most part nonobservant. Patriotism and "giving back" were the C. M. Loeb family's religion, and their names are deeply carved in patriotic, philanthropic American Jewish history.

—⁓—

The Children of Adeline Moses and Carl M. Loeb

1. **Margaret** (born May 22, 1899, St. Louis, Missouri; died December 31, 2001, Purchase, New York). Married Alan Horace Kempner (born July 4, 1897, Little Rock, Arkansas; died December 18, 1985) on June 1, 1920, at "Oaksmere" in Mamaroneck, New York. All three Kempner children were born in Pittsburgh, Pennsylvania: Alan Horace Kempner Jr. (born August 26, 1922; died June 18, 2004); Carl Loeb Kempner (born December 29, 1923; died September 15, 1998); Thomas Lenox Kempner (born July 14, 1927).

2. **John Langeloth** (born November 11, 1902, St. Louis, Missouri; died December 8, 1996, New York, New York). Married Frances Lehman (born September 25, 1906, New York, New York; died May 17, 1996, New York, New York) on November 18, 1926, New York, New York. All five children were born in New York, New York: Judith Helen, September 11, 1927; John Jr., May 2, 1930; Ann and Arthur (twins), September 19, 1932; Deborah, February 19, 1946.

3. **Carl Morris Jr.** (born August 10, 1904, St. Louis, Missouri; died August 13, 1985, Greenwich, Connecticut). Married Lucille H. S. Schamberg (born November 13, 1905, Philadelphia, Pennsylvania; died March 1, 1998, La Quinta, California), on January 30, 1929. All three children were born in New York, New York: Constance Margaret, September 13, 1930; Carl Morris Loeb III, May 5, 1933; Peter Kenneth, April 8, 1936; died November 16, 2004, New York, New York.

4. **Henry Alfred** (born March 30, 1907, New York, New York; died January 27, 1998, New York, New York). Married Louise Steinhardt (born April 11, 1915; died December 1, 2001) on September 14, 1934, in Armonk, New York. They had two daughters, Jean A., born August 28, 1938, and Elizabeth Louise, born September 22, 1939.

—w—

Obituaries of Adeline and Carl Loeb

New York Herald Tribune
Sunday, November 29, 1953

Mrs. C. Loeb Dies; Aided Charities

Mrs. Adeline Moses Loeb, wife of the investment banker, Carl M. Loeb, died yesterday at her home, 910 Fifth Ave. She also lived on Lincoln Ave., Purchase, N.Y.

Mrs. Loeb was born in Montgomery, Ala., and spent her early married years in St. Louis, before moving to New York in 1905. She was a member of the Daughters of the American Revolution. Her father, Capt. Alfred Huger Moses, fought in the Confederate Army during the Civil War.

Much of her life was devoted to helping others. During World Wars I and II she made surgical dressings and relief supplies for the wounded and displaced.

Mrs. Loeb was a member of many committees, among them the Vocational Adjustment Service, the Home Club for Girls and the Sisterhood of Temple Emanu-El. She was a member of the Women's Division of the Federation for Jewish Philanthropies.

In her last years her greatest efforts were spent in helping the blind. She was a board member of the New York Guild for the Jewish Blind and, with her husband, she was the donor of the new dining room in the Yonkers, N.Y. home of the guild. They also gave a recreation hall to the Kingsbridge Home for Aged and Infirm Hebrews.

A recent gift, also with Mr. Loeb, was the donation of funds to build the new boathouse in Central Park. She made numerous personal benefactions.

Surviving, besides her husband—with whom she observed her fifty-seventh wedding anniversary last week—are a daughter, Mrs. Alan H.

Kempner, and three sons, John Langeloth, Carl M. Jr. and Henry A. Loeb, all of New York; thirteen grandchildren, and ten great-grandchildren.

—◠◠—

New York Times
January 4, 1955

Carl Loeb 79, Banker, Is Dead
Head of New York Investment Firm;
Donated Boathouse for Lake in Central Park

Carl M. Loeb, head of the Stock Exchange investment banking and brokerage firm of Carl M. Loeb, Rhoades & Co., died yesterday in Mount Sinai Hospital. He had been ill there since Dec. 10, and had suffered periodic ailments during the last year. He was 79 years old and lived at 910 Fifth Avenue.

Mr. Loeb and his late wife, Mrs. Adeline Moses Loeb, were known for various philanthropic activities. These included the gift of a new boathouse on Central Park's Seventy-second Street Lake. That

$305,000 structure was opened last March 12 by Mayor Wagner, Parks Commissioner Robert Moses and Manhattan Borough President Hulan E. Jack.

Mrs. Loeb died Nov. 28, 1953, shortly after a family celebration marking the fifty-seventh anniversary of their marriage.

Born in Frankfurt, Germany

Mr. Loeb was born Sept. 28, 1875, at Frankfurt, Germany, a son of Adolf and Minna Loeb. He was 17 years old when his employer, a German concern that then was parent organization of the American Metal Company, sent him to work in its office at St. Louis. Five years later Mr. Loeb was naturalized as a United States citizen.

In 1904, having achieved a vice presidency in American Metal, he came to New York. He was elected president of that organization ten years later. In 1917 he had been made president of Climax Molybdenum Company.

In January, 1931, having retired from his other business connections, he founded the brokerage firm. He remained active in it until he became ill last month.

For many years Mr. Loeb was president of the Home for Aged and Infirm Hebrews and a trustee of the Federation of Jewish Philanthropies.

He also was a supporter of the New York Guild for the Jewish Blind, and a life trustee of Valeria House, a vacation resort in Peekskill, N.Y., for persons of medium income.

Gifts to Harvard, Syracuse

Mr. Loeb donated a collection of manuscripts of Heinrich Heine to the Houghton Library at Harvard. To Syracuse University, in 1948, he and Mrs. Loeb gave fifty-three acres and a number of buildings on the shore of Upper-Saranac Lake for use as a faculty rest home and a student art center.

It was in 1952 that Mr. and Mrs. Loeb learned of the need for a new boathouse on the Central Park Lake that was a feature of the view from their apartment. They pledged a gift of $250,000 for the purpose and later increased the amount to $350,000. The brick-and-limestone building, which also houses a cafeteria, was under construction when Mrs. Loeb died.

For this gift the Park Association awarded the couple its plaque for 1953, honoring Mr. Loeb and his late wife for "practical public-spirited philanthropy."

Mr. Loeb leaves a daughter, Mrs. Alan H. Kempner; three sons, John L., Carl M. Jr. and Henry A., thirteen grandchildren and ten great-grandchildren.

—⁂—

Margaret Loeb Kempner

MOTHER'S LIFE WITH FATHER

(From *Recollection: A Personal Memoir*)

Editor's note:

Adeline Moses Loeb would have been nothing less than delighted if she could have known that her oft-told stories of a proud Jewish heritage (sometimes so vividly embellished that her grandchildren weren't sure they were true) would come to light again some fifty-six years after her death. Her tales of seafaring ancestors, a great-grandmother born at sea, post–Civil War sagas of the South, her early life in Alabama and going from riches to rags (and if not rags, at least clothes she had to sew herself) and back to riches are all retold in this book.

But just who was Adeline Moses Loeb? What kind of a person was she? Was it Jewish genes that gave her so indomitable a spirit and made her so generous and loving a parent? The impersonal listing of her many philanthropies and her fortuitous marriage to the ultimately very successful Carl M. Loeb, founder of Loeb, Rhoades & Co. can be gleaned from their obituaries, but they do not provide the colorful, humanizing insights about the life, love, and marriage of two very strong individuals whom we find in the vignettes recounted by their only daughter, Margaret Loeb Kempner, in her unpublished book, *Recollection*. What follows here are excerpts from Mrs. Kempner's oral memoir recorded in September 1980.

The excerpt begins with the assumption that the reader knows that Adeline's father, Alfred Huger Moses, once a wealthy banker and real estate developer in Montgomery, and chief founder of Sheffield, Alabama, lost all his money and his standing in the community, and that in 1891 the entire family moved in markedly reduced circumstances to St. Louis,

49

Missouri. Why they settled in St. Louis is unclear, but it was lucky for Adeline that they did—it was there she would meet Carl M. Loeb, whose business acumen would make her wealthy once more.

Adeline was fourteen years old in 1891 when the family fortune toppled, and as a teenager she honed two marketable skills: teaching piano and typing. We pick up the story at this point in her life.

Mother got a job as a stenographer, which was very unusual in those days. She had lots of gumption. She learned how to type easily, as she played the piano well. I don't know if she ever learned shorthand. I do know she must have charmed her first boss, a Mr. Harris, for he wanted to marry her. My father must have "had something" for she chose a still-struggling young German who had little money, instead of Mr. Harris, an older and well-established man who later moved to Rolla, Missouri. Years later my father used to say, "If your mother had married Mr. Harris, you would be living in a hovel in Rolla, Missouri." (Mr. Harris lost his money and Father became very rich.) As the Loeb fortune grew and Father continued to speak of "what might have been," the imaginary Harris hovel grew progressively worse—Father even added pigs.

When Father moved to St. Louis [from New York City] he boarded with Mother's maiden aunts, Aunt Grace and Aunt Rose. He had been told that these ladies kept a high-class boarding house. Just exactly when Father met Mother I can't say, but she did visit her dear old aunties regularly. Father fell in love with her at first sight. Germans like the dark type, and Mother had big brown eyes, lovely white skin, and a marvelous smile. He found her beautiful and exciting. They married on November 12, 1896, when Father was twenty-one and Mother was nineteen. From that day on, Mother never worked again outside their home—Father supported her.

His superiors at American Metal gave them a railroad pass to New York City as a honeymoon gift, and one of the stories I always loved was their account of walking along Fifth Avenue and stopping at Henri Bendel's window. In it was a navy blue velvet picture hat with ostrich plumes. Father insisted that Mother try it on. She looked so beautiful in it that he bought the hat for $35, which in those

Adeline Moses Loeb almost always chose to be photographed wearing a hat and a neckpiece. Here she is as a young girl, thought to be "around eighteen" according to her daughter, Margaret Loeb Kempner.

—Thomas L. Kempner collection

Always proud of sewing her own clothes—a financial necessity in her teenage years—Adeline no doubt designed and made the balloon-sleeved gown in which she posed for a picture in about 1894. This was shortly before she met Carl Loeb at the boarding house of her aunts, Rose and Grace. Adeline and Carl married in 1896, when she was nineteen and he was twenty-one.

—Thomas L. Kempner collection

days was an enormous sum for a hat. He liked it; he wanted her to have it. In a way, I think that extravagant purchase typified his personality.

Mother was of medium height—5'4"—and weighed 127 pounds when they married. When she became stout in later years, Father used to tease her by saying he had only contracted for 127 pounds. Father had dark brown hair, a ruddy, healthy color, and brown eyes. Father had great charm. He was very bright, had a marvelous sense of humor, and was very attractive to women. He was always meticulously groomed, carried himself well, and remained young-looking until the day of his death at seventy-nine years of age in 1955.

Mother always underrated herself. She said Father was the big attraction, though she had great charm, too, and definitely had what today we would call "sex appeal." They were both unusual people. Mother always called Father "Mr. Loeb," a Southernism. When she was angry she called him "Carl." His good friends called him "C. M."

Shortly after they were married, Father took her to Germany to meet his parents and sister and to learn German. He left her there for seven months while he went back to America to work. When I think of it now, it seems almost incredible that Father left his lovely young bride for that length of time. In America she had been a pretty girl, but because she was dark, in Germany she was considered a great beauty. Everyone in Frankfurt fell in love with her. They called her "the beautiful American," and she had a marvelous time. Later, when she was annoyed at Father she used to say, "I should have eloped with the handsome Mr. Winkler"—one of her many admirers, a socially prominent German. She did not elope (witness the four of us children—Margaret, John, Carl and Henry), but returned to Father fluent in German. Mother and Father always remained very much in love, even though at times they fought like cats and dogs. They adored each other.

Mother and Father couldn't have been more different. Mother was 100 percent illogical. She used to drive my brother Carl, who was the most logical member of the family, crazy. He would say, "But Mother, I'll *prove* it to you." She didn't care at all. If she thought two and two made five, there was no arguing with her. In some ways, Father was easier for me to get along with than my

In 1913, while on one of their frequent trips to Germany to visit Carl Loeb's relatives, the lovely Adeline sat for her portrait. As usual, she chose a rather extravagant hat with a veil in which to have her picture taken.

—Ambassador John L. Loeb Jr. collection

mother because he was very logical. If you could prove to him you were right, he would listen. Mother wouldn't. If Mother believed something was a certainty, you could not change her mind.

After my parents returned to the United States, they moved to a house on Laclede Avenue, and there in St. Louis on May 22, 1899, I was born. Three and a half years later, on November 11, 1902, the eldest of my three brothers, John, was born. The fact that he was named John was interesting because Mother always said she called all of her best beaux "John." He was called John Langeloth in honor of Father's friend and top boss at American Metal Company. Twenty-two months later, Carl M. Loeb Jr. arrived on August 10, 1904. Henry was born March 30, 1907, in New York.

They moved to New York in 1907 when Father became vice president of the American Metal Company. Our first home was the Lenori on East 63rd Street. We all went to Horace Mann, which was a marvelous school. John Dewey of Columbia University's Teachers College was the inspiration for it. It was brilliant of my mother to send all of us there. In those days little girls went to Miss Jacoby's or Miss Something's—not nearly as good schools.

Mother was more difficult than Father. You couldn't argue with her—she was darling to me and wanted me to be happy, well-dressed, and everything I should have been, but it had to be her way—what she thought was best for me. In retrospect, it probably was. She was illogical, but she adored us. If any one of us was sick, she would break all of her dates, isolate herself, and spend her entire days nursing us. We knew we were the most important things in her life.

From the Lenori we moved to the Saint Urban on Central Park West and 86th Street. Central Park West was much more stylish in those days than Park Avenue, for the railroad tracks still ran down the middle of Park Avenue at ground level. Quite early on, my parents bought a five-story house at 41 West 85th Street, a half-block from Central Park. It was a wonderful house.

From 85th Street you walked up three steps into a marble hall, in the middle of which was a goldfish pond. The kitchen and the maids' dining room were a couple of steps down from street level. On the first floor there was a living room (seldom used); then you walked up a marble staircase to the second floor to the dining room and the music room. We children ate in the basement in the maids' dining room until I was fifteen.

The music room was Mother's favorite. She played the piano beautifully and sang, too. In the early days she played the piano often. She loved all the old songs: "Daisy, Daisy, Give Me Your Answer, Do," and of course, "Sweet Adeline," and she thought the piano should be played with "soul." The music room walls were lined with lavender brocade with green leaves and pink flowers woven into the material. There was a grand piano and opposite it a large marble bust of a woman—very Victorian. I remember my brother John, who had a rather bad temper, had a fight with Carl and started chasing him, threatening to crown him with that marble bust, which really could have been serious. The cook, known as "die grosse Marie," was the only one around strong enough to stop him. She saved Carl.

There were plenty of servants—the normal staff numbered five. They had a cook, a kitchen maid, a butler, and a parlor maid. It was very much like *Upstairs, Downstairs* [a British television series that ran from 1971 to 1975]. Mother had a maid who cleaned rooms, maided her, and pressed her clothes. There was a procession of German fräuleins. Father generally spoke English to Mother, but there was a lot of German heard as well. We nearly always had German help and

German fräuleins . . . or French mademoiselles. The latter never stayed too long, as we (and our poor French) were too much for them. We had more Germans because they were stronger and more able to take on the four of us children. Dinner consisted of five courses: soup, fish, meat, salad, dessert and coffee, and an appropriate wine with each course. There were no cocktails in those days—that came much later. Ladies did not drink hard liquor.

Mother was very much in charge of this large household. She always played a game, like the wife in *Life with Father* [a popular American television program broadcast from 1953–1955]. Mother, underneath the surface, was very strong. When we were very young, living in St. Louis, Father would come home and Mother would say, "Bow down, children, to your lord and master." We would bow down. She always pretended to do everything exactly the way Father wanted, but if she wanted it her way, it usually came out that way. Father might have steamed a little and shouted about it. She'd shout back, too, but she usually got her way. Perhaps she enjoyed a good fight.

Mother would always get herself up prettily for Father—she was very Southern in many ways. She had a habit of putting on her prettiest nightgown, fixing herself up, and putting on perfume when Father planned to visit her. (They had separate bedrooms.) Father would push a note under her door. After one of their dinner parties, Mother saw a note, got herself all fixed up, and then read the note. It read, "Fire the cook."

Mother loved the house to look attractive, but she was not acquisitive. Father was much more eager to have things; he wanted everything to be elegant. And Mother really didn't care that much about food; she was not really a gourmand. Father was. He liked good food, prepared well.

When Mother was young and unable to afford new clothes, she used to make her own, for she sewed very well. Father would come home and say, "Addie, how beautiful you look." Then she'd ask, "Do you like my dress?" When he told her he did, she'd tell him she made it herself and it cost forty-six cents. She didn't like to be extravagant, despite the fact that Father would have given her anything. She hated to spend a great deal of money on clothes. Later on when Mother got a bit

The summer of 1920 found the always dapper Carl Loeb happy to face the camera in his fashionable flat-crowned, beribboned straw "boater."

—Thomas L. Kempner collection

Later that same year of 1920, Adeline Moses Loeb, ready for winter in her handsome furs, posed on the steps of the Loeb house at 41 West 85th Street.

—Thomas L. Kempner collection

too plump, Father would insist that she shop for dresses at Bergdorf Goodman. So she did—and then made them over. That wasn't such a good idea—she'd usually add an inappropriate sash or a bow that did not belong.

Mother's home always had charm. She didn't care about antiques or the value of things. She wanted an effect. Their bedrooms were on a separate floor, as was the library, which we used a lot. It was fairly large, warm, and very livable. It had a big desk, a large sofa, and a number of comfortable chairs. That's where we spent the most time. Above the library were two bedrooms and two bathrooms. Early on, my youngest brother, Henry, and I slept in one bedroom; my two brothers in the other. As we grew older, all three boys shared the front room and I had a room to myself. I remember it was all pink—my choice.

Above our bedrooms was a room that mother called her infirmary, and whenever any one of us had a contagious disease, that child would be isolated there. There was no radio or television when we were young, so when we were sick she'd play cards and read to us by the hour. It must have been frightfully boring, but she did this for any one of us who became ill. She was a very devoted mother. When I was eighteen, I had scarlet fever, and Mother isolated herself with me for six weeks. In those days, one was quarantined. Mother was a wonderful nurse and would dress herself up in her Red Cross uniform, which became her. When Father wanted to tease her, he would call her his "Cross Red Nurse." During World War I, she did a lot of work for the Red Cross, holding surgical-dressing classes in her home and teaching a large group of women how to roll bandages.

Mother loved people. She was both gregarious and very well-liked. She became involved with various organizations. One was the Vocational Adjustment Service, which helped wayward girls. (A wayward girl at that time was one who had sex before marriage.) Her favorite charity was the New York Guild for the Jewish Blind. She spent many days there. She was never lazy; she was always up and out doing things.

Mother was very class-conscious—no fraternizing with the lower class. The servants addressed us children as "Miss Margaret," "Mr. John," and so forth from the time we were five. The maids wore uniforms chosen and supplied by Mother: blue or yellow in the morning, gray or black for dinner. With these they wore aprons and little caps, frilly ones in the afternoon and evening. They had to wear caps all the time. Actually, it was a becoming costume. I remember going to a costume party as a maid in a black uniform with sheer black stockings and a pretty dainty apron and cap.

At their formal dinner parties a butler and two maids were in attendance. In our house on 85th Street, everything had to be sent up by dumbwaiter, as the kitchen was several floors down. It must have been a real problem, but everything seemed to go beautifully—the food was hot, the wine cold. Help was plentiful in those days, and unless their jobs were done perfectly, they were fired. Plates were never stacked—they had to be removed from the table one at a time, and of course washed singly. There were no dishwashers for many, many years. It must have taken hours to wash those dishes. When dinner was over, the ladies adjourned to the drawing room while the men smoked their cigars.

Mother was very demanding about the way the staff did their jobs. There could be no finger marks. I remember if there was a finger mark on the door of the pantry, that was bad and she'd scold the maid. They had to do their work exactly as Mother wished. She wanted them to work certain hours and she wanted them to rest at certain hours. Someone was always on duty to answer bells, but they were given time off so they could rest. Certain jobs had to be finished in the morning or by a certain hour. Then they could rest or read or do whatever they wanted. They weren't supposed to deviate from her schedule.

My parents had all kinds of cooks. I think when we were young they had quite a number of German cooks. As we grew older, I remember Father had one famous French chef who had cooked on the Vanderbilt yacht. He cooked the best food I've ever eaten anywhere in my life. Every meal consisted of a very delicious and unusual entrée. Father liked his food perfectly prepared and not too rich. The vegetables had to be beautifully steamed and not cooked out. Mother preferred that too. They were quite famous for their cuisine. Mother loved her table to look beautiful, and she loved to arrange the flowers.

Father could always get a rise out of Mother until the day of her death—by criticizing her food, her costume, the help, almost anything. Sometimes Mother would be angry with all three of us—John, Father, and me. I remember, on one occasion, Father, who afterwards was sorry because Mother was really quite upset, apologized to Mother and wrote an apologetic verse:

> Just imagine Mother's dismay
> When Blighty came in the month of May [Margaret]
> Mother cannot bear to remember
> Another Blighty came in November [John]
> Now that all the damage is done
> Please forgive your devoted Hun

Thereafter John and I were known as "Blighties."

Every summer they'd rent a place in the country—originally in Lawrence or Woodmere, Long Island. In 1915 they rented a big place in Westchester, long before most of their group came up that way. Whenever Mother moved from one place to another, she would always go in with a maid, and together they'd line the shelves with paper and clean the house so that the night Father moved in, everything was perfect, with no disorganization. I think she was a frustrated housewife. She rather enjoyed housekeeping—she liked scrubbing shelves and fixing drawers.

Nobody but Mother gave orders. Even the butler did not. Believe me, if she wanted something done one way, that was it. Father was a business genius, but the game she played was of being a delicate flower, which she was not. She could have been the heroine of J. M. Barrie's *What Every Woman Knows* [a play of the 1930s in which the heroine guides her husband's career without his realizing it].

The Hochschilds (Harold Hochschild was one of Father's partners in the American Metal Company) had a camp at Blue Mountain Lake. We were invited up to visit practically every summer during the First World War—1914 to 1918. Fortunately, they had running water at Blue Mountain. In Europe, occasionally we stayed at hotels with no running water, so the help had to carry up pails of water for Mother. She was a stickler for cleanliness. I can remember, as a little girl, coming down right after my evening bath for inspection. Mother would tell me that I'd forgotten to wash behind my ears. Usually our hotel was on a lake, so we were excused from a bath, which delighted us. We swam, but Mother had to have her bath. She could not live without her bath every day. She never learned to swim and she was afraid of deep water. She would only wade into the water near the shore.

Mother and Father bought a Pierce Arrow in 1912. Dwyer, the chauffeur, drove us daily in it to Horace Mann. We were never allowed to go out alone; we were always chaperoned. And was I chaperoned! When beaux called on me, there was a maid in the next room.

My parents had a box at the Metropolitan Opera every Friday night. I hated the opera, but Mother had to fill that box, so I had to go too. We dressed in full evening regalia, and the ladies sat at the front of the box. I was not allowed to wiggle or move my head, lest the men in the back of the box could not see. The long Wagnerian operas were torture for me. I was about fifteen when this started. Mother would say, "I'll get a man for you." Usually it was Victor Wittgenstein, our music teacher, whom I liked. But he was ten years older than I was and seemed like an old man to me.

Mother and Father were both very musical. Mother went to the Philharmonic every Friday afternoon. They loved the theater and went to every good show in town. They belonged to the Theatre Guild, loved Gilbert and Sullivan, and never missed the Shakespeare productions. They had a rich cultural life, a rich intellectual life. Father was not only ambitious in business, but he made a point of being extremely well-read. He could quote Shakespeare and Goethe by the yard. He was well-versed in both English and German literature.

Mother had a kind of charming naiveté. Many years ago when my brother John was about nineteen, he and David Sulzberger had an argument about something at a Century Country Club dance, and John knocked David down. The next day Mother heard about it and was not at all pleased. She asked, "John, how could a son of mine, a Southern gentleman, do that?" John replied, "But Mother, I had to. He called me a son of a bitch." And Mother answered, "How could he? He doesn't even know me!"

Father did not discuss his business with us when we were children, and he certainly did not discuss business with females. One of his favorite remarks was "no petticoat interference." At the table, *en famille*, we were never allowed to talk about small stuff, such as what somebody wore the night before, or who went out with his little girlfriend, Ruth or Mary. Father thought that was a bore. He liked semi-intellectual conversation. He would say, "Tonight we'll discuss Abyssinia." Then he'd say, "Tomorrow night we'll discuss Afghanistan." We finally discovered he was going through the encyclopedia alphabetically. We learned something each night. He liked to tease us. He'd say, "Margaret, you're reading *The Mill on the Floss* by Adam Bede." Of course it's by George Eliot, and he would wait for me to catch the mistake. We might then discuss that book.

Father was socially ambitious for us; Mother wasn't at all. Mother had no pretensions. When one said "socially ambitious" in those days, one meant you

The Carl M. Loebs posed in a late afternoon sun sometime early in the 1940s for a photographic record of a small get-together with close friends and colleagues of long standing. Left to right: Theodore and Aline Bernstein, Carl and Adeline Loeb, Belle and Edwin Goodman, and Henry and Blanche Ittleson.

Theodore Bernstein and his son Ted Jr. were the first partners of Carl Loeb and his son John when they founded Carl M. Loeb and Co. in 1931. Aline Bernstein was the prominent Broadway scene and costume designer who founded the Metropolitan Museum's Institute of Costume Design. She was rather publicly known as the mistress of Southern writer Tom Wolfe from 1925 to 1931.

Edwin Goodman came to New York City in 1900, married Belle D. Lowenstein, and began his Manhattan career as a tailor for a firm on Union Square named Bergdorf and Vought. In 1906 he bought the company and renamed it Bergdorf Goodman. By 1928 he had built an emporium of high-end fashion on the site of the former William K. Vanderbilt mansion at Fifth Avenue and 58th Street. Bergdorf Goodman is still today synonymous with fashion and elegance, as is the name of Edwin Goodman, renowned not only for business acumen but for his personal attention to clients (including, of course, Adeline Loeb).

Carl Loeb's first friend in St. Louis had been Henry Ittleson, a fellow boarder in 1893 at the rooming house run by Adeline's Aunt "Ro" and Aunt Grace. In 1908 Henry founded what later became the hugely successful CIT (Commercial Investment Trust), the first car finance business in America. He and Blanche remained lifelong friends of the Loebs.

—Thomas L. Kempner collection

didn't go out with anybody who wasn't in your social circle. Later, Mother and Father became members of "Our Crowd." [Reference is to Stephen Birmingham's book, *Our Crowd.*] Mother felt that "Our Crowd" was a step down for her because, after all, she was a member of the Daughters of the American Revolution (DAR). Father was more realistic and worldly. He used to say, "Always remember, happiness can't buy money." His primary ambition was to be an enormously successful businessman, which he was, but he had social ambitions too.

Mother always worked very hard for charity as soon as we had grown up. She devoted a great deal of time to her favorite charity—the New York Guild for the Jewish Blind. She spent many, many hours sewing for the blind and raising money for them. They had a big ball on Thanksgiving Eve each year, so she used to get up at 6:00 AM every morning for weeks before the dance to write letters for the yearly benefit. She wrote and answered her letters personally; she never wanted a social secretary. Few people dared to turn her down. If they did, she took it as a personal affront. She was a great fund-raiser. She had so much, she felt she must share. She was very compassionate. Both of my parents, more power to them, taught us to feel that way.

Neither one was religious, though they belonged to Temple Emanu-El; they used to attend services on the Day of Atonement, Yom Kippur, for the memorial service, but they did not bring us up to be religious. We never observed Jewish dietary laws.

Both of my parents were intelligent. Mother was talented and charming. She was a very good mother, though contrary to what everyone thought, she was not easygoing. However, she was kind and she loved us dearly. She was attractive; she had a lovely face and was extremely musical. Most people liked and admired her. She assumed the role of the wife of a very prominent man with utter assurance. That is why my brothers resented very much Stephen Birmingham calling her a "Mrs. Malaprop" in his book *Our Crowd.* She spoke beautiful English in a very cultured voice. She was definitely *not* a "Mrs. Malaprop"; she was a stickler for grammar. Admittedly, at times she could be innocently naive, but that's not the same thing as misusing words.

Mother died very suddenly in 1953. She never took care of herself—she took care of everybody else instead. She hadn't told anyone that she had very high blood pressure; she just ignored it. She didn't want to stop anything she was accustomed to doing. She died the way she would have wished. She just dropped dead, alive to the minute before she died. She was fixing flowers and talking to Father. They had celebrated their fifty-seventh wedding anniversary only two weeks before.

Father, devastated by her death, died just over a year later.

Editor's Note:

Among many other Loeb philanthropies, the one that gave Carl M. Loeb the most pleasure was the Loeb Boathouse in New York's Central Park at the 72nd Street Lake, which, according to his son John, was one of his father's "favorite haunts." His children were "often his companions on his daily walks around the reservoir. In later years he took pleasure in strolling there with his grandchildren and great-grandchildren."

According to Margaret Kempner, their gift in 1952 of $350,000 to renovate the old boathouse (completed in 1954) came about because her parents were at a dinner party to which Robert Moses, the famously powerful and influential commissioner of parks, had been invited. The subject of restoring the boathouse came up, "whereupon Father decided he would like to make the gift."

However, a more telling story has surfaced, regaled by James Poll, of the famous William Poll Gourmet Food Shop on Lexington Avenue, and father of Dean Poll, the current concessionaire of the Loeb Boathouse. At the annual kick-off of the spring and summer season in 2007, James Poll recalled that his father's friend, Peter Pappas (the concessionaire who ran the boathouse from 1915 to 1955), told him the following tale, revealing that it was really Adeline, not Carl, who instigated the gift from the Loebs.

The pertinent series of events took place sometime in 1951. According to Poll, Peter Pappas, who provided rental boats for rowing on the lake, as well as snacks from a little food stand reminisced:

On the brisk day of March 12, 1954, the vision and generosity of Adeline and Carl M. Loeb were celebrated at a grand opening of the newly named Loeb Boathouse, attended by city officials and well-wishers. This view shows boats for rent, the new building, and a chilly crowd, looking east.

—New York City Department of Parks and Recreation

Manhattan Borough President Hulan Jack (far left) and Parks Commissioner Robert Moses (far right) seem to be enjoying a boat ride with Mayor Robert Wagner manning the oars. The two small girls in the center are Nancy Roosevelt (left), six-year-old daughter of Mr. and Mrs. Emlen Roosevelt of Oyster Bay, Long Island, and seven-year-old Nancy Olds, Mayor Wagner's granddaughter. A short while later the mayor picked up another customer, Deborah Loeb, the eight-year-old granddaughter of the Loebs.

—New York City Department of Parks and Recreation

This woman used to come walking by in the snow in the wintertime, early in the morning—an elderly lady. Practically no one else was out that early in the morning. I'd always call out and say, "Hello, Mama. Come over here. Let me buy you some hot coffee."

Peter Pappas didn't know who she was. Even if she'd told him, he wouldn't have known what the name Loeb meant anyway. One day she said to him, "You know, this boathouse looks terrible. We'll have to do something about it." He didn't give it any thought.

About two weeks later architects came in and started to take measurements and ask him questions. Peter Pappas said, "What are you people doing here? Who are you?" They said, "Well, we're going to build a new boathouse." Peter Pappas harrumphed, "That's strange. The parks commissioner didn't tell me about it. I would be the first one to know. I don't believe it.'" And the men said, "The parks department isn't building it. Mrs. Loeb is building it." That was how he found out who the lady he'd been giving coffee to was.

The Loeb Boathouse remains today a major New York City attraction in Central Park. Here the public can dine elegantly or casually, rent rowboats and bicycles, or take a ride in an authentic Venetian gondola.

With both parents gone, in 1959 the four Loeb children provided funding to New York University for the Carl and Adeline Loeb Student Center, with much of the money coming from a charitable trust their father had set up. Instead of splitting the trust and setting up separate foundations to give to their own favorite charities, they decided to give the entire philanthropic inheritance to New York University as a memorial to their parents.

On December 10, 1958, New York University President Carroll V. Newsom braved the cold with donor family members John L. Loeb, Margaret Loeb Kempner, and Henry A. Loeb as they laid the cornerstone of the Loeb Student Center, given in honor of their parents.

—New York University archives, photographic collection

The New York University Loeb Student Center was torn down in 2000, but the portraits of Carl and Adeline Loeb now hang in the new Kimmel Student Center. A plaque outside the Kimmel Center notes that "In recognition of the long-standing commitment and generosity of the Loeb family to New York University, the Student Club and Activities Center on the seventh and eighth floors has been named the Carl and Adeline Loeb Student Center."

PART TWO

THE LOEBS:
SONS AND DAUGHTERS OF
THE AMERICAN REVOLUTION

Ambassador John L. Loeb Jr.

Ambassador John L. Loeb Jr.

THE LOEBS: SONS AND DAUGHTERS OF THE AMERICAN REVOLUTION

AMONG THE CLEAREST OF MY CHILDHOOD memories is a beautifully framed document topped by a huge eagle hanging over my father's bed. It both awed and fascinated me, especially that enormous eagle. Not even his Harvard diploma was accorded so prominent a place in my father's most private room as that scroll bearing testimony to his membership in the Sons of the American Revolution (SAR). Being an American was something he felt very strongly about, coming as he did from a family of passionate patriots, immigrants to this land of hope and democracy. Belonging to the SAR, an organization uniquely dedicated to this country, was among the most meaningful associations in my father's life.

My father was a very persuasive man, but I don't believe it took much persuasion on his part to interest his history-loving mother, Adeline Moses Loeb, in becoming a member of the Daughters of the American Revolution (DAR), a step she took in 1928. Her only daughter, Margaret Loeb Kempner, followed suit in 1929, and my daughter, Alexandra Loeb Driscoll, became a member in 2002. The belief that Jewish women cannot be members of the DAR is a common misconception.

Founded in 1890, and later adopting the motto of "God, Home, and Country," with its avowed purpose of "cherishing, maintaining, and extending the institutions of American freedom, to foster true patriotism and love of country, and to aid in securing for mankind all the blessings of liberty," the DAR was right up Adeline's alley.

It took no persuasion at all from my father for me to join the Sons of the American Revolution and, later, Sons of the Revolution (officially Sons of the Revolution in the State of New York, or SRNY). These are two different groups with the same purpose and goals, the latter being connected to the historic New York City landmark, Fraunces Tavern®, where George Washington bade farewell to his officers in 1783. By the time I was twenty-two years old I had become an

Ambassador John L. Loeb Jr., a member of the Sons of the Revolution in the State of New York (SRNY), received that organization's Distinguished Patriot Award in February 1993.

—Lou Manna photographer
Sons of the Revolution in the State of New York

SAR member and, some twenty-four years later, just around the period of the 1976 American bicentennial, I became a member of SRNY.

Shortly after I joined SRNY, the Puerto Rican terrorist liberation organization FALN, or Fuerzas Armadas de Liberación Nacional, blew up the Anglers' Club, which abutted the Fraunces Tavern. The ensuing explosion left four people killed and a heavily damaged tavern. Not only SRNY members, but all those interested in New York City history, were appalled that the four-story neo-Georgian brick structure—still retaining portions of its original architectural detail dating back to 1719—was so greatly impaired.

Soon thereafter I was approached by a group of SRNY members, who said in essence, "We need to repair this area of our property that's been so badly blasted by the bomb. Would your family like to help us financially?" Then they made a suggestion we couldn't resist: If we funded the repair, the Sons would in some way honor my grandmother, through whose ancestry we Loebs had the genealogical credentials to join SRNY.

I liked the idea and so did my father. Together with representatives from SRNY we came up with the idea of naming one of the Fraunces Tavern Museum galleries after my grandmother. Today the Adeline Moses Loeb Gallery houses such exhibitions as "Heroes," paintings that spotlight some of the many people from diverse backgrounds who won America's independence. This particular exhibit includes paintings by Henry Hintermeister (*The Drill Master*), John Ward Dunsmore (*The Message from Lexington*) and Dennis Mallone Carter (*Molly Pitcher at the Battle of Monmouth*).

Amid a great deal of American Revolutionary history, a portrait of Granny Adeline by Gerald Brockhurst, given to the museum by her daughter, Margaret Loeb Kempner, hangs in perpetuity. The plaque beneath it reads in part:

Members of her family
have served in active duty
in every war since the
American Revolution

The stated purpose of the Fraunces Tavern Museum is to "educate the public and encourage exploration of Colonial, Revolutionary War, Early Republic and early New York history." When the museum director asked me what kind of an exhibition I would like to see in this new gallery I was more than ready with an answer, because the mission of the museum was perfect for what I had in mind.

I told the director, "For a long time I have wanted to mount an exhibit about the Jewish community in early New York. Here is the chance to tell a story that's never been really told, certainly not in the measure that it deserves." The director was polite about the idea and said (rather tepidly) that it was "interesting," but that she didn't really believe there would be enough material available to produce such an exhibit. "I think there is," I insisted, knowing from my own research how rich the mother lode of early American Jewish history was, just waiting to be mined. "Please look into it—I believe you'll find out there is a great deal of material that would make a fascinating exhibit." To make a long story short, she discovered that I was right. The SRNY board enthusiastically approved the idea, and ambitious plans were eagerly made for the exhibit, "The Jewish Community in Early New York, 1654–1800." It would take nearly three years to assemble, but when it finally opened the exhibit was an astounding success and ran from October 18, 1979, through April 30, 1980.

Twenty-two museums, synagogues, and individuals from all over the country shared their historical American Jewish treasures. The opening of the show was timed to coincide with the launch of the Adeline Moses Loeb Gallery and the reopening of the restored Fraunces Tavern Museum on October 3, 1979. President Jimmy Carter sent a congratulatory message saying, "The exhibition bears witness to the immense contributions the Jewish community has made in all facets of life—civic, cultural, economic, political, and military—right from the infancy of our country." Prime Minister Menachem Begin of Israel sent warm words for the dedication, as did Senator Jacob Javits. Former Mayor Abraham Beame, the first Jewish mayor of New York, said, "Three-hundred and twenty-five years ago this September, the first twenty-three Jews landed in New York City on the good ship *St. Charles.* From the very earliest days, the Jewish community, as illustrated by this gallery and this exhibition, has played a significant role in the history of our city. It is very appropriate that it be established here in Fraunces Tavern, which is so much a part of our city's history."

Lieutenant General Andrew J. Goodpaster, then superintendent of the U.S. Military Academy and former commander in chief of the U.S. forces in Europe, pointed out that 50% of the first graduating class of West Point was Jewish. (Only two cadets graduated and one of them was Simon Levy, a Jew.) Following him at the podium, I read my essay, "The Anatomy of Patriotism" (included in this book as an appendix). Kitty Carlisle Hart, chairman of the New York State Council of the Arts, was mistress of ceremonies.

By this time, Ann G. Perry had become the museum director, and under her aegis the show was guest-curated by Ellin M. Burke. A press release by Betsy Martin, then publicity director, bears quoting here:

> The exhibition shows that under Dutch rule and Peter Stuyvesant's governorship, the Jews met some opposition but were supported in their struggles by the Dutch West India Company. For example, the right to own land was at first prohibited to the Jews. However, their first private land purchase was made in 1675 and was recorded in the Asser-Levy Deed, owned by the Museum of the City of New York (MCNY), which is illustrated in the exhibition. Gradually the Jews became an integral part of life in New Amsterdam.
>
> On loan to the exhibition from the Chamber of Commerce is the Charter of 1768 illustrating the Jews' part in its formation. Also illustrated is a list of donors to the Church Steeple Fund at Trinity Church, dated 1711, which shows contributors, including several Jewish colonists [some of whom are noted as Adeline Moses Loeb's ancestors in Part III of this book].
>
> During the Revolution, Jewish merchants provided supplies to the troops and many fought in the militia. After the Revolutionary War the Jewish citizens' loyalty was commended by George

Washington in letters to Jewish congregations of New York and Philadelphia, thanking them for their role in the patriots' cause. On loan from Lilly Library of Indiana University, Bloomington, is the original letter written in 1803 to Lieutenant Colonel Jonathan Williams from Lieutenant Simon Levy, reporting for duty after graduating from West Point.

Toward the end of the seventeenth century, important individuals from the Jewish community began to emerge. Portraits in the exhibition highlight several of these prominent families revealing their elegant lifestyle. Portraits of Moses Levy and his wife, Grace Mears Levy [again, ancestors of Adeline Moses Loeb] depict one of the earliest successful merchant families. The pair of paintings are from the Museum of the City of New York.

Also on loan from the Museum of the City of New York is a miniature of Gershom Mendes Seixas, who was the first American-born Jewish religious leader. It was Rabbi Seixas who led most of the congregation to Connecticut and then to Philadelphia during the British occupation in 1776.

From the American Jewish Historical Society there is a portrait of Bilhah Abigaill Franks, attributed to Duyckinck, and excerpts of letters to her son in England. The letters are rich in detail and provide insight into the family's social attitudes, as well as lend personal interpretation to the exhibition. Abigaill Franks's daughter Phila married Oliver DeLancey, the son of Stephen DeLancey, who built what is now known as Fraunces Tavern. [Oliver, however, was not a reputable character, as revealed in Judith Endelman's genealogical study of Adeline Moses' ancestry in the last section of this book.] Another painting from the collection of the American Jewish Historical Society is a portrait of Jonas Phillips attributed to Charles Willson Peale. A merchant in European goods, Jonas Phillips served in the Philadelphia Militia during the American Revolution.

The religious life of the Jewish community is explored through objects on loan from several congregations and cultural institutions. From the New-York Historical Society is a porcelain plate showing the Mill Street Synagogue in 1750, only a few blocks from Fraunces Tavern Museum. Religious objects in the exhibition include the beautiful silver *Rimonim* bells by Myer Myers, lent by Mikveh Israel in Philadelphia. *Rimonim* are ornamental bells that decorate the wooden poles of the Torah.

A Torah arrangement from the Congregation Shearith Israel includes tin bells or *Rimonim*, a silver Torah pointer, and an Omer Scroll that computes the days between the holidays. Among objects on loan from The Jewish Museum are a glass Star of David and a seventeenth-century Purim Megillah, which tells the story of the Purim holiday.

Artistic contributions from the first Jewish colonists are represented by Myer Myers, the first Jewish artist born in America. A renowned silversmith, Myer Myers created works used in every facet of New York's society. He crafted elegant pieces for both Jewish and Christian households. Religious objects were made for both his congregation and Christian churches. Works by Myer Myers included in the exhibition are a tankard with the Hamilton Coat of Arms from the Philadelphia Museum of Art, a sauceboat and two salvers from Bernard and S. Dean Levy, Inc., a sugar bowl with the Goelet family crest from the Brooklyn Museum, a candlesnuffer from The Jewish Museum, and a circumcision set from the American Jewish Historical Society. An ornate silver tea kettle made in 1745 by Paul de Lamerie, decorated with the Franks family crest, is from the collection of the Metropolitan Museum of Art.

The exhibit was a terrific hit. Radio, television, and newspapers rained positive publicity. The public loved it; the little museum was at times almost overwhelmed

On these two facing pages are highlights from the exhibition "The Jewish Community in Early New York, 1654–1800" held at the Fraunces Tavern Museum on Pearl Street from October 18, 1979, to April 30, 1980.

"*Rimonim*," also called "Torah Finials" and "The Tin Bells." These decorative pieces are used to cover the posts on Torah scrolls. The bells announce the passing by of the holy books as they are marched around the congregation every Sabbath and holiday. Fourteen inches high, they were the work of the famed colonial silversmith Myer Myers. Lent for the exhibit by Congregation Mikveh Israel, Philadelphia.

"Eternal Lamp," or "Sabbath Lamp," used in the synagogue, above the Ark (closet) where the Torah Scrolls are kept. This brass piece, about 32 inches high, was created around 1730 by an unknown artist. Lent by Congregation Shearith Israel, New York.

"Mogen David," or "Star of David," stained glass decorative pieces by an unknown artist in the early nineteenth century. Lent by The Jewish Museum of New York.

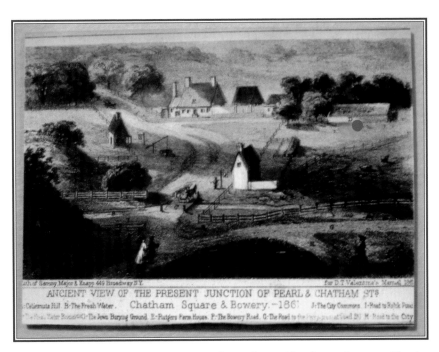

"Ancient View of the Present Junction of Pearl & Chatham Streets, Chatham Square & Bowery, 1861," from an original print from *D. T. Valentine's Manual 1861*. The blue dot shows the location of "The Jews Burying Ground," now known as the Chatham Square Cemetery or the Olive Street Cemetery of Congregation Shearith Israel. It is the oldest remaining Jewish burial ground in New York. Lent by the New York Historical Society.

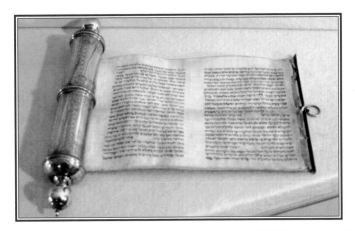

A "Purim Megillah," a single scroll of the complete Old Testament Book of Esther, which is read in its entirety on the holiday of Purim. This particular liturgical parchment scroll has an etched, inlaid silver case and was created by an unidentified artist in the late seventeenth century; it was lent by The Jewish Museum.

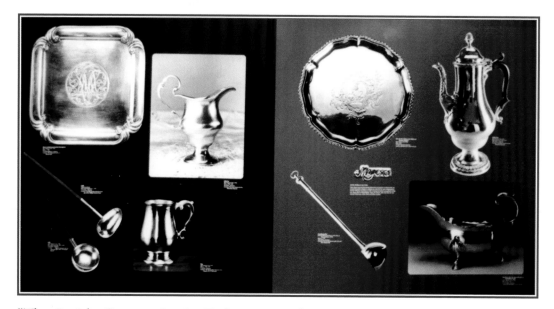

"The Jewish Community in Early New York, 1654–1800" began with a hugely successful run at New York's Fraunces Tavern Museum in October 1979. A photographic version (seen here) toured various cities in the South the following year. The show was then expanded, remounted, and renamed "The Jewish Community in Early America, 1654–1830" for a December 1980 opening at the DAR national headquarters in Washington, D.C.

—Ambassador John L. Loeb Jr. collection

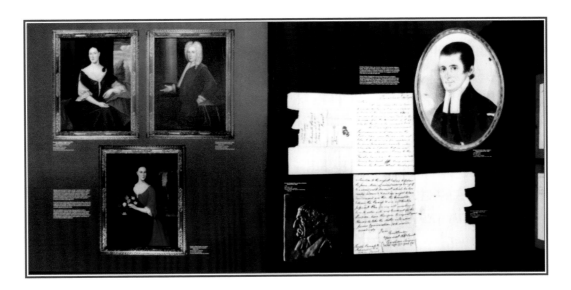

The exhibit drew artifacts from twenty-two museums and synagogues as well as numerous individuals from all around the country. It included silver work by the colonial silversmith Myer Myers, portraits by Thomas Sully, and a great number of religious items, such as silver *Rimonim* bells that decorate the wooden poles of the Torah.

Enjoying a more recent encore at the Museum of the City of New York in 2005 with yet another name variation—"Tolerance and Identity: Jews in Early New York, 1654–1825"—the exhibit played a role in the year-long 350th-anniversary celebration of the arrival of Jews in America.

—Ambassador John L. Loeb Jr. collection

Introduced by DAR President General Patricia Shelby, President Gerald Ford addressed an enthusiastic crowd of over 3,000 at the December 10, 1980, opening of "The Jewish Community in Early America, 1654–1830," the first major loan exhibition ever held at the DAR Museum Gallery in Washington, D.C.

—Anne Day photographer
Ambassador John L. Loeb Jr. collection

John L. Loeb and former First Lady Lady Bird Johnson were among the guests who enjoyed a gala dinner held after President Ford's address.

—Anne Day photograher; Ambassador John L. Loeb Jr. collection

Christians and Jews were refugees in the same new land at approximately the same time; both Christians and Jews, as they settled in the New World, insisted on the separation of church and state. Both Christians and Jews, from our Puritan beginnings, recognized a common bond: They shared a common religious heritage and a common dedication to the application of the principle that all people are created in the image of God, that they are entitled to the freedom and respect incident to their divine origins, and they are obligated to conduct themselves toward others in full recognition of the kinship of all people.

The applause for President Ford's speech was thunderous.

Following his address at the DAR opening of "The Jewish Community in Early America, 1654–1830," President Gerald Ford was "introduced" to the portrait of Adeline Moses Loeb by her grandson, Ambassador John L. Loeb Jr., a member of both the Sons of the American Revolution (SAR) and the Sons of the Revolution in the State of New York (SRNY). President Ford, too, was a member of Sons of the American Revolution, and his mother was a member of the DAR.

—Photo courtesy of the National Daughters of the American Revolution

A series of lectures about the exhibit and related Jewish history were held at the DAR museum on Sunday afternoons in the weeks following. The first speaker was Rabbi Harold S. White of Georgetown University. He was followed by Rabbi Malcolm Stern, president of the Jewish Historical Society of New York and past president of the American Society of Genealogists. At the time, Rabbi Stern was updating his monumental book, *First American Jewish Families: 600 Genealogies, 1654–1988,* first published in 1960, which proved to be a revelation to more than a few Jews—quite a few of whom had been reared as Christians and had not previously known of their Jewish heritage. Few books on genealogy have enjoyed quite so much titillating gossip as this one that included newly discovered Jews.

The last speakers were Linda Simmons of the Corcoran Gallery of Art and Donald Fennimore of the Henry Francis du Pont Winterthur Museum. When the exhibit and the lectures ended in 1981, I felt a strong sense of having accomplished what I'd set out to do: to make known more universally the very important part that Jewish people played in early America. I knew that Granny Loeb would have been pleased.

That might have been the end of the story, but it wasn't. From 2000 to 2001 both Fraunces Tavern Museum and Fraunces Tavern restaurant underwent major renovations, giving both a true eighteenth-century ambience. This necessitated closing down much of the building during the reconstruction and redecoration. Following the completion of the repairs, a reopening of the Adeline Moses Loeb Gallery was scheduled, ironically enough, for September 12, 2001, the day after 9/11 and the infamous bombing of the World Trade Center. The reopening and reception were accordingly rescheduled for November 15, 2001. The revised invitation read as follows:

> Fraunces Tavern Museum has safeguarded and protected American Revolutionary history and the flag for the past ninety-five years. The Museum, just ten blocks from the World Trade Center, was among the many historic landmarks in Lower Manhattan fortunate enough to remain untouched. The New York Fire Department, instrumental in rescuing Fraunces Tavern Museum from fire earlier this year (June 29, 2001), suffered devastating losses in the recent World Trade Center disaster. It is fitting that New York firefighters be honored and also share in the proceeds from this event.

The reopening of the Adeline Moses Loeb Gallery was memorably poignant, and sentiments of patriotism were never more proudly evident. *New York Post* columnist Steve Dunleavy's article about the reopening of the Fraunces

Tavern restaurant in October 2001 gave voice to the way most of us felt at the gallery opening:

> Two floors above me, on December 4, 1783, George Washington said his farewell to arms—and the men who risked their lives for these United States of America gave him a thunderous salute. At Fraunces Tavern, the landmark of patriotism that once stood in the shadow of the World Trade Center, hearts are still broken, but spirits are unshattered. It officially reopens today as a symbol of pride, patriotism, of course, and yes, damn it, downright defiance . . . this is the heart of patriotism—and it can help mend all our hearts.

It was an evening of good food, laughter mixed with tears, and a feeling shared by the crowd in the Adeline Moses Loeb Gallery that mirrored Dunleavy's comment in his column, "Osama, you sure as hell picked on the wrong city." We were already rebounding from the devastating blow to our country. Remembering George Washington and his troops at Fraunces Tavern helped to reinforce our courage and determination.

Even the 2001 event at the Adeline Moses Loeb Gallery was not the end of the ripple effect from that first exhibit at Fraunces Tavern Museum in 1979. In 2005 I engaged the interest of Susan Henshaw Jones, president and director of the Museum of the City of New York, in mounting a similar exhibit to help observe the yearlong 350th anniversary celebration of the arrival of Jews in America. With lead financial support from Susan and Roger Hertog and me, plus additional funds from fourteen other foundations and individuals, the exhibit "Tolerance and Identity: Jews in Early New York, 1654–1825" at the MCNY extended the breadth and scope of the original 1980 exhibit. It ran from May 10 through October 2, 2005. Curated by Dr. Sarah Henry and Dr. Deborah Waters, the show was designed by Jack Diamond of Diamond and Schmitt Architects and again received wonderful press and ongoing accolades that continue to warm my heart.

"Facing the New World: Jewish Portraits in Colonial and Federal America," an exhibit running from September 21 through January 11, 1998, at the Jewish Museum, inspired Ambassador John L. Loeb Jr. to sponsor an Internet exhibit based on the same concept. The Loeb database now has 200 portraits and miniatures featured on the Web sites of the American Jewish Historical Society (AJHS.org) and on Loebjewishportraits.com. It is expected to grow to include as many as 400 pictures.

The face of Grace Mears Levy (1694–1740), the seven-times great-aunt of Ambassador Loeb, looks down on him, actress Anne Jackson (Mrs. Eli Wallach), and actor Eli Wallach, who were among those attending the opening of the 1997 Jewish Museum exhibit. The show went on to the Maryland Historical Society and ran in the late winter and early spring of 1998.

—Ambassador John L. Loeb Jr. collection

One of the most insightful commentaries on the Museum of the City of New York exhibit came from *New York Times* reviewer, Edward Rothstein, on May 23, 2005. He led his article with a description of the pathetic little group of twenty-three Jews, ejected from their home in Brazil, robbed at sea by pirates, and stripped of most of their belongings, to be met in New York by an unwelcoming Peter Stuyvesant, who pleaded with the Dutch West India Company to deny them permanent residence. Governor Stuyvesant was afraid that opening the doors to Jews might result in something even worse—the admission of Lutherans and Papists! But wiser heads prevailed, and his superiors wrote the belligerent Stuyvesant instructing him to "allow everyone to have his own belief, as long as he behaves quietly and legally and gives no offense to his neighbor and does not oppose the government."

Further into his article, Rothstein wrote an eloquent description of the exhibit and its manifestation of Jewish history in America:

> Ultimately it is a tale of successful immigration. The exhibition "Tolerance and Identity," in its portraits and displays, in its accounts of first synagogues and its samples of early correspondence, shows how dynasties of Jewish families took root. Some of these family trees lost branches through assimilation, some through tragedy. But over time they flourished at the center of New York's cultural, political, and religious life of the 18th and early 19th centuries, writing, engaging in commerce and politics, donating books to the first public library, joining the first New York Chamber of Commerce. . . . It gave the Jews their first home in exile. And for all the flaws and failings, something similar was offered to other immigrant groups over the course of 350 years—which is why this anniversary is more important than it might seem.

How true! The admission of Jews to America was most emphatically "more important than it might seem."

—⁓⁓—

PART THREE

THE ANCESTORS
OF ADELINE MOSES LOEB

Judith E. Endelman

CHAPTER ONE

HISTORICAL OVERVIEW

IN A COUNTRY AS YOUNG AS the United States, it is unusual to find a family whose ancestors have been in America for over three hundred years. When that family is Jewish, it is even more unusual. There cannot be more than a handful of Jewish families who can make such a claim. The number of Jews who lived in America prior to the nineteenth century was small— approximately 1,300 to 1,500 Jews lived in America at the time of the first federal census in 1790.[1] Of this handful of families, many died out, migrated, intermarried, or were otherwise lost to history. The family of Adeline Moses Loeb has not been lost to history, even though they were probably in America for a century before the first census was taken.

Our knowledge of the family's past is most certainly not due to it having been sedentary and unadventurous. The generations prior to Adeline Moses Loeb lived in Germany, England, several West Indian islands, various cities in America—New York, Newport, Charleston, Savannah, Montgomery, Sheffield, and St. Louis—as well as smaller towns in the South and the East. They changed their places of residence with almost every successive generation. Several members of the family seem to have been born with wanderlust. Jacob and Hannah Phillips, for example, lived with their growing family in Newport, Rhode Island; New York City; rural South Carolina; the Dutch island of St. Eustatius; the French island of Martinique; and finally, Charleston, South Carolina.

The history of the Moses family is more than a mere listing of names and dates. Beyond the historical record and the fact that the Moses family can be traced to the late seventeenth century, there is another remarkable characteristic about this particular family history. Each generation is uncannily representative of the American Jewish experience of its respective period. In addition, the members of this family seemed always to be among the vanguard of their time. They were risk takers who struck out, moved on, and ventured where others dared not tread.

ANCESTORS OF
ADELINE MOSES

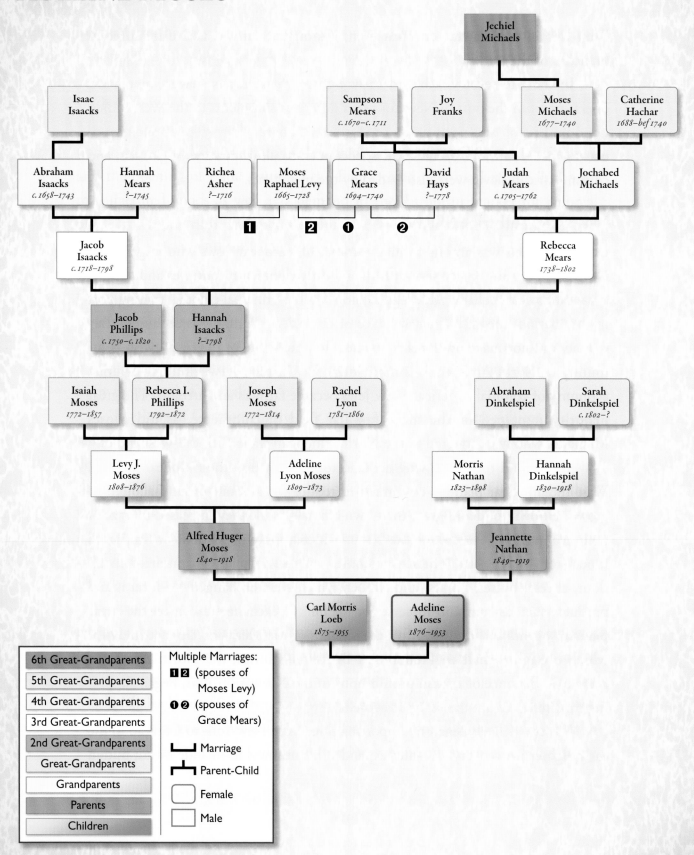

Jechiel Michaels

Isaac Isaacks

Sampson Mears
c. 1670–c. 1711

Joy Franks

Moses Michaels
1677–1740

Catherine Hachar
1688–bef 1740

Abraham Isaacks
c. 1658–1743

Hannah Mears
?–1745

Richea Asher
?–1716

Moses Raphael Levy
1665–1728

Grace Mears
1694–1740

David Hays
?–1778

Judah Mears
c. 1705–1762

Jochabed Michaels

1 **2** **❶** **❷**

Jacob Isaacks
c. 1718–1798

Rebecca Mears
1738–1802

Jacob Phillips
c. 1750–c. 1820

Hannah Isaacks
?–1798

Isaiah Moses
1772–1857

Rebecca I. Phillips
1792–1872

Joseph Moses
1772–1814

Rachel Lyon
1781–1860

Abraham Dinkelspiel

Sarah Dinkelspiel
c. 1802–?

Levy J. Moses
1808–1876

Adeline Lyon Moses
1809–1873

Morris Nathan
1823–1898

Hannah Dinkelspiel
1830–1918

Alfred Huger Moses
1840–1918

Jeannette Nathan
1849–1919

Carl Morris Loeb
1875–1955

Adeline Moses
1876–1953

Legend

| 6th Great-Grandparents |
| 5th Great-Grandparents |
| 4th Great-Grandparents |
| 3rd Great-Grandparents |
| 2nd Great-Grandparents |
| Great-Grandparents |
| Grandparents |
| Parents |
| Children |

Multiple Marriages:

1 **2** (spouses of Moses Levy)

❶ **❷** (spouses of Grace Mears)

└─┘ Marriage

└┬┘ Parent-Child

▢ Female

▢ Male

peas, meat, ham, bacon, and kosher meat (an ecumenical combination of products, to say the least). He had various North American Jewish partners. Like Jacob Mears in Jamaica, he lived in Curaçao for several years and oversaw the business from there. In 1730 Michaels was the largest importer among the Curaçaoan Jews, and was one of the few Ashkenazi Jews in a business dominated by Sephardim. He died in Curaçao in 1740 and was buried in the famous Jewish cemetary there.

Sampson and Joy Mears

Sampson Mears and his brother Jacob were active in many areas of West Indian trade. Like Moses Michaels, they were Ashkenazi Jews in a field where nearly all of the Jewish participants were Sephardic. The two Mears brothers first made their mark as shipowners and merchants in London. Jacob Mears moved to Jamaica and was there during the earthquake of 1692, trading in "Wheat flower, Indico [indigo, a blue dye], Negroes and such like Comodities." Jacob Mears co-owned the sloop *Dolphin* with Colonel Charles Sadler and his son John Sadler. Sampson Mears served as his brother's agent in England, and he and his family returned to London to watch over their London activities, while Jacob continued to oversee their business affairs in Jamaica.[4]

The earliest Jewish immigrants to London from Central Europe joined the Spanish and Portuguese congregation in Bevis Marks Synagogue. In 1690 the growing Ashkenazi community established its own congregation in nearby Duke's Place. In 1704 a group of Jews with ties to Hamburg, including Mears, attempted to set up a *bet midrash* (prayer and study hall) in a private home near the Duke's Place Synagogue. Concerned by this potential competition, the leadership of the Duke's Place Synagogue and the Sephardic community persuaded (perhaps bribed) the Court of Aldermen of the City of London to prevent establishment of the *bet midrash*. Three years later, however, in 1707, the leader of the Hamburg group, Marcus Moses, did open a synagogue in his home.[5]

Sampson and his wife, Joy Mears, never settled in North America, but their three children did. Sampson Mears died in London around the year 1711. Seven years later, his daughter Grace was married off to Moses Levy, a widower and one of colonial New York's wealthiest Jews. A few years after Grace Mears's marriage, her brother Judah migrated to New York. Sometime before 1734, Judah Mears married Jochabed Michaels, daughter of Moses and Catherine Michaels, thus uniting the Mears and Michaels families, from whom Adeline Moses Loeb is descended.

Judah and Jochabed Mears

Judah Mears may have been attracted to New York by the business ties available there through his sister's marriage to Moses Levy. Judah was a merchant shipper, like his father, Sampson Mears. He was probably active in providing West Indian sugar planters with provisions, like his father-in-law, Moses Michaels. By the early eighteenth century, New York was a relatively tolerant community with no significant restrictions against Jews. Even the rights and privileges granted to London Jews did not compare with the civil liberties enjoyed by New York Jewry. New York Jews were quick to take advantage of these civil privileges. Like many others, Judah Mears applied for and received the status of a freeman of New York City in 1738. Unlike Germany, where Jews were not permitted to own land, colonial New York imposed no such restrictions, and Judah Mears owned property in Manhattan and Huntington, Long Island. Sampson Mears's decision to migrate from Germany had been a fortunate one, for he and his children prospered in the less restrictive atmosphere of the Anglo-American world.

Jacob and Rebecca Isaacks

In 1760, Rebecca, the daughter of Judah and Jochabed Mears, married Jacob Isaacks, the New York–born son of another German immigrant and merchant shipper, Abraham Isaacks.[6] Abraham Isaacks was not only an overseas merchant, but a landowner as well. He owned several properties, including a 120-acre farm in Somerset County, New Jersey. His son Jacob preferred to remain in commerce, an area of economic life with which he was more familiar. When his father died in 1743, Jacob sold all of his father's property.

New York was not the only North American community to have a Jewish settlement in the late seventeenth century. A small group of Jews settled in

Newport, Rhode Island, in 1658. The Newport Jewish community experienced its greatest growth and prosperity between 1740 and 1770—decades that marked the period of Newport's greatest economic prosperity. Boston's dominance as the principal port of entry for English goods was undermined during the long period of military tension between France and England (1743–1760), which caused heavy losses in men and ships. Philadelphia, New York, Providence, and Newport, as well as other ports, all captured some of Boston's business.

Newport's ships collected and discharged cargo along the whole American coast and into the Caribbean. Most of the earnings of Newport's merchants came from trading, carrying, and insurance services. Rhode Island was also the principal center of the American slave trade. Its merchant shippers carried rum to Africa to buy slaves, whom they then sold to planters in Virginia and the Carolinas. Jacob Isaacks was one of a number of New York Jewish merchants attracted to Newport. At the community's peak, there may have been as many as a thousand Jews living in Newport.

Jacob Isaacks's business career was diverse. He owned ships, sent trading ships of provisions to the West Indies, and insured other carriers. He sold African slaves as well as such imported goods as English tea and West Indian rum in Newport.

With the final cessation of hostilities between France and England in 1763, the French were virtually excluded from North America. The British now turned their attention to their own colonists, authorizing their colonial agents to use stricter methods to prevent smuggling and to enact a series of new taxes. All of these actions badly hurt Newport's economy. Overseas trade was no longer as profitable as it had been, and Jacob Isaacks was one of several Jewish merchants who filed for bankruptcy in 1771–1772. Isaacks left the field of overseas trade and tried to make a living locally by selling African slaves, imported goods, and real estate.

In 1776 the British occupied Newport and, like most of the Jewish community, Jacob Isaacks and his family fled the city. Although the Isaacks family returned to Newport after the Revolutionary War, neither Isaacks nor his adopted city ever regained their former prosperity.

St. Eustatius harbor, c. 1760

In the 1760s, Sampson Mears, Adeline Moses Loeb's five-times great-grandfather, settled in the Dutch colony of St. Eustatius, a small island east of Puerto Rico that had attracted a Jewish community dating back to 1725. Seafaring Jews, merchant shippers, and traders were drawn to the island because it was a free port, and they became a substantial part of the island's white population. The island's Jewish community continued to grow throughout the eighteenth century, and in 1739 a synagogue, Honen Dalim, was founded.

Jewish families in the West Indies were frequently linked with families in the North American colonies through business as well as through marriage, and sometimes through both.

Ruins of Honen Dalim Synagogue – Oranjestad, St. Eustatius

Mikvé Israel-Emanuel (Snoa) Synagogue (second building 1730) – Willemstad, Curaçao

The Caribbean

Early Jewish Communities and Congregations (1620s–1790s)

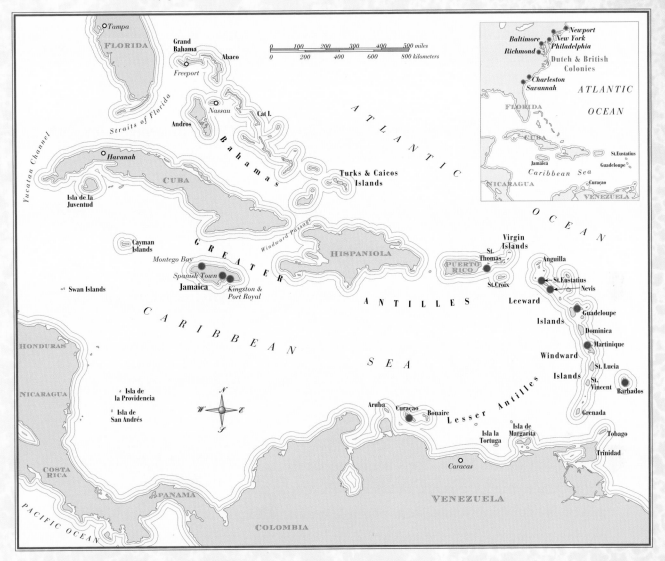

Island	Jewish Community Founded	Congregation Name	Congregation Established
Barbados	c. 1628	Nidhei Israel	1654
Curaçao	1651	Mikve Israel-Emanuel	1651
Guadeloupe	1654		
Jamaica	1530	Kahal Kadosh Neveh Shalom	1662
		Shaar Hashamayim	1692
		Kahal Kadosh Mikveh Yisrael	1796
		also Montego Bay and Port Royal	
Martinique	c. 1620		
Nevis	c. 1671	Charlestown	c. 1679
St. Eustatius	c. 1720	Honen Dalim	1739
St. Thomas	1781	St. Thomas	1796

Spanish Colonies (Marranos/Hidden Jews) — CUBA

British, Dutch, or French Colonies — Colonies

Island Group — **Bahamas**

Island — **Martinique**

Jewish settlement ● — *Kingston*

Other major settlement ○ — *Freeport*

The Newport synagogue, which had been dedicated in 1763, reopened after the war, but the Jewish community soon dwindled to a handful of families. Independence from Britain had disrupted the trade patterns established during the colonial period. The younger generation of Newport Jews relocated to New York and other cities with greater economic prospects. When George Washington visited Newport on August 17, 1790, he received a message of welcome from Congregation Jeshuat Israel, but the synagogue was in serious decline. The last surviving member of the original Jewish community of Newport moved to New York in 1822.[7]

Jacob and Hannah Phillips

Hannah, the eldest daughter of Jacob and Rebecca Mears Isaacks, was married in Newport in 1785 to Jacob Phillips, an immigrant from England who had settled in South Carolina and served in South Carolina's militia during the Revolutionary War. Like all of her nine siblings (excluding those who died in infancy), Hannah and her new husband did not remain in the declining port city of Newport but moved on to areas of greater economic promise.

Undoubtedly the family's fortunes suffered from the economic dislocation and depression of the postwar years, and they tried to make a living in several places—New York, St. Eustatius, South Carolina, and Martinique. Jacob Phillips was the last of the Moses-Loeb family ancestors to make a living in the West Indian trade. After the death of his wife in Martinique in 1798, Jacob Phillips moved his family to Charleston, South Carolina. Thus, he was responsible for moving the family from the mercantile and increasingly industrial North to the plantation economy of the South. The family would remain in the South for three generations before moving back to the North in the late nineteenth century.

Isaiah and Rebecca Moses

In 1807 Jacob Phillips's fifteen-year-old daughter Rebecca married Isaiah Moses, a thirty-five-year-old widower with four young children. The match resembled that of her great-grandfather's sister Grace Mears to Moses Levy some ninety years earlier, and was probably arranged for similar reasons. The limited resources of the bride's family could not attract a better husband for their daughter, so she contented herself with an older—albeit well-to-do—widower with young children. In addition to caring for four stepchildren, Rebecca bore twelve children herself, all of whom lived to adulthood—remarkable in a period of high infant mortality. Like his father-in-law, Jacob Phillips, Isaiah Moses was an immigrant, although from Germany, not England. He probably settled in South Carolina sometime after the end of the Revolutionary War.

The Jews in the Southern states had accommodated themselves to the plantation economy by providing a variety of commercial services to plantation owners as jobbers, brokers, auctioneers, and peddlers. Although few Jews became plantation owners, they accepted the Southern ideal of gentility (and the practice of slaveholding) represented by plantation life. Even the most successful lawyer, politician, or merchant hoped to end his days as a plantation owner.

Isaiah Moses, who began his career as a shopkeeper on Charleston's King Street, was no different. Around 1819 he purchased a moderate-sized plantation at St. James, Goose Creek, near Charleston, where he cultivated rice. After the failure of the plantation in 1841, Isaiah Moses continued to buy and sell slaves, and he leased out his bondsmen on an annual basis, a common source of income for white Southerners.

Levy and Adeline Moses

In 1832 Levy J. Moses, the eldest son of Isaiah and Rebecca Moses, married Adeline L. Moses, another Charleston native. The men of the first five generations of this family were all in business for themselves. Throughout his working life, however, Levy Moses was an employee. In the growing economy of the nineteenth century, simple partnerships were no longer adequate for amassing the additional capital needed for expansion, and many Southern Jews developed large brokerage and auctioneering firms. Levy Moses worked for one of these firms as a bookkeeper and a notary public.

The nine children of Levy and Adeline Moses were all born in Charleston, but they did not stay there. A planter aristocracy dominated the city and it offered few economic opportunities outside the agricultural sector. Shortly before the outbreak of the Civil War, their sons Joseph and Alfred left Charleston for Montgomery, Alabama. Their younger brothers Mordecai and Henry soon joined them, and three of the brothers (Joseph may have been too old) served in the Alabama Regiment during the Civil War. After the war, the brothers entered the real estate and insurance business in Montgomery. The firm of Moses Bros. profited in real estate development and speculation to such an extent that the remainder of the family—their youngest brother Judah, their sisters, and parents—also moved to Montgomery.

Alfred and Jeannette Moses

As Moses Bros. prospered, Alfred Moses, the leading member of the firm, began to look beyond the city of Montgomery for property to develop. It was probably on one of these scouting trips through the South that he met and married Jeannette Nathan of Louisville, Kentucky, the eldest daughter of German immigrants. The couple was married in Louisville in 1871 and returned to Montgomery, where all of their five children were born.

Alfred Moses' career as a real estate developer suggests the hectic pace of industrial development in the South in the late nineteenth century as the South attempted to convert its slave-centered agrarian economy to a more industrial one that would be able to compete with the North. Alfred Moses, like many other investors, sought a project that would duplicate the phenomenal success of Birmingham, an industrial city that had provided tremendous profits for its initial developers. Unfortunately, Alfred Moses' project—the founding of Sheffield in northern Alabama—was not another Birmingham. Like the majority of the boomtowns of the late nineteenth century, Sheffield was a failure—Alfred Moses and Moses Bros. were ruined. After nearly one hundred years of residence in the South, the Moses family moved north again, this time to St. Louis, Missouri.

Carl and Adeline Loeb

Alfred Moses did not prosper in St. Louis, but his daughter Adeline's marriage in 1896 to Carl M. Loeb (a recent German immigrant) brought success to the family once again. Carl Loeb was born in 1875 in Frankfurt am Main. In 1892, Metallgesellschaft, then the German parent company of the American Metal Company, sent Carl Loeb (at the age of seventeen) to work in their St. Louis office. He soon met and (at the age of twenty-one), married nineteen-year-old Adeline Moses. By 1904 he was made a vice president of the American Metal Company, and the couple moved to New York City. In 1914 he became president of the firm. By 1917 he was also one of the founders and developers of the Climax Molybdenum Company and became its first president. In 1929, at odds with the board of directors, he left American Metal Company and ostensibly retired. His son, John Langeloth Loeb, said of him in 1959, "He had too much energy and too much wisdom to stay on the sidelines for long. In 1931 he formed the investment banking firm of Carl M. Loeb and Co., now Carl M. Loeb, Rhoades & Co. Later my brother Henry joined us and two of Father's grandsons."[8] Through later mergers of Loeb, Rhoades with Hornblower Weeks Noyes and Trask in 1978 and Shearson Hayden Stone, Inc. in 1979, Shearson Loeb Rhoades was for a time the second largest brokerage house in the country.

The succeeding chapters of this book tell the history of ten families that make up seven generations of the Moses family. The story begins with the founding generation of Sampson Mears and Moses Michaels, whose children's marriage—Judah Mears and Jochabed Michaels—began the ancestry of Adeline Moses Loeb. Eight of the families profiled are direct ancestors, while two chapters profile collateral relatives. Grace Mears, elder sister of Judah Mears, was the second wife of Moses Levy, one of the most prominent Jewish merchants in New York at the time. Samson Mears, the only son of Judah Mears, struggled to make a living during the Revolutionary War. These two couples—Moses and Grace Mears Levy and Samson and Hannah Robles Mears—lived through turbulent periods of our nation's history. The details of their lives open a window into the hardships of life during the early years of our country.

The generations of Adeline Moses Loeb provide us with American history at its most intimate—not dry recitations of facts and figures, but history populated

the restrictive atmosphere of German life—factors that encouraged many ambitious young Jews to leave Germany—probably account for the migration of Sampson and Jacob Mears from Hamburg to London in the late seventeenth century.

In London, the Mears brothers became merchant shippers. Sampson Mears watched over the brothers' affairs from London while Jacob set up operations in Jamaica. He is reported to have been there during the earthquake of 1692. Sampson seems to have lived in Jamaica only briefly (his eldest child, Grace, was born in Spanishtown, Jamaica, in 1694, but he was in London in 1699). The brothers actively traded between London, the West Indies, and North America, dealing in "Wheat flower, Indico, Negroe slaves, and such like Comodities [*sic*]," as well as Madeira wine, gold, silver, and various other goods. Jacob co-owned the sloop *Dolphin* with Colonel Charles Sadler and his son John Sadler; Sampson served as the ship's agent from London.[1]

In the spring of 1699 the *Dolphin* set out from Jamaica to Madeira to buy wines. The sloop had been troubled by a leak and the owners directed the master, Isaac Adderly, to run the *Dolphin* to another port if the leak reappeared, rather than return to Jamaica. Two days out, the leak did reappear and Adderly decided to sail for Bermuda to have it repaired. In Bermuda, the crew fell prey to the despotic governor of Bermuda, Samuel Day, who confiscated the sloop's sails and refused to clear the vessel for sail once the repairs were completed. The brothers' relentless battle for release of the sloop, its crew, and cargo continued for over two years. Their petitions to the Crown and their documentation of Day's unreasonable actions ultimately led to Day's dismissal by the Board of Trade in London.[2]

This case reveals the degree to which Jewish merchants were treated as equals to other merchants. (The Mears brothers did not act only for themselves. There were other non-Jewish owners of the *Dolphin* who do not appear in the case at all.) Although they did not hide their identity, the fact that the Mears brothers were Jewish is not referenced in the court proceedings. The Board of Trade, to which they made their appeal, did not care about a plaintiff's religion—its primary concern was trade. At the time, only Great Britain and Holland would have recognized the Mears brothers as merchants and not *Jewish* merchants.

The Mears brothers understood the importance of trade between England and the colonies. Thus, they made their complaint with confidence that it would be addressed. And it was.[3]

The Mears brothers' business activities were not confined to merchant shipping. Sampson, the brother who remained in London, sold cloth, loaned money to the gentry, and dealt in diamonds and other precious jewels.

Court cases preserved in the Public Record Office provide a window into the business practices of eighteenth-century Anglo-Jewish merchants. Members of the British aristocracy often hired Jewish merchants to procure expensive merchandise such as precious gems, diamonds, jewelry, and watches for them, and to lend them money. When a client couldn't pay his bill or make good on the loan, these disputes often ended up in court, as did several cases involving Jacob Mears in the early eighteenth century.[4]

Jews had lived in England as early as the late eleventh century, when Jewish merchants from northern France crossed the English Channel, following the Norman Conquest of 1066. However, in 1290 Edward I expelled the Jewish community, which numbered about two thousand.

The modern Anglo-Jewish community dates from the 1630s, when merchants of converso origin (the descendants of baptized Jews from Spain and Portugal) began settling in London, attracted by its growing international economic importance. Other openly Jewish and converso merchants and their families followed. Although their residence was technically illegal, the government and religious authorities turned a blind eye. In the winter of 1655-1656 a series of events resulted in the emergence of a permanent, government-tolerated Jewish community.

Radical Puritans were the first to propose the readmission of Jews to England, convinced that England would then play an active role in bringing about the millennium and the End of Days. A key aspect of this belief was the conversion of Jews. In the 1640s, with the coming of the English Civil War, the belief in conversionist millenarianism spread. Some who shared the view that the coming of the millennium was at hand (perhaps to occur as soon as 1655 or 1656) urged the immediate readmission of the Jews to hasten the coming of the End of Days.

Reports of the growth of this pro-Jewish sentiment reached Amsterdam. Menasseh ben Israel, a communal rabbi and a Portuguese New Christian by birth, responded to these developments with great interest. As the child of parents who had suffered at the hand of the Inquisition, he wanted to find new lands of refuge for Jewish settlement. He was also a messianist who imagined that the return of the Jews to England would hasten the coming of the messiah. In 1650 he published *The Hope of Israel*, which marked the beginning of a campaign to obtain government permission for the Jews to openly resettle in England. These campaigns and petitions went on for several years. Although no formal order of readmission was ever issued by the British government, in March 1656 the Council of State granted permission for a group of Spanish Jews to gather privately for Jewish worship and acquire a burial ground in London. Following this, an openly Jewish community began to emerge.[5]

The Mears family lived in Goodman's Fields, an area just outside the eastern border of London that became increasingly popular for middle-class Jews. Although the earliest Jews to settle in London were primarily exiles from the Iberian Peninsula, the Mears family was part of a growing Ashkenazi community. By 1700 the Ashkenazim had formed their own synagogue, later known as the Great Synagogue of London. A small group of Ashkenazim, including Sampson Mears, attempted to form a second synagogue and study house in the home of Abraham Nathan in St. Mary Axe in 1704. Moses Hart, then president of the Great Synagogue, was uneasy about this development, believing that the new institution "would undermine the position of the existing Ashkenazi synagogue . . . and . . . increase anti-Jewish feeling among the general population." Hart appealed to the head of the Sephardic community, Abraham Mendez, for support, and the two approached the Court of Aldermen hoping they would deny the new group permission to organize. The court held a hearing on the matter on March 22, 1704. After listening to the arguments of both parties, the court denied the group permission to form the new synagogue and ordered them to forfeit £500 each—one-half payable to the queen and one-half to the poor—if they violated the ban. At the end of 1706, Marcus Moses successfully petitioned to have the ban overruled. In the following year, 1707, he opened the new synagogue in his home. The congregation became known as the Hambro Synagogue, a nod to the organizers' Hamburg origins.[6]

Sampson Mears died in 1711—his burial place is unknown—and letters of administration were granted to his widow "Joy Meers of the parish of St. Botolph, Aldgate, London" on April 24, 1711.[7] Jacob Mears outlived his brother Sampson by several years and continued to conduct business in both Jamaica and London.

Although Sampson and Joy Mears never settled in North America, all three of their children did. Grace, the eldest daughter, who married Moses Levy of New York in 1718, was the first to settle in North America. Both her brother Judah and younger sister Tabitha followed her there. Sampson and Jacob Mears had done business with Moses Levy for several years. His marriage to Grace may have helped settle a suit that Joy Mears had brought against her future son-in-law in 1717.

Joy Mears and Moses Hart, representing Jacob Mears (who was in Jamaica), filed the lawsuit against Moses Levy in London. The Mears brothers had done business with Levy, then a resident of New York, between 1705 and 1707, and at one point had shipped him goods to sell valued at £112 9s. 7½d. The litigants alleged that Levy had promised either to pay for or return the goods to London, but he had never done so. Levy claimed that he had never had any dealings with the Mears brothers. The Mears complaint stated that "Witnesses who could and would prove the truth of . . . the premisses [sic] are either dead or beyond the seas or gone into places remote and unknown . . . so that your Orators are remediless in the premises of the Common Law and are only relievable by the aid of this Court."[8]

The suit demonstrated some of the risks inherent in the overseas trade. If a New York merchant chose not to pay a bill or to claim he never received a certain shipment from Jamaica or London, there was little that could be done beyond embarrassing him into payment by taking the matter to court.

It is not known if Moses Levy ever paid the debt, but within the year he had married Joy Mears's eldest daughter, Grace, and taken her back to live with him in New York. Grace was then twenty-four, well beyond the typical age of marriage at the time. Levy, one of New York's wealthiest Jews, was a fifty-two-year-old widower with five children. Although Levy was less than an ideal husband (he was five years older than her father), Grace probably had little choice in the matter, as he was most likely the best husband that Joy Mears, with limited resources, could provide for her daughter. Did Levy agree to marry Grace so that Joy and Jacob Mears would drop the charges against him? The answer is lost to history.

DESCENDANTS OF
SAMPSON MEARS & JOY FRANKS

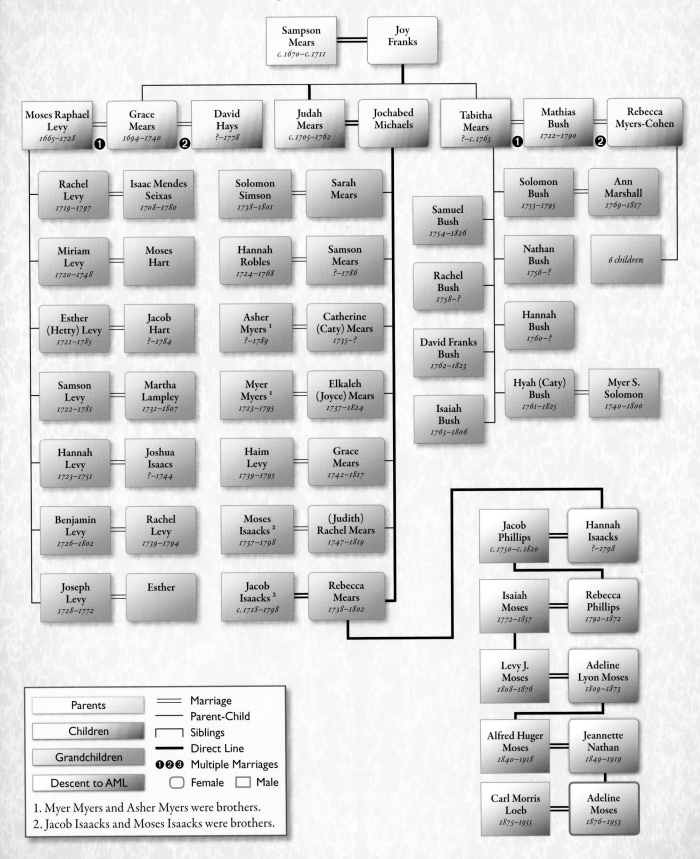

Sampson Mears *c. 1670–c. 1711* — Joy Franks

Moses Raphael Levy *1665–1728* ❶ — Grace Mears *1694–1740* ❷ — David Hays *?–1778*

Judah Mears *c. 1705–1762* — Jochabed Michaels

Tabitha Mears *?–c. 1763* ❶ — Mathias Bush *1722–1790* ❷ — Rebecca Myers-Cohen

Rachel Levy *1719–1797* — Isaac Mendes Seixas *1708–1780*

Miriam Levy *1720–1748* — Moses Hart

Esther (Hetty) Levy *1721–1785* — Jacob Hart *?–1784*

Samson Levy *1722–1781* — Martha Lampley *1731–1807*

Hannah Levy *1723–1751* — Joshua Isaacs *?–1744*

Benjamin Levy *1726–1802* — Rachel Levy *1739–1794*

Joseph Levy *1728–1772* — Esther

Solomon Simson *1738–1801* — Sarah Mears

Hannah Robles *1724–1768* — Samson Mears *?–1786*

Asher Myers [1] *?–1789* — Catherine (Caty) Mears *1735–?*

Myer Myers [1] *1723–1795* — Elkaleh (Joyce) Mears *1737–1824*

Haim Levy *1739–1795* — Grace Mears *1742–1817*

Moses Isaacks [2] *1737–1798* — (Judith) Rachel Mears *1747–1819*

Jacob Isaacks [2] *c. 1718–1798* — Rebecca Mears *1738–1802*

Samuel Bush *1754–1826*

Rachel Bush *1758–?*

David Franks Bush *1762–1823*

Isaiah Bush *1763–1806*

Solomon Bush *1753–1795* — Ann Marshall *1769–1817*

Nathan Bush *1756–?*

Hannah Bush *1760–?*

Hyah (Caty) Bush *1761–1825* — Myer S. Solomon *1740–1800*

6 children

Jacob Phillips *c. 1750–c. 1820* — Hannah Isaacks *?–1798*

Isaiah Moses *1772–1857* — Rebecca Phillips *1792–1872*

Levy J. Moses *1808–1876* — Adeline Lyon Moses *1809–1873*

Alfred Huger Moses *1840–1918* — Jeannette Nathan *1849–1919*

Carl Morris Loeb *1875–1955* — Adeline Moses *1876–1953*

Legend:
- Parents
- Children
- Grandchildren
- Descent to AML
- ══ Marriage
- — Parent-Child
- ⌐ Siblings
- ━ Direct Line
- ❶❷❸ Multiple Marriages
- ◯ Female ☐ Male

1. Myer Myers and Asher Myers were brothers.
2. Jacob Isaacks and Moses Isaacks were brothers.

The Children of Sampson and Joy Franks Mears

1. **Grace** (born 1694, Spanishtown, Jamaica; died October 14, 1740, New York City). Married Moses Raphael Levy (born 1665, Germany; died June 14, 1728, New York) in 1718, in London, England. Levy was a widower and a wealthy New York merchant. They had seven children: Rachel, Miriam, Esther, Samson, Hannah, Benjamin, and Joseph. After Levy's death, Grace married David Hays (born New Rochelle, New York; died June 1778) on April 28, 1735. Hays was also a widower and New York merchant.

2. **Judah** (born c. 1705, London, England; died June 7, 1762, St. François, Guadeloupe, West Indies). Married Jochabed Michaels, daughter of Moses and Catherine Michaels, in the 1730s, in New York. Judah came to America about 1728 and was a New York merchant. They had seven children: Catherine (Caty), Elkaleh (Joyce), Rebecca, Grace, (Judith) Rachel, Sarah, and Samson. The marriage of Judah Mears and Jochabed Michaels united the Mears and Michaels families. **Adeline Moses Loeb is a direct descendant of their daughter, Rebecca.**

3. **Tabitha** (died c. 1763). Married Mathias Bush (born May 10, 1722, Prague; died March 29, 1790, Philadelphia, Pennsylvania). They lived in Philadelphia, Pennsylvania. Tabitha and Mathias Bush had eight children: Solomon, Samuel, Nathan, Rachel, Hannah, Hyah (Caty), David Franks, and Isaiah. When Tabitha died, Mathias married Rebecca Myers-Cohen in 1764.[9]

1. Friedman, "Jacob Mears and Simon Valentine," 77–82; Cohen, "Sampson and Jacob Mears," 234–35; Complaint of Thomas Wood.
2. Cohen, "Sampson and Jacob Mears," 234–39.
3. Cohen, "Sampson and Jacob Mears," 241–42.
4. Complaint of Jacob Mears; Complaint of John Vaughn.
5. Endelman, *The Jews of Britain*, 18–26.
6. Roth, *The Great Synagogue*, 36–37; Hart, "The Family of Mordecai Hamburger," 57–59.
7. Alexander, *Notes*, 92.
8. Complaint of Matthew Brandon.
9. Stern, *First American*, 28, 104, 154, 190; Alexander, *Notes*, 93–94.

CHAPTER THREE

MOSES MICHAELS
(1677–1740)

and

CATHERINE HACHAR MICHAELS
(1688–before 1740)

MOSES MICHAELS AND SAMPSON MEARS shared a similar northern German background. However, Sampson Mears came from the city of Hamburg, while Moses Michaels was from Herzfeld, a small town in Westphalia, a region of northwestern Germany that borders Holland.

When Moses Michaels left Herzfeld, he probably first went to Amsterdam or London before continuing his journey to New York. When he arrived in New York City in the late seventeenth or early eighteenth century, it was a brawling young frontier town, and he was one of the first Ashkenazi Jews to settle there.

We do not know precisely when Moses Michaels came to New York City or the date and location of his marriage to Catherine Hachar. However, by 1707 the couple were married residents of New York. In that year, Jacob de Porta, a Sephardic Jew, brought a suit against them in Mayor's Court. De Porta claimed that Moses and Catherine Michaels owed him £18. The Michaels swore "upon their oath that the said Katherine [*sic*] while she was solo [unmarried] did not assume upon herself to pay unto the said Jacob the . . . sum of £18 or any part thereof. . . ." De Porta lost the suit.[1]

Moses and Catherine Michaels lived in the South Ward, the location of Congregation Shearith Israel, which had been founded around 1706. The Jewish population of New York City was small. Twenty Jews were listed in the unpublished assessment list of February 1734 out of a total population of about 10,000. Moses Michaels is listed as one of thirty-seven dues-paying members of the congregation in the earliest known records of the synagogue, which date from 1720. The synagogue records for the years 1721–1727 have not been located, but between 1728 and 1730 Moses Michaels made numerous contributions to the construction of the first synagogue building. In a gesture of neighborliness, Michaels was one of seven Jews who contributed to a fund to build a steeple for Trinity Church in 1711.[2]

New York City in the early eighteenth century was little more than a trading post. The city lived by trade and commerce, its merchants trading primarily in the commodities of upstate New York, neighboring New Jersey, and the Connecticut Valley. They shipped the products of these interior regions—particularly flour, pork, and furs—to plantations on the Southern Coast as well as to the West Indies.

Moses Michaels was attracted to the flourishing North American trade with the West Indies. As the demand for sugar on the European market increased, sugar planters increased the amount of sugar they raised, thus reducing the amount of land allocated for growing their own personal food and livestock. They became increasingly dependent on imported foods from the North American colonies. The West Indian planters imported meat, flour, cheese, butter, horses, and timber in exchange for island produce such as rum and molasses, or for bills of exchange drawn on the sugar planters' agents in London. After the signing of the Treaty of Utrecht in 1713, which brought a temporary end to French and British hostilities, the North American traders defied various restrictive British Navigation Acts, such as the requirement that all colonial produce be exported on English vessels or colonial-owned ships with English captains. The North American traders began supplying the French and Dutch islands as well, as they sought additional markets where they could sell their surplus products.

Moses Michaels's foreign-born status placed additional restrictions on his economic activities. Aliens in England and in the English colonies could not hold land or other real property, own or hold a share in a British sailing ship, or engage in the colonial trade. They also had to pay special alien duties, such as discriminatory customs rates and special port fees. These alien-born Jews could not become naturalized citizens by the expensive means of sponsoring a private bill through

Parliament because every petitioner was required to receive the sacrament in the Church of England and to swear the oaths of supremacy and allegiance "upon the true faith of a Christian." The only alternative for a foreign-born Jew like Moses Michaels was to be made a free denizen by the purchase of royal letters patent, a costly measure and one that did not confer all the benefits of naturalization. Endenization gave one the right to engage in colonial trade, for example, but did not grant exemption from alien duties.[3]

Michaels undertook the expensive process of endenization in 1713, and thus gained the right to engage in the British colonial trade. However, as far as we know, he traded principally between New York and the Dutch island of Curaçao. He became one of the leading Jewish merchants in Curaçao, particularly in the importation of flour from New York, a business largely in Jewish hands. Like his in-law Sampson Mears, he was one of only a handful of Ashkenazim in a field of trade made up almost entirely of Sephardic Jews.

The earliest reference to Michaels's business activity dates from 1717, although he was certainly active before that date. In 1717 Michaels and his partner, the Sephardic Abraham Ulloa Sr., were shipping flour from New York to Curaçao. They must have been well-established flour exporters by then, because that year the government secretary on the island, Guillermo Heldewier, asked the two men to declare the price of flour for the week. The partners also shipped candles, bread, and butter from New York, as well as flour.[4]

The Jewish traders in the West Indies usually worked with continental partners, and Moses Michaels was no exception. Between 1720 and 1721 he and Michael Asher of Boston exported flour, meat, bread, butter, peas, ham, and bacon from New York to Curaçao. Between 1731 and 1732 he conducted business with his son Michael Michaels as "Moses Mikal and Zoon." In 1735 he imported flour as "Cruger, Marton and Michael."[5]

Moses Michaels maintained his New York residence at least until 1730, but he must have traveled frequently between New York and Curaçao, maintaining residences in both places. He was probably already well-established in Curaçao by 1718. In that year he refused to pay a supplemental tax of one-half percent levied

Novum Amsterodamum, c. 1643
unknown artist — courtesy of The New York Public Library

N ew York City in the early eighteenth century was little more than a trading post, and most of the city's Jews survived as peddlers, artisans, or small shopkeepers. Those who aspired to greater wealth strove to enter the highly competitive world of the merchant shipper, where fortunes could be made.

Congregation Shearith Israel, Mill Street Synagogue (1730)

Moses Michaels and Catherine Hachar, Abraham Isaacks and Hannah Mears, Judah Mears and Jochabed Michaels, Jacob Isaacks and Rebecca Mears, some of Adeline Moses Loeb's ancestors, were among the founders or early members of Shearith Israel, New York City's first Jewish congregation. The influence of her forebears on the mercantile, philanthropic, and cultural fabric of the city continues to this day.

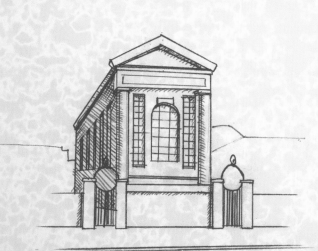

Congregation Shearith Israel, Crosby Street Synagogue (1834)

New York, New York

c. 1755–1790

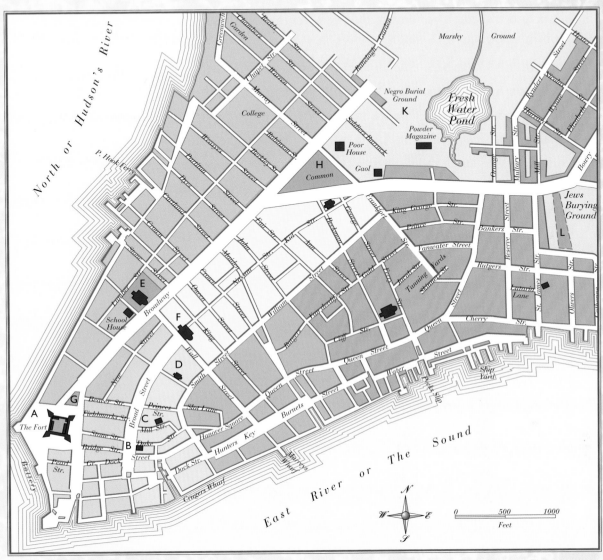

Buildings are not to scale. Placement is approximate.

Public Buildings

A. The Fort
B. Fraunces Tavern
C. Shearith Israel Synagogue (1730)
  [Mill Street Synagogue]
D. Old Dutch Church
E. Trinity Church
F. City Hall

Parks & Cemeteries

G. Bowling Green
H. The Common
K. Negro Burial Ground
L. Jewish Burial Ground (1682)

Private Homes & Businesses

Abraham Isaacks & Hannah Mears;
  also Jacob Isaacks & Rebecca Mears
  [South Ward]

Moses Michaels & Catherine Hachar
  [South Ward]

Judah Mears & Jochabed Michaels
  [East Ward]

Moses Raphael Levy & Richea Asher;
  later with Grace Mears; also his brother
  Samuel Levy [Dock Ward]

Grace Mears & David Hays [Dock Ward]

Gershom M. Seixas & Family [Dock Ward]

South Ward
North Ward
East Ward
West Ward
Dock Ward
Montgomeries Ward

on aliens by the Dutch West India Company, arguing that he was a resident of the island and therefore not required to pay the tax. It is not known whether he ever paid the extra tax.[6]

After 1730 there are no further references to Michaels in New York, and it is likely that he abandoned his New York residence around that time. It may have been during that period that his wife Catherine died. All of his children, however, remained in New York. Until his death in 1740, Michaels continued to ship goods from New York to Curaçao, paying customs duty on a shipment of butter, peas, and kosher meat only a few days before he died in Curaçao on January 25, 1740. He was buried in the Sephardic cemetery, then the only Jewish cemetery on the island.[7]

The discovery of his tombstone by I. S. Emmanuel corrected an old and well-established error in Michaels's lineage. Genealogists identified Moses Michaels as a son of Asher Michaels de Paul and Rebecca Valentine, and therefore a brother of Michael, Rachel, and Richea Asher. Why he had chosen to use a different last name than his brother and sisters was a puzzle, but the birth and death dates all seemed to fit and the descent was accepted. In addition, Moses Michaels was in business with his "brother" Michael Asher between 1720 and 1721, which seemed to confirm the genealogy. However, as Moses Michaels's tombstone clearly indicates, he was the son of Yehiel, not Asher, a name that he changed in English to "Michael" or "Moses Michaels." His tombstone is written in English, Hebrew, and Spanish, but only in Hebrew does it identify his German origins.[8]

Three days before he died, Moses Michaels wrote his will in Dutch. It was written in Curaçao but filed in New York, presumably because all of the heirs were there. (Four daughters, a son, and his son's wife had all died earlier.) His will freed his slave Piro but gave "two negroes, Tham and Prins," to his remaining children and heirs.

The executors of his estate were Levy Maduro and Cohen Henriques, well-known Jewish residents of Curaçao. For four weeks in December 1740, they published a notice in Dutch and English in the *New York Weekly Journal* that "all persons having charge against said estate to deliver vouchers in six months from the first day November 1740."[9]

With the death of Michaels in 1740, Jacob Ribero and Isaac Levy Maduro became the leading Jewish importers of New York produce, but this business, particularly the shipment of flour from New York, gradually passed out of Jewish hands.

In the 1730s Jochabed, a daughter of Moses and Catherine Michaels, married Judah Mears, the only son of Sampson and Joy Mears, in New York. The family of Adeline Moses continues through this union.

—ᚹ—

DESCENDANTS OF
MOSES MICHAELS & CATHERINE HACHAR

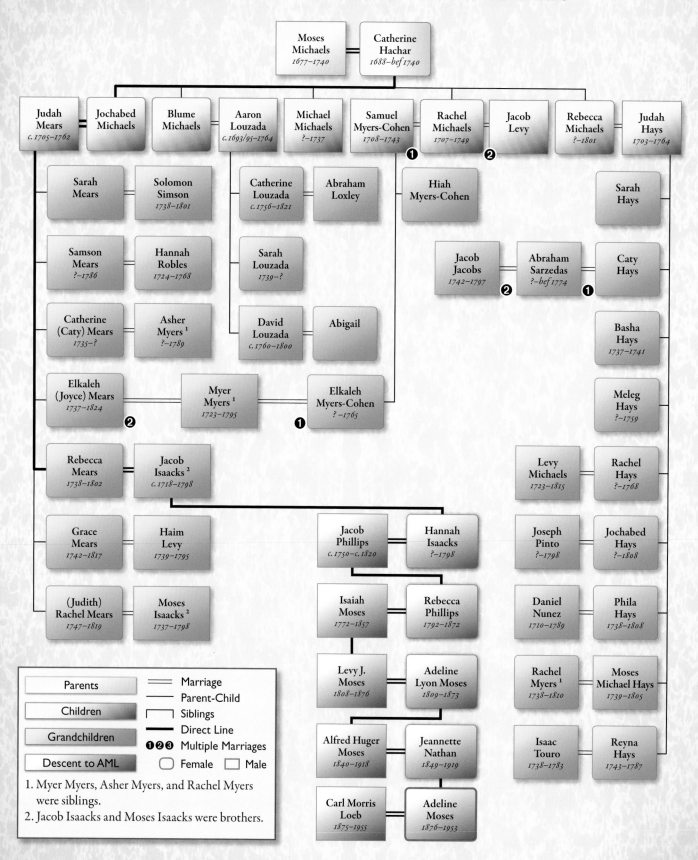

Moses Michaels *1677–1740* — **Catherine Hachar** *1688–bef 1740*

Judah Mears *c. 1705–1762* | **Jochabed Michaels** | **Blume Michaels** | **Aaron Louzada** *c. 1693/95–1764* | **Michael Michaels** *?–1737* | **Samuel Myers-Cohen** *1708–1743* ❶ | **Rachel Michaels** *1707–1749* ❷ | **Jacob Levy** | **Rebecca Michaels** *?–1801* | **Judah Hays** *1703–1764*

Sarah Mears — **Solomon Simson** *1738–1801*

Catherine Louzada *c. 1756–1821* — **Abraham Loxley**

Hiah Myers-Cohen

Sarah Hays

Samson Mears *?–1786* — **Hannah Robles** *1724–1768*

Sarah Louzada *1739–?*

Jacob Jacobs *1742–1797* ❷ — **Abraham Sarzedas** *?–bef 1774* ❶ — **Caty Hays**

Catherine (Caty) Mears *1735–?* — **Asher Myers** [1] *?–1789*

David Louzada *c. 1760–1800* — **Abigail**

Basha Hays *1737–1741*

Elkaleh (Joyce) Mears *1737–1824* ❷ — **Myer Myers** [1] *1723–1795* — **Elkaleh Myers-Cohen** *?–1765* ❶

Meleg Hays *?–1759*

Rebecca Mears *1738–1802* — **Jacob Isaacks** [2] *c. 1718–1798*

Levy Michaels *1723–1815* — **Rachel Hays** *?–1768*

Grace Mears *1742–1817* — **Haim Levy** *1739–1795*

Jacob Phillips *c. 1750–c. 1820* — **Hannah Isaacks** *?–1798*

Joseph Pinto *?–1798* — **Jochabed Hays** *?–1808*

(Judith) Rachel Mears *1747–1819* — **Moses Isaacks** [2] *1737–1798*

Isaiah Moses *1772–1857* — **Rebecca Phillips** *1792–1872*

Daniel Nunez *1710–1789* — **Phila Hays** *1738–1808*

Levy J. Moses *1808–1876* — **Adeline Lyon Moses** *1809–1873*

Rachel Myers [1] *1738–1810* — **Moses Michael Hays** *1739–1805*

Alfred Huger Moses *1840–1918* — **Jeannette Nathan** *1849–1919*

Isaac Touro *1738–1783* — **Reyna Hays** *1743–1787*

Carl Morris Loeb *1875–1955* — **Adeline Moses** *1876–1953*

Legend

Parents	══ Marriage
Children	— Parent-Child
Grandchildren	☐ Siblings
Descent to AML	▬ Direct Line
	❶❷❸ Multiple Marriages
	◯ Female ☐ Male

1. Myer Myers, Asher Myers, and Rachel Myers were siblings.
2. Jacob Isaacks and Moses Isaacks were brothers.

The Children of Moses and Catherine Hachar Michaels

1. **Rachel** (born 1707; died August 20, 1749, New York). Married Samuel Myers-Cohen (born February 1708; died September 21, 1743) as his second wife, sometime after 1732. They had two daughters: Elkaleh (first wife of Myer Myers—see Chapter Four) and Hiah. After Samuel's death, Rachel married Jacob Levy in 1744.

2. **Rebecca** (died April 8, 1801, Boston, Massachusetts). Married Judah Hays (1703–1764), a New York merchant, between the years 1734 and 1735. They had nine children: Meleg, Basha, Phila, Moses Michael, Caty, Reyna, Rachel, Sarah, and Jochabed.

3. **Jochabed**. Married Judah Mears (born c. 1705, London, England; died June 7, 1762, St. François, Guadalupe, West Indies), a New York merchant and son of Sampson and Joy Mears. He arrived in New York from London around 1728. Judah and Jochabed Mears had seven children: Catherine (Caty), Elkaleh (Joyce), Rebecca, Grace, (Judith) Rachel, Sarah, and Samson. The marriage of Jochabed Michaels and Judah Mears united the Mears and Michaels families. **Adeline Moses Loeb is a direct descendant of their daughter, Rebecca.**

4. **Blume**. Married Aaron Louzada (born 1693/95, London, England; died December 27, 1764, Bound Brook, New Jersey), before 1740. Aaron was a merchant of New York and New Jersey, who came to New York in 1717. They had three children: Sarah, Catherine, and David.

5. **Michael** died unmarried, March 1737, in New York, before his father.[10]

1. *Porto v. Michael*, 302–4.
2. Hershkowitz, *Wills,* 59; Hershkowitz, *Letters,* xix; Marcus, *Studies,* 50; "Earliest Extant," 19–25; Alexander, *Notes,* 99.
3. Hershkowitz, "Some Aspects," 15–16; Ross, "Naturalisation," 59–72.
4. Emmanuel, *Precious Stones,* 261–63.
5. Ibid.
6. Ibid.
7. Ibid., 263.
8. Ibid., 260.
9. Hershkowitz, *Wills,* 59–61; Emmanuel, *Precious Stones,* 264–65; Hershkowitz, *Wills,* 60; Emmanuel, *Precious Stones,* 260, 265.
10. Stern, *First American,* 104, 179, 190, 193, 223; Hershkowitz, *Wills,* 39, 60, 65.

CHAPTER FOUR

JUDAH MEARS
(c. 1705–1762)

and

JOCHABED MICHAELS MEARS
(dates unknown)

THE MARRIAGE OF JUDAH MEARS, the only son of Sampson and Joy Mears, to Jochabed Michaels, one of the four daughters of Moses and Catherine Michaels, united two families of similar backgrounds and accomplishments. Sampson Mears and Moses Michaels were both born in Germany and migrated to the West—London and New York City. All of their children were born in one of these two cities. The origins of their spouses—Joy Franks Mears and Catherine Hachar Michaels—are not known. Judah Mears was born in London. Jochabed Michaels was most likely born in New York City.

Sampson Mears and Moses Michaels were both active in the West Indian trade. Sampson Mears, in business with his brother Jacob, traded between London and Jamaica. Moses Michaels shipped merchandise between New York and Curaçao. Like his father and father-in-law, Judah Mears was active in the West Indian trade, supplying West Indian sugar planters with produce from the North American colonies. Judah Mears probably left London for New York some time after 1718, the year his elder sister Grace married the widower Moses Levy, one of colonial New York's wealthiest Jews. His sister's marriage provided him with powerful New York in-laws who could help establish him in business. Mears was in partnership with Jacob Franks, another prosperous merchant and the husband of Abigaill Levy Franks (Moses Levy's eldest daughter by his first wife). He served as one of the executors of Moses Levy's estate in June 1728.

The letters of Abigaill Franks (who was Grace Mears Levy's stepdaughter) are among the few surviving letters written by an eighteenth-century woman of New York. Her correspondence from 1733 to 1748, written primarily to her son Naphtali in London, provide a window into everyday life—the customs, gossip, and personalities not revealed in the dry legal and business contracts and other documents that constitute most of the source material for this period. In 1734 Abigaill Franks wrote to her son Napthali in London about a Mears-Franks business loss:

> Mears and your Father have had a Quarle they don't speak to Each other I cant say but I think Your Father Sometimes to hasty Something it relates to the Affair of the Brig that was Lost However I never Interfere in these matters I was Very Sorry when they had this quarle for I sate by a Silent Listener he is now at Phil[adelphia] where I Suppose he will meet with Polly Colly I wish Your Uncle may relent I cant think of him but with some sampthy of his Unhappiness.[1]

In addition to his shipping business in New York, Judah Mears had business interests in Princeton, New Jersey. He also owned at least two pieces of real estate—a home in Manhattan on Whitehall Slip and a home in Huntington, Long Island. He had certainly achieved a measure of prosperity in colonial America.[2]

Jews in America gained religious, civil, and economic rights earlier and with greater ease than did their European or British brethren. Jews in England, for example, could not become freemen of the City of London without the swearing of a Christian oath. Without taking the oath, a Jew could not operate a retail business in the city. Beginning in 1785, the ban was extended to baptized Jews as well. In contrast, a few years after the first Jews had arrived in New Amsterdam, they were granted burgher rights (citizenship) by the Dutch. Before the end of the seventeenth century, the English authorities (England gained control of New Amsterdam in 1664) had relaxed all restrictions against Jewish participation in retail trade and real estate, as well as other former limitations on Jewish economic activity. Jews were permitted to become freemen of New York City, which gave them the right to

Portraits formerly identified as
Judah Mears (d. 1762)
and
Jochabed Michaels Mears (dates unknown)

The two pictures above from the collection of John L. Loeb Jr. are photographic copies of oil paintings currently owned by the Jewish Museum. These two well-dressed colonial citizens have for many years been identified as Jochabed Michaels Mears and her husband, Judah Mears, a successful merchant shipper of the eighteenth century. They were the four-times great-grandparents of Adeline Moses Loeb.

The portraits were a gift to the museum by Dr. Harry G. Friedman in about 1959 and were attributed to the popular colonial painter Jeremiah Theus. The Jewish Museum has recently undertaken verification of the identity of both the artist and the subjects who posed for him, and as a result of its research, their identity is now questioned. While we cannot therefore be certain of the identity of these subjects, their appearance is typical of Jews of the class and period of Jochabed and Judah Mears. The identity of the artist is also unverified, although it is believed that these portraits were painted in the eighteenth century.

—Ambassador John L. Loeb Jr. collection

A Southwest View of Newport, *1795*
artist Samuel King, engraver L. Allen — courtesy of The New York Public Library

THE NEWPORT JEWISH COMMUNITY (established in 1658) enjoyed its greatest growth and prosperity between 1740 and 1770—decades that paralleled the city's economic growth, thanks to its increasing importance in the shipping industry.

During this time the members of Newport's Congregation Jeshuat Israel had become financially secure enough to build and support their now famous Touro Synagogue, the oldest synagogue existing in this country. Its congregation is still active.

Touro Synagogue (1763) of Congregation Jeshuat Israel

Newport, Rhode Island

The Newport Community, c. 1777

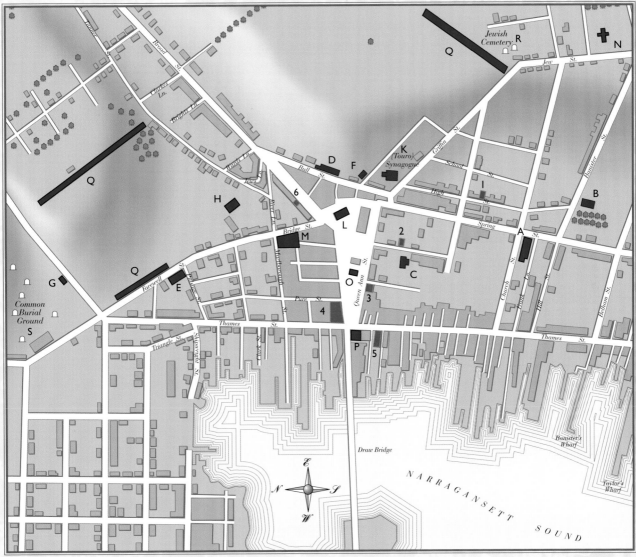

Buildings are not to scale. Placement is approximate.

Public Buildings

A. Trinity Church
B. 1st Congregational Meeting House
C. 2nd Congregational Meeting House
D. 1st Baptist Meeting House
E. 2d Baptist Meeting House
F. 3d Sabbatarian Baptist
    Meeting House
G. 4th Baptist Meeting House
H. Friends Meeting House
K. Jews Synagogue (Touro)

L. Courthouse
M. Gaol (Jail)
N. Redwood Library
O. Town School House
P. Brick Market
Q. Rope Walks

Parks & Cemeteries

R. Jewish Burial Ground (Touro)
S. Common Burial Ground

Homes & Businesses

1. Rev. Isaac and Reyna Hays Touro
    Judah, Abraham, Rebecca Touro
2. Dr. Ezra Stiles
3. Moses Levy
4. Jacob & Abraham Rodrigues
    de Rivera
5. Aaron Lopez
6. Moses Michael Hays

practice retail trade, to vote, and to hold public office. In 1740, Parliament enacted a law that allowed Jews to become naturalized citizens after seven years of residence in the colonies. They only had to swear allegiance to the Crown and were excused from taking the oath "upon the true faith of a Christian." Thus, a Jew in the colonies could become a "natural born Subject of Great Britain," which entitled him to own property, own shares in English ships, trade with the colonies, and pay lower customs duties than his English cousins.[3]

On May 30, 1738, Judah Mears became a freeman of New York City with full economic and political rights. Three years later, on September 29, 1741, he was elected constable of the East Ward, a dubious honor, because constables were required to patrol the streets to ensure the safety of the ward. The "lucky" candidate did not greet his election to this office with any great enthusiasm. Those who could, often bought their way out, paid fines, or hired others to serve in their place. For example, when Moses Levy and Jacob Franks were elected constables in 1719 and 1720, both refused to serve and were each fined £15. Judah Mears served his term in 1741, but when he was elected constable of the North Ward on September 30, 1751, he petitioned for exemption on the grounds that he had already served once within the last ten years.[4]

While fulfilling his duties as constable of the East Ward, Judah Mears was assaulted by Oliver DeLancey. DeLancey, who was considered to be a "dandy" and a "tough," was a member of one of New York's most prominent Protestant families. During the American Revolution, he served in the British Army as a high-ranking Loyalist officer. A month before the street attack on Mears, Oliver DeLancey had secretly married Phila Franks, eldest daughter of Jacob and Abigaill Franks. Neither an indictment for his assault on Mears, who was his father-in-law's business partner, nor his marriage to Phila Franks encouraged DeLancey to mend his ways. Seven years later, in 1749, DeLancey and some of his friends reportedly attacked a poor Jew and his wife, broke their windows, and swore they would lie with the woman. They then warned the Jewish couple not to press charges. Later that same year DeLancey was said to have stabbed and killed a Dr. Colchoun in a drunken brawl.[5]

Judah Mears married Jochabed, the daughter of Moses and Catherine Michaels, in the 1730s. They had seven children, of whom the eldest was probably born in March 1735 or 1736. Jochabed Michaels Mears was an unpopular woman. Her sister-in-law (Grace Mears Levy) disliked her (as in-laws often do), but she inspired negative reactions from others as well. In June 1734, in a letter to her son in London, Abigaill Levy Franks described how some of her relatives felt about Jochabed Mears, who was her stepmother's sister-in-law:

> There is something in Agitation with Mears and his mate You certainly will be Surprised to hear [of] my mother [Grace Mears Levy] and Josey [Jochabed Mears] friendship. The Latter lives in huntington She came to town the week after her sister was marrid when my Mother went to See her And Saluted her with as much kind[ness] as the dearest friends could doe they was frequently together and I have of a night Seen 'em walk with Mears between that I have actuly blushed for it to think what has been Said amongst 'em tho' all this friendship is but Outwardly for I am told my Mother Spares Jose as Little as Ever if you Say anything to Uncle Nat[han Levy] abouth this desire him Not to write it back Again as from me tho' Tell him in Conformity I hope he will recant all the Cruell Things he has Said I think he Showed a Vast deall of Weekness If it be true as Mrs. Levey Tells me He has Sat Whole Eavenings at Is[aac] Levy's Railing at Josey.[6]

Although relations between Jochabed Mears and Grace Levy were poor, when Grace died in 1740, leaving six children under the age of twenty-one, the Mears family took in Grace's daughter Hannah to live with them until she married Joshua Isaacs in December 1741.[7]

Like most of the Jewish merchants of colonial New York, Judah Mears was an active member of Congregation Shearith Israel and served as *parnas* (president) from 1741 to 1742. As an executor of his brother-in-law Moses Levy's estate, in

1728, Mears and the other executors arranged for Levy's two lots on Gold Street to be sold to the synagogue, which needed them for a cemetery. Mears himself contributed funds to the synagogue to help pay for its purchase of Levy's lots.[8]

In addition to the usual mention in the Shearith Israel records of donations to the congregation, Judah Mears's name appears in the minutes regarding a controversy with his brother-in-law Judah Hays, which took place in the summer of 1760. The conflict rose over the seemingly simple matter of finding seats in the women's section for their daughters, but it quickly grew into a public incident.

Lack of seating was a problem for the synagogue, particularly in the severely limited accommodations in the women's gallery. During a Sabbath service in June of 1760, Judah Mears went into the women's gallery and asked his niece, Miss Josse Hays (daughter of Judah and Rebecca Michaels Hays) to leave the seat that he claimed belonged to his daughter. Judah Hays then filed a complaint against Judah Mears, and at a congregational meeting on June 24, 1760, Judah Mears was fined 40 shillings "in order to prevent for the future any person assuming to themselves the authority of determining the property of seats in the Sinagogue . . . ." The two young women were asked to return to their former seats. This did not satisfy Judah Hays, and at the next meeting (July 17, 1760)

> . . . it was agreed to procure some method to pacify Mr. Judah Hays, in respect to a seat for his Daughter . . . by lengthening the bench on which Mrs. Hays Sets in Synagogue, there might be a seat found for Miss Hays.

After two more meetings, the congregation eventually levied a fine against Judah Hays, which resolved the dispute.[9]

In 1760 Judah Mears sold his Manhattan home on Whitehall Slip. Two years later, he died while traveling in the West Indies, as reported in the Shearith Israel records:

On 26 Sivan 5523 [June 7, 1762] departed this life at the Cape François Judah Mears of the Congregation. The news was brought about the time of Rosasana [Rosh Hashanah] by some acquaintances that came from that place and verificated after that by letters from that place.[10]

The British occupied Cape St. François, Guadeloupe, the largest island in the French Antilles, in 1762. However, the following year it was returned to France by the terms of the Treaty of Paris, which ended the Seven Years War. There was a small Jewish colony on Guadeloupe with whom Mears may have been involved in business, although the circumstances of his death and the location of his grave remain unknown.

—◊—

Descendants of
Judah Mears & Jochabed Michaels

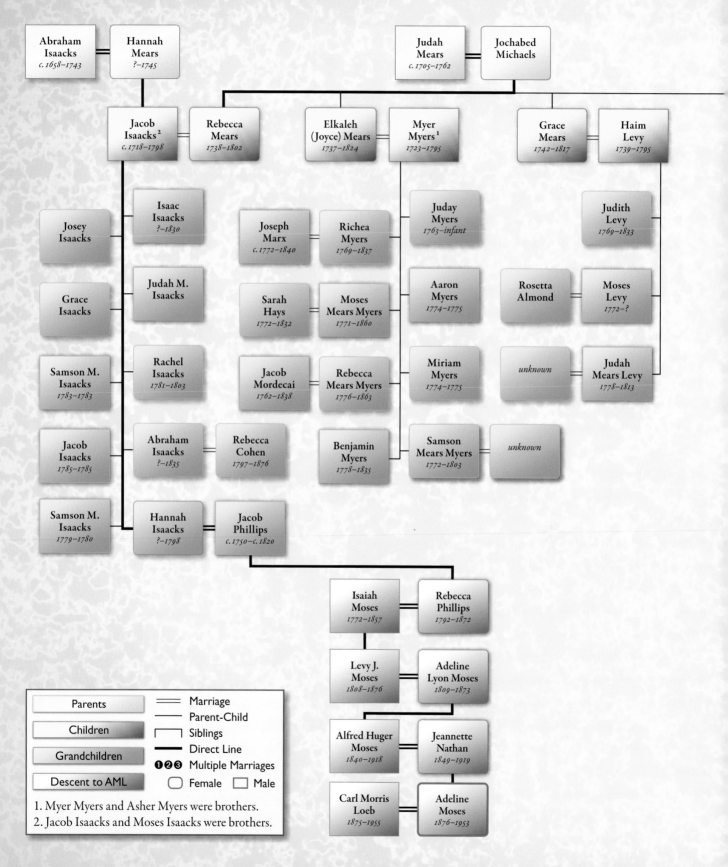

Abraham Isaacks *c. 1658–1743*
Hannah Mears *?–1745*
Judah Mears *c. 1705–1762*
Jochabed Michaels

Jacob Isaacks [2] *c. 1718–1798*
Rebecca Mears *1738–1802*
Elkaleh (Joyce) Mears *1737–1824*
Myer Myers [1] *1723–1795*
Grace Mears *1742–1817*
Haim Levy *1739–1795*

Josey Isaacks
Isaac Isaacks *?–1830*
Joseph Marx *c. 1772–1840*
Richea Myers *1769–1837*
Juday Myers *1763–infant*
Judith Levy *1769–1833*

Grace Isaacks
Judah M. Isaacks
Sarah Hays *1772–1832*
Moses Mears Myers *1771–1860*
Aaron Myers *1774–1775*
Rosetta Almond
Moses Levy *1772–?*

Samson M. Isaacks *1783–1783*
Rachel Isaacks *1781–1803*
Jacob Mordecai *1762–1838*
Rebecca Mears Myers *1776–1863*
Miriam Myers *1774–1775*
unknown
Judah Mears Levy *1778–1813*

Jacob Isaacks *1785–1785*
Abraham Isaacks *?–1835*
Rebecca Cohen *1797–1876*
Benjamin Myers *1778–1835*
Samson Mears Myers *1772–1803*
unknown

Samson M. Isaacks *1779–1780*
Hannah Isaacks *?–1798*
Jacob Phillips *c. 1750–c. 1820*

Isaiah Moses *1772–1857*
Rebecca Phillips *1792–1872*

Levy J. Moses *1808–1876*
Adeline Lyon Moses *1809–1873*

Alfred Huger Moses *1840–1918*
Jeannette Nathan *1849–1919*

Carl Morris Loeb *1875–1955*
Adeline Moses *1876–1953*

Legend:
- Parents
- Children
- Grandchildren
- Descent to AML
- ══ Marriage
- — Parent-Child
- ⊐ Siblings
- ▬ Direct Line
- ❶❷❸ Multiple Marriages
- ◯ Female ▢ Male

1. Myer Myers and Asher Myers were brothers.
2. Jacob Isaacks and Moses Isaacks were brothers.

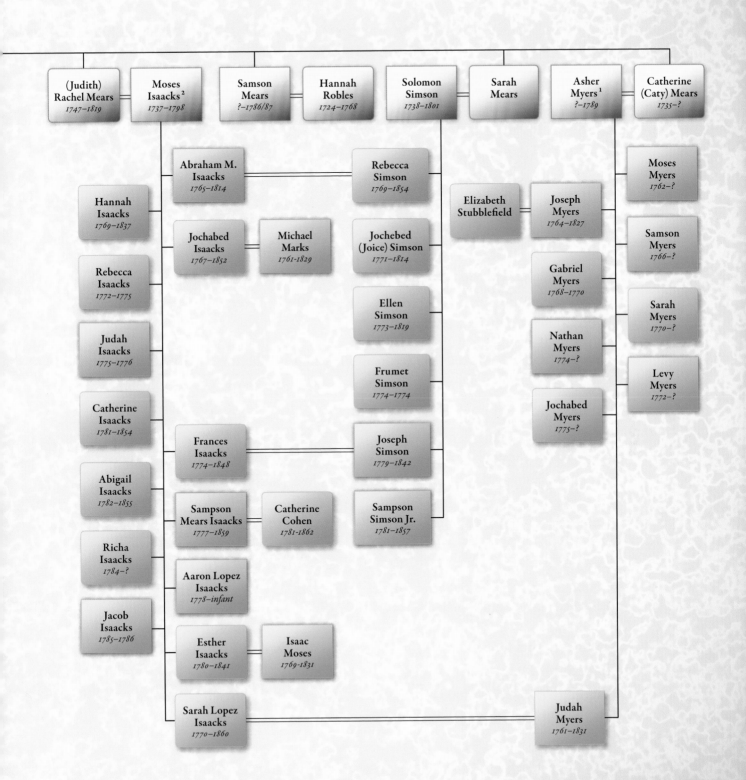

(Judith)
Rachel Mears
1747–1819

Moses
Isaacks [2]
1737–1798

Samson
Mears
?–1786/87

Hannah
Robles
1724–1768

Solomon
Simson
1738–1801

Sarah
Mears

Asher
Myers [1]
?–1789

Catherine
(Caty) Mears
1735–?

Abraham M.
Isaacks
1765–1814

Rebecca
Simson
1769–1854

Elizabeth
Stubblefield

Joseph
Myers
1764–1827

Moses
Myers
1762–?

Hannah
Isaacks
1769–1837

Jochabed
Isaacks
1767–1852

Michael
Marks
1761–1829

Jochebed
(Joice) Simson
1771–1814

Gabriel
Myers
1768–1770

Samson
Myers
1766–?

Rebecca
Isaacks
1772–1775

Ellen
Simson
1773–1819

Nathan
Myers
1774–?

Sarah
Myers
1770–?

Judah
Isaacks
1775–1776

Frumet
Simson
1774–1774

Jochabed
Myers
1775–?

Levy
Myers
1772–?

Catherine
Isaacks
1781–1854

Frances
Isaacks
1774–1848

Joseph
Simson
1779–1842

Abigail
Isaacks
1782–1855

Sampson
Mears Isaacks
1777–1859

Catherine
Cohen
1781–1862

Sampson
Simson Jr.
1781–1857

Richa
Isaacks
1784–?

Aaron Lopez
Isaacks
1778–infant

Jacob
Isaacks
1785–1786

Esther
Isaacks
1780–1841

Isaac
Moses
1769–1831

Sarah Lopez
Isaacks
1770–1860

Judah
Myers
1761–1831

The Children of Judah and Jochabed Michaels Mears

1. **Catherine (Caty)** (born March 10, 1735). Married Asher Myers (died May 7, 1789), a brazier [a worker in brass]. He was made a freeman of New York City, September 30, 1755, and elected constable. Active in synagogue affairs, he was elected *parnas* in 1765 and 1771. Asher and Catherine Myers had nine children: Judah, Moses, Joseph, Samson, Gabriel, Sarah, Levy, Nathan, and Jochabed.

2. **Elkaleh (Joyce)** (born July 15, 1737; died July 19, 1824, Richmond, Virginia). Married (as his second wife) Myer Myers (born 1723; died December 12, 1795, New York), on March 18, 1767, in New York. Joyce was named for her grandmother, Joy Mears. Myer Myers was the noted gold- and silversmith and brother of Asher Myers (who married her sister Catherine, above). Myers was made a freeman of New York on April 29, in 1745/46. Myer and Elkaleh (Joyce) Myers had eight children: Juday, Richea, Moses Mears, Samson Mears, Aaron, Miriam, Rebecca Mears, and Benjamin.

3. **Rebecca** (born 1738; died 1802, Charleston, South Carolina). Married Jacob Isaacks (born c. 1718, New York; died March 20, 1798, Newport, Rhode Island) on October 8, 1760 in Newport, Rhode Island. Isaacks was a merchant and sometime inventor who developed a process of obtaining fresh water from salt water. Jacob and Rebecca Isaacks had ten children: Samson M., Rachel, Samson M., Jacob, Hannah, Isaac, Abraham, Judah M., Josey, and Grace. **Adeline Moses Loeb is a direct descendant of their daughter, Hannah.**

4. **Grace** (born 1742; died March 4, 1817). Married Haim Levy (born 1739; died July 12, 1795) on July 28, 1768, in Newport, Rhode Island. Grace was named for Judah Mears's sister Grace. Haim and Grace Levy had three children: Judith, Moses, and Judah Mears.

5. **(Judith) Rachel** (born April 20, 1747, New York City; died June 6, 1819, New York City). Married Moses Isaacks (born March 25, 1737, New York; died August 31, 1798, New York) on August 30, 1764, in Philadelphia, Pennsylvania.

Moses was the youngest brother of Jacob Isaacks; the two brothers were in business together in Newport, Rhode Island. Moses and Rachel Isaacks had fourteen children: Abraham Mears, Jochabed, Hannah, Sarah Lopez, Rebecca, Frances, Judah, Sampson Mears, Aaron Lopez, Esther, Catherine, Abigail, Richa, and Jacob.

6. **Sarah.** Married Solomon Simson (born September 1738; died January 17, 1801, Yonkers, New York) on October 26, 1768. The couple lived at 31 Broad Street in New York. Son of Joseph Simson, a well-known New York merchant, Solomon was also a prominent merchant in partnership with his brother Samson, and owned a store on Stone Street in Manhattan. Solomon was active in politics and congregational affairs. He and Sarah Simson had six children: Rebecca, Jochebed (Joice), Ellen, Frumet, Joseph, and Sampson, Jr.

7. **Samson** (born New York City; died 1786/87, St. Eustatia). Married Hannah Robles, a widow (born 1724; died January 18, 1768, St. Eustatia). Samson, the only son of Judah and Jochabed Mears, was named for his paternal grandfather. A gold- and silversmith in New York, in the 1760s he migrated to St. Eustatia, became active in the West Indian trade, and met Hannah Robles. Samson and Hannah Mears had no children.[11]

—⚬—

1. Hershkowitz, *Letters*, 28.
2. Hershkowitz, *Wills*, 39; Marcus, *Colonial*, 333.
3. Faber, *A Time for Planting*, 17–18.
4. Alexander, *Notes*, 93; Hershkowitz, "Some Aspects," 13.
5. Hershkowitz, *Letters*, 116–17; Hershkowitz, *Wills*, 39.
6. Hershkowitz, *Letters*, 31.
7. Hershkowitz, *Letters*, 81; Stern, *First American*, 124.
8. Pool, *Portraits*, 15; Hershkowitz, *Wills*, 39.
9. Pool, *Old Faith*, 270–71.
10. Alexander, *Notes*, 94.
11. Stern, *First American*, 120, 165, 190, 217, 272; Hershkowitz, *Wills*, 67, 139–41, 201.

CHAPTER FIVE

MOSES RAPHAEL LEVY
(1665–1728)

and

RICHEA ASHER LEVY
(d. 1716)

GRACE MEARS LEVY HAYS
(1694–1740)

IN 1718 GRACE MEARS MARRIED the widower Moses Levy, one of New York's wealthiest merchants. Although not a direct ancestor of Adeline Moses Loeb (that honor resides with her brother Judah), Grace is significant for two reasons. Her late marriage to the wealthy merchant and widower Moses Levy probably brought her brother Judah from London to New York. Once in New York, this familial connection allowed Judah entrée to the most prominent social and business circles in the city. Moreover, Grace and Moses Levy left a significant documentary record. The traces of their lives help us imagine what life was like for the earliest Jewish residents of New York, including Grace's brother Judah Mears.

Moses Levy was born in Germany in 1665, the son of Isaac (died February 24, 1695) and Beila Levy (died April 29, 1697). Sometime in the late seventeenth century, Moses migrated west with his brother Samuel Zanvil (1666/67–1719). The two brothers settled in London before setting out for New York, where they were among the very earliest Jewish residents of the city. Moses Levy became a freeman of New York on June 5, 1695, only forty-one years after the first boatload of Jews arrived in what was then New Amsterdam. Moses Levy remained a resident of New York for the rest of his life, although he made frequent trips to London. Both of his marriages took place there, several of his children were born there, and a number of his London business partnerships were established there.

Moses Levy became a freeman of New York. However, since New York was still a British colony, he was subject to the economic restrictions placed on aliens by Great Britain. (Parliament did not enact a naturalization law until 1740, which would have allowed him to become a naturalized citizen.) To gain the right to engage in colonial trade and other privileges, Levy purchased royal letters patent in England in 1713 to become a free denizen (an alien admitted to certain rights of citizenship).[1]

The Jewish community of early eighteenth-century New York was not prosperous. Most of New York's Jews survived as peddlers, artisans, or small shopkeepers. Those who aspired to greater wealth strove to enter the ranks of the highly competitive world of the merchant shipper, where fortunes could be made.

Moses Levy was among the most successful of New York's merchant shippers. By 1701 he and his brother Samuel owned a home and land in the Dock Ward, located in the southeastern edge of lower Manhattan. Like other successful Jewish merchants, he was a frequent contributor to Congregation Shearith Israel, and at the time of his death in 1728 was serving as *parnas* (president) of the synagogue. In 1711, along with six other well-to-do Jews, including Moses Michaels, he contributed to the fund to erect a steeple for Trinity Church.* Perhaps nothing makes Moses Levy's prosperity and status as clear as his large oil portrait, painted sometime in the 1720s by an artist of the Hudson River School. Levy is portrayed as a substantial man, wearing a long gray wig and a blue velvet waistcoat. An elegant greyhound seated in the foreground adds a note of prosperity; a ship in the background symbolizes his status as an affluent merchant shipper. The companion painting of his second wife, Grace Mears Levy, shows an ample, prosperous-looking woman dressed in silk and velvet. These portraits depict a successful colonial gentleman and his lady.[2]

Moses Levy's first wife was Richea Asher, whom he married in London in 1695. His brother Samuel married Richea's sister Rachel. These two sisters, Richea (birth date unknown) and Rachel (born 1691), and their brother Michael (born 1686) were the children of Asher Michaels de Paul and Rebecca Valentine Asher, who

---

*   In 2009 Trinity Church is still located at the corner of Broadway and Wall Street, although in a building dating from 1846.

Moses Raphael Levy (1665–1728)   Grace Mears Levy (1694–1740)

At the time these elegant portraits were painted, the twice-married Moses Levy was an affluent merchant-trader and the father of twelve children—five by his first wife. His second wife, Grace Mears (the five-times great-aunt of Adeline Moses Loeb) brought a very small dowry to the marriage, and there had been a less-than-generous prenuptial agreement, so when Grace Levy's much older husband died, the thirty-four-year-old widow was left little money. For a time she engaged in business for herself, evidencing the sort of genetic "gumption" during financial challenges that more than 200 years later were attributed to her five-times great-niece, Adeline Moses Loeb.

—No longer attributed to Gerardus Duyckinck (1695–1746)
Now listed as "artist unknown," c. 1720–1728
Oils on canvas
Museum of the City of New York

were residing in New York by 1680. Rachel and Michael Asher were born in New York, but Richea—the eldest—was probably born abroad. European Jews did not have last names at this time and were known simply as Michael ben (son of) Asher, for example. When the Asher children and their mother needed a last name in New York, they took the father's first name of Asher as their family name, a common practice.

Moses and Richea Levy resided in London for several years after their marriage. Their three eldest children were born there: Bilhah Abigaill in 1696, Asher in 1699, and Nathan in 1704. They must have moved back to New York shortly after Nathan's birth as their last two children, Isaac and Michael, were born in New York in 1706 and 1709 respectively. When Richea died in New York on September 29, 1716, her children ranged in age from seven to twenty. At the time of her death, her eldest child and only daughter, Bilhah Abigaill (known as Abigaill) was already married and a mother herself.

In 1718, two years after Richea died, Moses Levy married Grace Mears in London. Grace Mears, the eldest child of Sampson and Joy Mears, was born in 1694 in Spanishtown, Jamaica. Grace may have spent her first five years in Jamaica, but her family had returned to London by 1699. Her uncle Jacob arranged her marriage to Levy, since her father was no longer living. On her wedding day, Grace Mears was twenty-four years old, well beyond the average age of marriage.

Although Grace Mears married one of New York's wealthiest Jews, there was a drawback: her husband was a fifty-two-year-old widower with five children. Grace probably had little choice in the matter, as he was most likely the best match the limited resources of her widowed mother, Joy Mears, could manage for her daughter. Grace's dowry of £350 was small, an indication that she brought little money to the marriage. If she survived her husband, she would receive £300 of "Great Britain money, 150 ounces of silver, and his [Levy's] best Negro slave."[3]

Grace's marital life could not have been happy. Her marriage took her from a comfortable London home to the brawling frontier community of New York. There are indications that the marriage was made to settle a suit brought against Moses Levy by Joy Mears and her brother-in-law Jacob Mears. If true, this settlement could not have made for a happy union. Grace's not-so-young husband went on to

Rachel Seixas (Mrs. Isaac Mendes Seixas)
(1719–1797)
Rachel was the eldest daughter of Grace Mears and Moses Raphael Levy, and the mother of eight children, including Gershom Mendes Seixas. The Loeb family is related to the Seixas family through Judah Mears, Grace Mears Levy's brother.

—Attributed to John Wollaston
Oil on canvas, c. 1750
American Jewish Historical Society,
Newton Centre, Massachusetts, and New York, New York

Gershom Mendes Seixas
(1745–1816)

This grandson of Grace Mears and Moses Levy—and son of their oldest daughter Rachel Seixas (see portrait on page 147)—figured large in colonial religious history. A Shearith Israel hazan (a synagogue official who conducts the religious portion of a service) during the American Revolution, he vigorously opposed the British monarchy and persuaded the congregation to close the synagogue during the British occupation of New York. He returned there only after the war. He was one of fourteen religious leaders represented at George Washington's inauguration, and was appointed to the Board of Regents at King's College (now Columbia University) in 1784.

—Unknown artist
Miniature, oil on ivory, c. 1770
E. Norman Flayderman collection

David G. Seixas
(1788–1865)

The eldest son of Gershom Mendes Seixas (see portrait on facing page), David G. Seixas was a pioneer in educating the deaf, founding the Pennsylvania School for the Deaf in 1820, which still flourishes today in Philadelphia. Having an inventive mind, Seixas—a lifelong bachelor—was both a merchant and manufacturer and is credited with producing an improved sealing wax, a less expensive printer's ink, and a process of lamination. He was a veteran of the War of 1812.

—John Carlin, 1813–1891
Graduate of the Pennsylvania School for the Deaf
Miniature on ivory, c. 1820
Pennsylvania School for the Deaf, Philadelphia, Pennsylvania

Joshua Isaacs Jr.
(1744–1810)

Joshua was a grandson of Moses and Grace Mears Levy, and the son of their daughter Hannah. Born in the West Indies, he took the American oath of loyalty in 1780 and served thereafter in a Pennsylvania militia. Eventually marrying in that state, he and his wife, Justina Brandly Lazarus, moved to New York, where they were major supporters of Shearith Israel Synagogue.

—Unknown artist
Oil on canvas, New York, c. 1781
Museum of the City of New York

Frances Isaacs (1783–1854) was a daughter of Joshua Isaacs Jr. (see portrait on facing page) and sister of Solomon J. Isaacs (see below). In 1840 she married Harmon Hendricks, whose New Jersey-based company launched the copper manufacturing industry in America and whose clients included metalsmith Paul Revere and steamboat inventor Robert Fulton. The Hendricks marriage produced thirteen surviving children.

—Unknown artist
Oil on canvas, New York, c. 1800–1805
Museum of the City of New York

Solomon J. Isaacs (1786–1855) lived with his sister Frances Isaacs Hendricks (see above) and her family, and worked for many years alongside his brother-in-law Harmon Hendricks in the pioneering American copper manufacturing business in Soho, New Jersey. Extremely adept in the field, he is given great credit for the success of a company that arguably helped lay the foundation for this country's industrial revolution. A longtime bachelor, at the age of forty-four, he married Elkalah Kursheedt, with whom he had ten children. Like all of the Isaacs family, they were active and generous members of the Shearith Israel congregation.

—John Wesley Jarvis (1780–1840)
Oil on canvas, c. 1815
The Jewish Museum, New York City

amicably, but they were apparently unsuccessful. On December 5, 1735, Grace and David Hays filed a suit in Chancery Court. The suit alleged that Nathan and Isaac Levy had kept funds from her and that they had mismanaged her investments so badly that she and her new husband were now in debt. There is no record of a court decision, so the case must have been settled out of court.[7]

Grace's complaint and her eventual suit did nothing to make her more beloved by her stepchildren. Here Abigaill Franks comments on the incident to her son in London in June 1737:

> . . . she is a base Vile woman and her Action has Allways bin of a Piece tho I think in this Last Affaire She has Out done her Usall Outdoeings of Malice and Craft if you See Uncle Asher pray Give my Love to him and Tell him if As he thinks he has been Ill Used and wishes revenge on his brothers he has a Sufficient one in the plague My father has Intailed opon Us here in New York by that woman.[8]

For a few years during their brief marriage, David and Grace Hays lived outside of New York City, possibly in Westchester County, since many members of the Hays family lived there. They moved back to the city only a few months before Grace died, according to Abigaill, who again reveals continued animosity to her stepmother in another letter to her son:

> David Hays and family Are Come to Live in town again She Letts her child[ren] come to our house but with her Self I have noe Confab[ulation] nor I hope never Shall for I don't Love her.[9]

Grace died in New York on October 14, 1740, at the age of forty-six, and was buried in the Chatham Square Cemetery of Congregation Shearith Israel. In 1856 her grave was transferred to the congregational plot at 21st Street and Sixth Avenue in New York, where it remains today. In death, her stepdaughter Abigaill

Bilhah Abigaill Levy Franks (Mrs. Jacob Franks)
(1696–1756)

Tart of tongue and a shrewd observer of life around her, the oldest daughter of Moses
Levy by his first wife (Richea Asher) has given a rare and candid window on the American
colonial Jewish world through her frequent and chatty letters to the eldest of her thirteen
children. Over thirty letters from Abigaill to Naphtali Franks, her London-based son, are
in the collection of the American Jewish Historical Society in New York City.

—Attributed to Gerardus Duyckinck (1695–1746)
Oil on canvas, New York, c. 1735
Crystal Bridges Museum of American Art, Bentonville, Arkansas

Mary "Polly" Pearce Levy (1762–?)   Judge Moses Levy (1756–1826)

Moses Levy, like his father Samson Levy and brother Samson Levy Jr., married out of Judaism, embracing the Episcopal religion of his wife. Admitted to the bar in 1778, Moses Levy became a prominent magistrate and a trustee of the University of Pennsylvania, and at one time served in the Pennsylvania legislature. He was a grandson of Moses and Grace Mears Levy.

—Mary Pearce Levy by Charles Wilson Peale (1741–1827)
Oil on paper mounted on canvas, 1808
Montclair Art Museum, Montclair, New Jersey

—Judge Moses Levy by Rembrandt Peale (1778–1860)
Oil on canvas, 1820
Montclair Art Museum, Montclair, New Jersey

Sarah Coates Levy (1776–1854)   Samson Levy Jr. (1761–1831)

Samson Levy Jr., another grandson of Moses and Grace Mears Levy, led quite a different life from his religiously observant cousin, Gershom Mendes Seixas. Marrying Sarah Coates, a Philadelphia gentile, Samson became a Christian and enjoyed an elite social life in that city. (His father was on the original list of the Assembly, an exclusive social club in Philadelphia.) Reputed to be a witty and intelligent lawyer, Samson Levy Jr. was one of the founders of the Pennsylvania Academy of the Fine Arts and the brother of Judge Moses Levy (see facing page).

—Both portraits by Thomas Sully (1783–1872)
Oils on canvas, companion pieces painted in 1808
Montclair Art Museum, Montclair, New Jersey

looked more kindly and was almost sympathetic to her stepmother's difficult situation. Abigaill wrote to her son in November, 1740:

> Mrs. Hays Death has been Very Sudden if there be Such a thing as Dying of a broken heart, it was her Case Noe one Ever had Soe much reason to resent her Conduct for the fellow she Marrid treated her Exceeding Ill and She was Slighted by all her acquaintance Soe that her Cup was filled up with bitterness and to a woman of her Spirit I am amazed she bore it Soe Long Sam[son] Hetty and Joe goe to Phila[delphia] Hannah is to be with Mrs. Mears and Little Miriam is to be put at board Some Where.[10]

Grace's tombstone was described in 1856 as defaced and illegible. However, in his 1952 book, *Portraits Etched in Stone*, David de Sola Pool was able to decipher much of the English and Hebrew inscriptions:

Hebrew: Tombstone/ of the modest woman Grace
Daughter of Samson Mear who died [26 Tishri]
———year 5501/———days of ———-
May her soul be bound up in the bond of life.

English : ———think this stone
———Be thy fate
———e you give a
———call of heavn
———of Grace ye wife of
[David Hays] formerly wife of Moses
[Levy who] departed from this scene of
———to eternal bliss Octr ye 14 1740
In the [4]6th year of her age.[11]

—ɯ—

Descendants of
Moses Raphael Levy & Richea Asher & Grace Mears

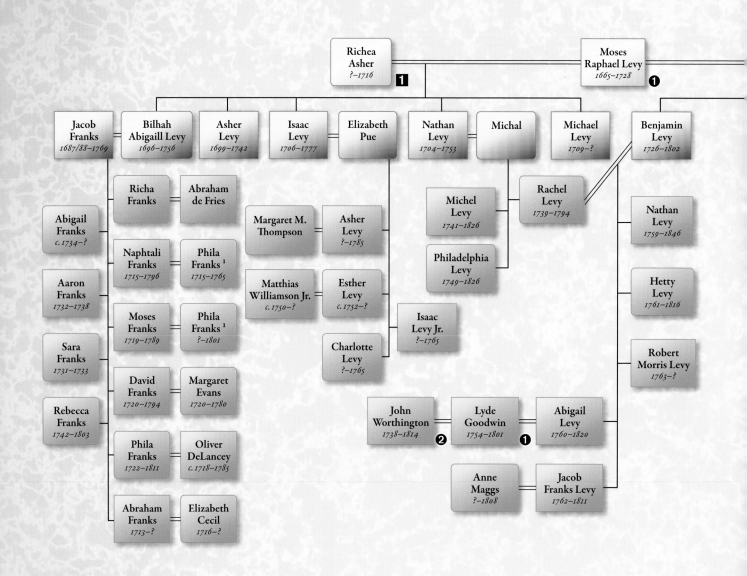

Richea Asher
?–1716 **1**

Moses Raphael Levy
1665–1728 **1**

Jacob Franks
1687/88–1769

Bilhah Abigaill Levy
1696–1756

Asher Levy
1699–1742

Isaac Levy
1706–1777

Elizabeth Pue

Nathan Levy
1704–1753

Michal

Michael Levy
1709–?

Benjamin Levy
1726–1802

Richa Franks

Abraham de Fries

Abigail Franks
c. 1734–?

Margaret M. Thompson

Asher Levy
?–1785

Michel Levy
1741–1826

Rachel Levy
1739–1794

Nathan Levy
1759–1846

Naphtali Franks
1715–1796

Phila Franks [1]
1715–1765

Aaron Franks
1732–1738

Matthias Williamson Jr.
c. 1750–?

Esther Levy
c. 1752–?

Philadelphia Levy
1749–1826

Hetty Levy
1761–1816

Moses Franks
1719–1789

Phila Franks [1]
?–1801

Sara Franks
1731–1733

Charlotte Levy
?–1765

Isaac Levy Jr.
?–1765

Robert Morris Levy
1763–?

David Franks
1720–1794

Margaret Evans
1720–1780

Rebecca Franks
1742–1803

Phila Franks
1722–1811

Oliver DeLancey
c. 1718–1785

John Worthington
1738–1814 **2**

Lyde Goodwin
1754–1801 **1**

Abigail Levy
1760–1820

Abraham Franks
1713–?

Elizabeth Cecil
1716–?

Anne Maggs
?–1808

Jacob Franks Levy
1762–1811

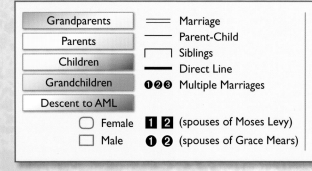

Grandparents	══ Marriage
Parents	— Parent-Child
Children	⌐ Siblings
Grandchildren	▬ Direct Line
Descent to AML	❶❷❸ Multiple Marriages

⬭ Female **1** **2** (spouses of Moses Levy)
▢ Male ❶ ❷ (spouses of Grace Mears)

1. The two Phila Franks noted above are granddaughters of Moses Hart (see Chapter 2), president of the Great Synagogue in London. Their fathers, Isaac and Aaron Franks were both brothers of the Jacob Franks shown above, making the ladies first cousins to each other and to their husbands.

2. The eight children of Tabitha Mears and Mathias Bush are shown in Chapter 2.

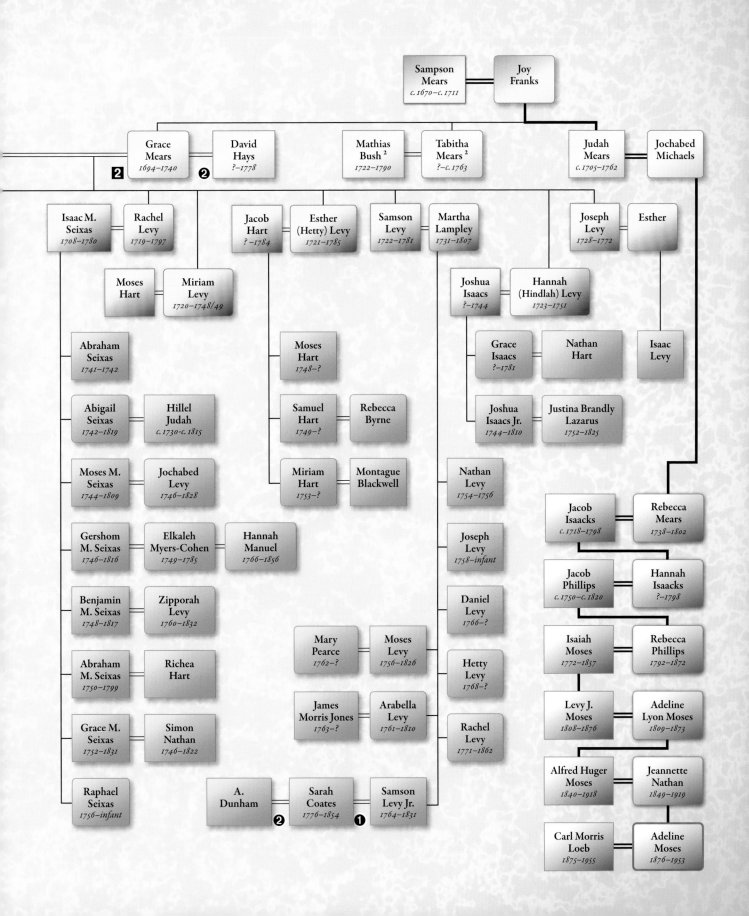

The Children of Moses and Richea Asher Levy

1. **Bilhah, known as Abigaill** (born November 26, 1696, London; died May 16, 1756, New York). Married Jacob Franks (born 1687/88, London; died January 16, 1769, New York) in 1712 in New York. Jacob was a successful New York merchant. Jacob and Abigaill Franks had ten children: Naphtali, David, Phila, Sara, Abigail, Aaron, Rebecca, Richa, Abraham, and Moses.

2. **Asher** (born February 2, 1699, London; died 1742, Philadelphia, Pennsylvania). He met with financial reverses in London and was declared bankrupt in 1732.

3. **Nathan** (born February 18, 1704, New York; died December 21, 1753, Philadelphia, Pennsylvania). Married Michal, who died of insanity. Nathan was a Philadelphia merchant. Nathan and Michal Levy had three children: Rachel, Michel, and Philadelphia. Rachel married Benjamin Levy, son of Moses Raphael Levy and his second wife, Grace Mears.

4. **Isaac** (born July 19, 1706, New York; died March 1777, Philadelphia, Pennsylvania). Married Elizabeth Pue. Isaac was a merchant in New York, Boston, and Philadelphia. Isaac and Elizabeth Levy had four children: Asher, Isaac Jr., Charlotte, and Esther.

5. **Michael (Jechiel)** (born July 10, 1709, New York; died in Jamaica). He was a New York merchant and part owner of the brig *Prince Frederick*.

The Children of Moses and Grace Mears Levy

1. **Rachel** (born February 27, 1719, London, England; died May 12, 1797, New York City). Married Isaac Mendes Seixas (a Sephardic Jew, born September 5, 1708, Lisbon, Portugal; died November 3, 1780, Newport, Rhode Island) in May 1740, in New York. Isaac Mendes Seixas was in New York before 1738, endenized in New York, November 4, 1745. Isaac and Rachel Mendes Seixas had eight children: Abraham, Abigail, Moses Mendes, Gershom Mendes, Benjamin Mendes, Abraham Mendes, Grace Mendes, and Raphael.

2. **Miriam** (born February 11, 1720, New York City; died February 4, 1748/49, New York). Married Moses Hart of New York. (She, like her siblings, moved from the family home when her mother died in 1740.)

3. **Esther (Hetty)** (born February 28, 1721, New York City; died June 26, 1785, England). Married Jacob Hart of Stamford, Connecticut (later a Newport Tory, who died November 3, 1784, in England). Esther went to Philadelphia to live with her brothers Samson and Joseph when her mother died. Jacob and Esther Hart had three children: Moses, Samuel, and Miriam.

4. **Samson** (born August 19, 1722, New York City; died March 22, 1781, Philadelphia, Pennsylvania). Married Martha Lampley (born 1731; died 1807), widow of James Steel Thompson, on November 3, 1752. Martha and Samson Levy had eight children: Moses, Nathan, Joseph, Arabella, Samson Jr., Daniel, Hetty, and Rachel.

5. **Hannah (Hindlah)** (born September 22, 1723; died April 3, 1751). Married Joshua Isaacs (died July, 1744) in December, 1741. When her mother died in 1740, she went to live with her aunt and uncle, Judah and Jochabed Mears. Hannah and Joshua Isaacs had two children: Joshua Jr. and Grace.

6. **Benjamin** (born September 5, 1726, New York City; died February 3, 1802, Baltimore, Maryland). Married Rachel Levy (born 1739, Philadelphia, Pennsylvania; died November 11, 1794, Baltimore, Maryland, daughter of his

half-brother, Nathan) in 1758. Benjamin became a settler of Newport, Rhode Island. He and Rachel Levy had five children: Nathan, Abigail, Hetty, Jacob Franks, and Robert Morris.

7. **Joseph** (born June 12, 1728, New York City; died 1772, South Carolina). Married Esther in 1772 in South Carolina and died the same year. He had become a freeman of New York on November 7, 1752. Joseph and Esther Levy had one son: Isaac.[12]

—m—

1. Stern, *First American*, 154; Pool, *Portraits*, 198–99; Hershkowitz, "Some Aspects," 15–16.
2. Hershkowitz, *Wills*, 36; Pool, *Portraits*, 199–200; Alexander, *Notes*, 99.
3. Complaint of Matthew Brandon; Pool, *Portraits*, 226.
4. Hershkowitz, *Wills*, 36–39; Pool, *Portraits*, 197–98.
5. Hershkowitz, *Letters*, 28, 47, 59.
6. Hershkowitz, *Wills*, 47; Pool, *Portraits*, 226; Hershkowitz, *Letters*, 58–59.
7. Hershkowitz, *Wills*, 36–39; Hershkowitz, *Letters*, 58–59.
8. Hershkowitz, *Letters*, 58–59.
9. Ibid., 72.
10. Pool, *Portraits*, 255–56; Hershkowitz, *Letters*, 81.
11. Pool, *Portraits*, 225.
12. Stern, *First American*, 124, 154, 265; Hershkowitz, *Wills*.

CHAPTER SIX

SAMSON MEARS
(d. 1786/87)

and

HANNAH ROBLES MEARS
(1724–1768)

EVERY LIFE IS LIVED IN A CONTEXT of social and political change that shapes the life experience. For some, these events might be experienced as a kind of soft background music. For others, the vectors of geography, politics, and economy seem to ricochet through their lives with astonishing ferocity. Such was the case for Samson Mears, the older brother of Rebecca and a direct ancestor of Adeline Moses Loeb. Samson's life provides a dramatic and personal perspective on the devastating impact of the War of Independence on everyday life. Although the war continuously frustrated his ability to make a living, Samson remained a loyal American patriot.

Samson Mears, named for his paternal grandfather, was born in New York sometime in the mid-eighteenth century (exact year unknown). He began his business career as a gold- and silversmith in New York. The following advertisement from the *New York Mercury* of November 29, 1762, announced the opening of his shop:

> Samson Mears, goldsmith Has Open'd his Shop in Pearl-street, in the house Mr. Andrew Brested, formerly lived, where he intends to carry on the gold and silversmiths business, after the newest and neatest fashion, and all Commands he is favoured with, will be executed with the most thankful Dispatch.[1]

Within a few years, however, Samson Mears had abandoned his craft. In the 1760s he settled in the Dutch colony of St. Eustatius, a small island east of Puerto Rico, which had a Jewish community dating back to 1725. The island's Jewish community continued to grow throughout the eighteenth century, and they founded a synagogue, Honen Dalim, in 1739. Jews were attracted to the island because it was a free port, and the Jewish population became a substantial part of the island's white population.

In St. Eustatius, Mears married Hannah Robles, a Sephardic widow, but their married life was brief. On January 18, 1768, his forty-four-year-old wife died and was buried in the St. Eustatius cemetery. Her epitaph reads:

[To the]
[M]emory of
Mrs
[Ha]nnah Mears
Wife of Mr.
Samson Mears
who departed this
life Jan[ry] the 18th
A.D. 1768 aged 44 years[2]

Samson Mears remained in St. Eustatius for another eight years after his wife's death, returning to New York City shortly before the British occupation of the city in 1776.

The exact nature of Samson Mears's economic activity on St. Eustatius is not known. He continued to maintain business associations with North American Jewish shippers, including Aaron Lopez, one of the most prominent colonial merchants, for whom he acted as an agent. In September 1775, for example, when the brig *Minerva*, jointly owned by Aaron Lopez and Francis Rotch, was preparing to sail from Newport, Rhode Island, the ship's captain, John Lock, was instructed not to return directly to New England, but to stop enroute at the

Dutch West Indies, possibly because the owners feared the outbreak of war between Great Britain and the colonies. If he stopped in St. Eustatius he was to seek aid from Samson Mears.[3]

In another incident, Samson Mears provided help to Virginia planters who were attempting to get a shipment of grain through the British blockade of Boston harbor. The ship was driven off course by bad weather and took refuge at St. Eustatius, where a pro-American merchant sold the cargo without charging a commission. The proceeds were then turned over to Samson Mears, who sent a bill of exchange to Boston, drawn on Isaac Moses of New York, who honored the draft.[4]

The Jews in the West Indies and in the North American colonies were linked through business, marriage, and family. When one community needed support for their synagogue, for example, it was a common practice to appeal to their coreligionists in other communities for aid. In 1772 Samson Mears was serving as treasurer of Honen Dalim when a hurricane leveled their building. Mears and the other synagogue officers wrote to the Jewish communities of Amsterdam, Curaçao, and New York for assistance in rebuilding their synagogue. New York and Amsterdam quickly responded with contributions. In November 1772, Mears, David R. Furtado, and Judah Benjamin wrote to the Curaçao congregation that the building was nearly finished.[5]

In 1776 Samson Mears returned to New York from St. Eustatius. He was in New York City when the British occupied the city in August of that same year. Most of the Jewish community fled the city and many resettled in Connecticut where they spent the duration of the war. Samson Mears settled in Norwalk, Connecticut, along with three of his sisters and their husbands: Joyce and Myer Myers, the well-known silversmith; Catherine and Asher Myers, a metalsmith; and Sarah and Solomon Simson, a merchant. Even in Connecticut, the refugees were not safe from British fire. In October 1777, Samson Mears and other Norwalk residents petitioned the Connecticut authorities for an armed vessel to patrol Long Island Sound and protect them from the British raids of the Connecticut harbor and river towns.[6]

During the four years that Samson Mears lived in Connecticut from 1776 to 1780, he made a living as a horse-and-wagon peddler in the Connecticut countryside. He bought his merchandise from Aaron Lopez, the wealthy merchant shipper of Newport, who was carrying on an extensive interstate trade during the war years by means of coastal shipping and overland wagon. Mears bought velvet and woolens, men's clothing, tobacco and snuff, spermaceti candles, iron wire, and salt from Lopez. He peddled these products or traded them for items Lopez wanted, such as flaxseed and flour.

His reduced circumstances, coupled with the disruption of the war, continued to frustrate Mears. Deliveries were delayed for weeks; inflation was rampant. Often by the time the goods arrived, prices had risen, the market was oversupplied, and the value of paper money had depreciated. Transportation was also difficult—Mears had to drive his horse and wagon over muddy, rut-filled roads to reach such Connecticut towns as Leicester, Newport, and New London. He was often away for weeks at a time, returning to find his family distraught because they had never received his letters.[7]

The restrictions on trade enforced by neighboring states brought business almost to a standstill. Mears wrote restively to Aaron Lopez on July 4, 1779:

> I confess I never was more perplexed in what to employ my self than I am now; sick and tired of an idle life and wh't to persue with any appearance of stability and advantage to take me out of it. I am at a loss, and now appears new difficulties arising to the southward and eastward by the threatening restrictions on trade that adds to the confusion of the times. Is there nothing abroad that I can serve you and Mr. Rivera in?[8]

In his eagerness to take on a more challenging (and profitable) occupation, Mears proposed to return to St. Eustatius to form a company based there and in Amsterdam to speculate in Continental currency. He invited Lopez and his father-in-law, Jacob Rivera, to participate. However, the British began a fresh attack on the Connecticut towns bordering the Long Island Sound on July 5, 1779, and temporarily halted Mears's plans. On July 11, General Tryon's company burned the houses, barns, and churches of Norwalk, plundering and exhibiting "cruel, barbarous, inhumane and unmerciful conduct and behaviour." Mears wrote to Lopez on July 20, 1779, "To describe the scene with all its horrors and the distress of its inhabitants would require a much abler pen than mine . . ." He and others—Myer and Asher Myers, and Moses Isaacs—had to flee, leaving behind "a considerable part of furniture and other valuable effects in our respective dwellings that has, to the great distress of some of our families, been consumed with the houses."[9]

Eventually, Samson Mears and his relatives found accommodations in Wilton, a few miles up the Norwalk River, safely away from Long Island Sound. The comparative tranquility of Wilton did not quell Mears's restlessness. In November 1779, he was preparing "to leave the continent in persuit of better fortune than I have met on it." In 1780 Samson Mears left North America and returned to St. Eustatius. Nothing more is known about his life there. Like his father Judah and his grandfather Moses Michaels, Samson Mears died in the West Indies. In 1786 or 1787 he died in St. Eustatius, leaving no will. Letters of administration were granted to his brother-in-law, Solomon Simson, in New York on February 19, 1787.[10]

So ended a life marked by loneliness and frustration. Except for the few years of his childless marriage, Samson Mears spent his adult life alone. Hampered by the era's political upheavals, financial success eluded him. Whatever fortune Samson Mears earned came from overseas trade. In 1788 the Marine Society of New York acknowledged this by making Mears a posthumous honorary member.[11]

Samson and Hannah Mears had no children.

—m—

1. Gottesman, *Arts and Crafts,* 52.
2. Emmanuel, *Netherland Antilles,* 1055.
3. Chyet, *Lopez,* 145–48.
4. Hühner, "Jews of New England," 84; Marcus, *Colonial,* 141–42.
5. "Earliest Extant," 79; Emmanuel, *Netherland Antilles,* 522; Phillips, "Items Relating," 149–51.
6. Marcus, "Connecticut Jewry," 11; Hühner, "Jews of New England," 92.
7. Marcus, "Connecticut Jewry," 12–13.
8. Ibid., 46.
9. Hühner, "Jews of New England," 161.
10. Marcus, "Connecticut Jewry," 48; *Collections of the New York Historical Society,* 348.
11. Pool, *Old Faith,* 471.

CHAPTER SEVEN

JACOB ISAACKS
(c. 1718–1798)

and

REBECCA MEARS ISAACKS
(1738–1802)

JUDAH AND JOCHABED MICHAELS MEARS had six daughters and one son, Samson, whose life was described in the previous chapter. Their daughter Rebecca married Jacob Isaacks in Newport, Rhode Island, on October 8, 1760, when he was forty-two and she was about twenty-two. The descent of Adeline Moses Loeb is traced through this union.

The backgrounds of Jacob Isaacks and Rebecca Mears were remarkably similar. Both were born in America, probably in New York City. Rebecca's mother, Jochabed Michaels Mears, was also native-born, but her father, Judah Mears, had migrated from England. Jacob's father, Abraham, was born in Emden, a North Sea port in what is now the state of Lower Saxony in northwestern Germany. It is not known where his mother, Hannah Mears Isaacks (undoubtedly a relation of Judah Mears), was born. Both Rebecca's and Jacob's fathers were merchant shippers. Both families were Ashkenazi and active members of Congregation Shearith Israel of New York City.

Jacob, the oldest child in a family of six, was born about 1718. Rebecca's birth date and birth order in her family are unknown, but she was probably born around 1738, making an age difference of about twenty years between Jacob and Rebecca Isaacks. An age difference this great was not uncommon in Jewish marriages at the time. The small number of Jews in the American colonies limited the availability of eligible mates for marriage. Deaths of their wives during childbirth often left widowers with children who needed a mother.[1]

Jacob's father, Abraham Isaacks, migrated to New York from Emden around 1697 or 1698. He was made a freeman of the City of New York on August 6, 1723, and two years later, on September 29, 1725, was elected constable of the South Ward. He was naturalized under the Plantation Act of 1740. This act allowed for the uniform naturalization of all aliens in the British colonies after seven years of residence and permitted Jews to swear allegiance to the Crown and be excused from taking the oath "upon the true faith of a Christian."[2]

Like many New York Jews of the early eighteenth century, Abraham Isaacks was active in overseas trade. He worked closely with the successful merchant Nathan Simson, and he took charge of handling his American affairs after Simson returned to London. Abraham Isaacks was also a man of property. He owned a house and lot on Pearl Street in Manhattan, land in Oyster Bay, Long Island, and "120 acres of good land with a good dwelling house, store house, barn, two barracks, and orchard" in Griggstown on the Millstone River in Somerset County, New Jersey. Following his death, his son Jacob sold all of these properties.[3]

Abraham Isaacks was an active member of Congregation Shearith Israel. His name appears in the earliest written records of the congregation, which date from 1720. In that year, Abraham Isaacks was one of the thirty-seven active, dues-paying members. Even at this early date, Ashkenazim already outnumbered Sephardim in this "Sephardic" synagogue. In 1728 Abraham Isaacks was one of the signers of a petition presented to the New York Common Council to permit the establishment of a Jewish cemetery on land purchased by the congregation from the executors of Moses Levy's estate. He contributed £1 8s. toward the purchase of the property.

Isaacks also participated in the purchase of land for the building of a synagogue for Shearith Israel, which was consecrated on the seventh day of Passover, 1730. That same year, he donated £3 to Shearith Israel in honor of his eldest son Jacob, perhaps in commemoration of his bar mitzvah. In 1732 Abraham Isaacks served as *gabay* (treasurer) of Shearith Israel. In 1733 and again in 1737 he was *parnas* (president) of the congregation.[4]

At one time, Isaacks apparently planned to settle in England, perhaps to join his colleague Nathan Simson in business there. In March 1731, the following notice appeared in the *New York Gazette:*

> This is to give notice that Abraham Isaacs of the City of New York, merchant, is bound to Great Britain and all persons that have any demand on him are desired to and receive the same, and those who are indebted to him are desired to come and settle their accounts immediately in order to prevent trouble.[5]

It is not known if Abraham Isaacks ever left for England. He died in New York on September 24, 1743, and was buried in the Shearith Israel Cemetery. His tombstone (in Hebrew) reads as follows:

> Here lies buried
> The venerable and honored married man
> Rabbi Abraham son of Isaac* (whose memory is a blessing)
>   From the City of Emden in Friesland
> He died on the first of the middle days of Sukkot and was buried
> The same day in the year 5504 [September 24, 1743]
> May his soul be bound up in the bond of life.[6]

Abraham Isaacks died intestate and letters of administration were granted to his widow Hannah on October 6, 1743. When she died two years later, her husband's affairs were still not settled and new letters were granted to their eldest son (Jacob) on September 24, 1745. The estate of Abraham Isaacks was not settled for another thirteen years and required several court visits. At the time of Abraham Isaacks's death, John Merritt held a promissory note of Abraham Isaacks dated

---

*   Rabbi is an honorific title only. Isaacks took his father's name Isaac as his last name when he migrated to America.

April 14, 1743, for £285 lawful money of New York plus interest. On September 18, 1755, Merritt sued Jacob Isaacks for £6,000 current money of New England. The case was heard once in New York and twice in the Inferior Court of Common Pleas of Rhode Island. The Privy Council in London finally heard the case on February 17, 1758, finding in favor of Jacob Isaacks.[7]

When his father died in 1743, Jacob Isaacks was probably a resident of Newport. Although there was a small Jewish settlement in Newport as early as 1658, the Newport Jewish community experienced its greatest growth and prosperity between 1740 and 1770—decades that coincided with the era of Newport's greatest economic prosperity. During the long period of war and uneasy peace between France and England from 1743 to 1763, Boston's position as the principal port of entry for English goods was undermined. Ports in Philadelphia, New York, Providence, and Newport all captured some of Boston's business.

In the 1740s, Newport ships collected and discharged cargo up and down the American coast and into the Caribbean. Rhode Island was also the principal center of the American slave trade. The ships of the colony carried rum to Africa and traded for slaves, whom they then sold to planters in Virginia and the Carolinas. During this period, a number of New York Jewish merchants were attracted to Newport and, like Jacob Isaacks, decided to make it their home. At the height of Newport's prosperity, there may have been as many as a thousand Jews living there.[8]

Jacob Isaacks remained a resident of Newport from the early 1740s until his death in 1798, except for a brief period during the Revolutionary War when the British occupied the town and Isaacks and his family were forced to flee. He was active in every aspect of community life—community welfare, the war effort, the synagogue, the Freemasons, and Jewish social life. His economic career was similarly wide-ranging. He was at various times a shipper, an insurance agent, a real estate broker, a scientist-inventor, and a moneychanger. He sold everything from sugar, rice, and tea to houses, property, ships, and Negro slaves. Diversity in business was typical of the times.

American Jewry in the eighteenth century enjoyed greater political, social, and economic freedom than did Jews in England or in the European countries, all of which restricted Jewish economic and political activity in some way. America's Jews were quick to take advantage of these freedoms, and they acclimated themselves with relative ease to American life. The life and career of Jacob Isaacks give testimony to how comfortable and how much at home America's Jews felt.

When Isaacks felt his rights as a citizen had been violated, he was quick to protest and take his case to the proper authorities. This happened many times during his long career. The first such incident occurred shortly after he had moved to Newport, where he was declared a "stranger" by the town authorities and ordered to pay a special tax assessed on nonresidents conducting business in Rhode Island. In 1742, fourteen "transient persons and Strangers," including five Jews, were assessed from £3 to £10 by the town of Newport. Of the fourteen who were assessed, three of them—Jacob Isaacks, Abraham Hart, and Issachar Pollock—objected to the designation of "stranger" and refused to pay the tax. Town Constable Dyre then seized various silks, linens, and rugs belonging to the three in lieu of payment. Isaacks, Hart, and Pollock then brought action against Dyre in the Superior Court of Common Pleas and submitted various proofs of their Rhode Island residency. However, the Supreme Court found that their residency in the colony was not long enough to exempt them from payment of the tax.[9]

This incident did not sour Isaacks on his adopted city, and he maintained an interest in civic affairs and a dedication to the improvement of his community. In August 1762 he signed a petition along with seventy-seven other Newport residents, protesting what they considered to be an unfair form of assessment. In 1763 Isaacks was the only Jew among 150 Newport citizens who petitioned the Rhode Island General Assembly to establish government hospitals to provide inoculation against smallpox. In 1768 he signed yet another petition, this time asking the General Assembly to authorize a lottery, the proceeds of which would be used to pave a street in Newport.[10]

Jacob Isaacks's sense of civic responsibility extended beyond his home of Newport. As a young man, he volunteered to serve with the British forces fighting the French in North America during King George's War (1744–1748). He served as a private in Captain Samuel Lumbart's Tenth Company of the Seventh Massachusetts Regiment in the expedition sent by the Colony of Massachusetts Bay to capture Louisbourg in Nova Scotia from the French in 1745. By the time of the Revolution, thirty years later, Isaacks, a patriot, was too old to serve in the Revolutionary Army, but he aided the war effort by loaning three four-pounders (cannons) to Rhode Island.[11]

When British forces occupied Newport on December 8, 1776, only a handful of residents remained in the town. Most of the Jewish community had fled, including Jacob Isaacks and his family. They returned to Newport at the war's end. In making preparations to leave Newport in December 1776, Jacob Isaacks had stored eighty-six casks of white and spermaceti oil with a Martin Luther in Warren, Rhode Island. After the war, Isaacks went to reclaim his oil and found it missing. He learned that in July 1778 the Council of War had ordered the casks removed from Bristol County to Providence. Beyond that, there was no record of what had happened to the oil or, if it had been sold, what had become of the money. In October 1781 the Rhode Island Assembly, acting on the petition of Jacob Isaacks, appointed a committee to investigate the incident. Unfortunately, no report of the committee has ever been found.[12]

In addition to the loss of eighty-six casks of oil, Isaacks also suffered a more personal humiliation. After the Rhode Island Whigs returned to power in Newport, Isaacks and four other Jews were accused of being Tories. The reasons behind this accusation are unknown. Perhaps it was felt that Isaacks should have done more to aid the American cause, or perhaps it was just a case of political revenge or commercial rivalry.[13]

Jacob Isaacks was a major force in the development of Newport's Jewish communal institutions. While still a resident of New York, in 1736 he was granted a license as a ritual *shohet* (slaughterer) by David Mendez Machado, then the hazan (cantor) of Congregation Shearith Israel. When Isaacks moved to Newport a few years later he, along with Zachariah Polack, provided kosher meat for the community and they both acted as officiants of the synagogue, which was initially maintained in a private home.[14]

This very rare silk prayer shawl (*tallit*), nine feet long, dates back to before 1743, and possibly as early as the 1600s. It once belonged to the five-times great-grandfather of Adeline Moses Loeb. Abraham Isaacks (died 1743) was a wealthy merchant in New York City and a prominent member of Shearith Israel in the 1700s, and at one time he served as the *parnas* (president) of the congregation. The *tallit* is now owned by the American Jewish Historical Society, the gift of a family descendant, Judith Alexander Weil Shanks, author of *Old Family Things*.

—Courtesy of the American Jewish Historical Society
New York, N.Y. and Newton Centre, Mass.
Photo by Henri Silberman

Jacob Isaacks remained a contributing member of Shearith Israel in New York until 1759, when the Newport Jewish community decided to build a synagogue. Just as when the St. Eustatius congregation needed funds to rebuild its hurricane-damaged building, the Newport community turned to its coreligionists in the older, established communities of New York, Jamaica, Curaçao, Surinam, and London for help in raising the funds necessary to build a synagogue.

An East Perspective View of the City of Philadelpha, in the Province of Pennsylvania, in North America, Taken from the Jersey Shore, *1752*
1778 engraving based on the work of artist George Heap — courtesy of The New York Public Library

On July 4, 1788, the people of Philadelphia held a parade and public feast to celebrate the ratification of the U. S. Constitution by the Pennsylvania Commonwealth. Clergy of many denominations were among the participants. In his reminiscences of the parade, Dr. Benjamin Rush, a signer of the Declaration of Independence, noted ". . . the Rabbi of the Jews, locked in the arms of two ministers of the gospel, was a most delightful sight."

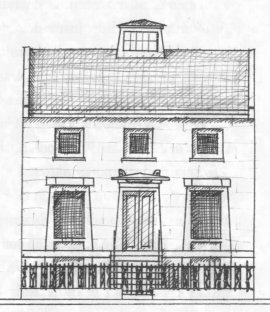

Mikveh Israel (1825)–Cherry Alley

Mikveh Israel's Second Synagogue (1860)

Naphtali Phillips, a third cousin through marriage to Adeline Moses Loeb, had participated in the parade as a teenager. He later wrote that "the arrangers of the fête, with a thoughtfulness that gives evidence of their high regard for their Jewish fellow citizens, prepared a special kosher table for the Jews . . . [who] could not partake of the meals from the other tables."

Philadelphia, Pennsylvania

c. 1776–1790

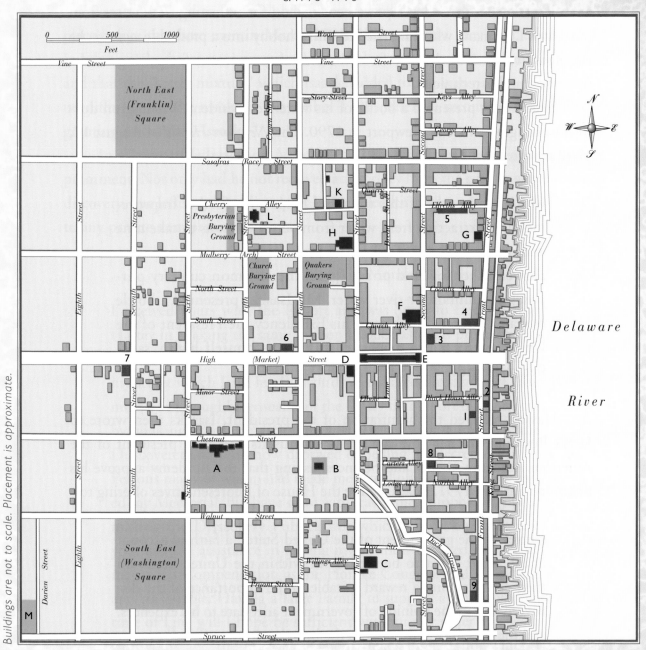

Public Buildings ■

A. Independence Hall/
   Congress Hall/Old City Hall
B Carpenter's Hall
C. St. Paul's Church
D Gaol (Jail)
E. Courthouse
F. Christ Church
G. Quaker Meeting House
H. New Presbyterian Meeting House

K. Mikveh Israel Synagogue (1782)
   (Cherry Street Synagogue)
L. German Lutheran Church

Parks & Cemeteries ■

M. Mikveh Israel Cemetery (1740)
   (Spruce Street Cemetery)

Private Homes & Businesses ■

1. Isaac Franks (broker)
2. Samuel Hays (broker)

3. Israel Jacobs Store
4. Hyam Salomon
5. Jacob I. Cohen, Jacob R. Cohen,
   Elazar Levy, Joseph Levy, Moses
   Mordecai, Levy Rosenthal
6. Michael Gratz and Family
7. Simon & Hyman Gratz business
   (Graff House)
8. Levy Franks Business
9. Daniel Gomez Dry Goods

Descendants of
Jacob Isaacks & Rebecca Mears

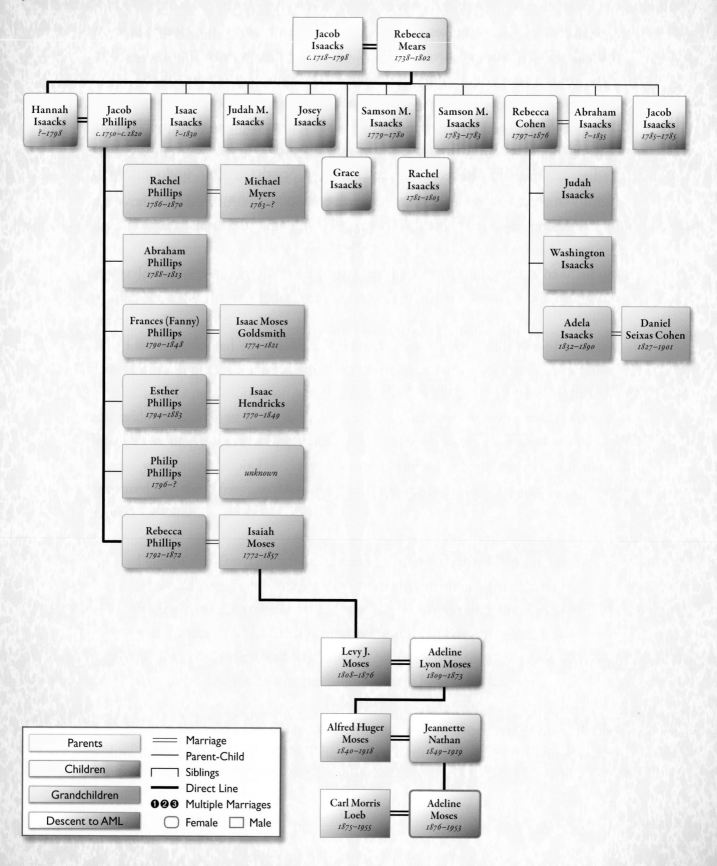

The Children of Jacob and Rebecca Mears Isaacks

1. **Samson M.** (born December 27, 1779; died in infancy, January 20, 1780).

2. **Rachel** (born 1781, Charleston, South Carolina; died September 22, 1803, Cheraw, South Carolina).

3. **Samson M.** (born June 13, 1783; died in infancy, June 29, 1783).

4. **Jacob** (born 1785; died in the same year).

5. **Hannah** (born Newport, Rhode Island, or Jamaica; died March 8, 1798, Martinique, West Indies). Married Jacob Phillips (born c. 1750, England; died c. 1820, Charleston, South Carolina) on August 13, 1785, in Newport, Rhode Island. They had six children: Rachel, Abraham, Frances (Fanny), Rebecca, Esther, and Philip. **Their daughter Rebecca married Isaiah Moses. They were the great-grandparents of Adeline Moses Loeb.**

6. **Isaac** (died March 3, 1830, Havana, Cuba).

7. **Abraham** (born Rhode Island; died February 25, 1835, Montgomery, Alabama). Married Rebecca Cohen (born November 2, 1797, Charleston, South Carolina; died March 3, 1876, Nyack, New York). They had three children: Judah, Washington, and Adela.

8. **Judah M.** (died Charleston, South Carolina).

9. **Josey.**

10. **Grace.**[31]

—⁂—

family legend, every Friday evening his grandchildren came to his bedside to receive a Sabbath blessing from him. He died about 1820.[7]

Jacob Phillips was the last representative of the Moses family to make a living in the West Indian trade. His death brought an end to a lifestyle that had characterized the family for nearly 150 years. The men of the first four generations of the family were immigrants or sons of immigrants. They were well-traveled, cosmopolitan men who were equally at home in London, Charleston, New York, or Curaçao. They maintained strong ties with the London commercial world—their business associations were international—and they were as much a part of the West Indian world as they were of the American scene. International political events had a profound and personal effect on the family fortunes of these first generations, particularly the war between France and Great Britain, national acts regulating international trade, and the American War of Independence.

In contrast, the lives of the next three generations were lived almost entirely in the South. These men had no connection with overseas trade but made their living in the Southern regional economy. Isaiah Moses, the next in line after Jacob Phillips, was a plantation owner and shopkeeper in South Carolina. His son, Levy Moses, was a bookkeeper and notary public in Charleston. His son, Alfred Moses, was a lawyer, banker, and real estate developer in Alabama.

The history of the Moses family began with the marriage of Judah Mears to Jochabed Michaels in the 1730s and continued through three female descendants. The Mears's daughter Rebecca married Jacob Isaacks; the Isaacks's daughter Hannah married Jacob Phillips; the Phillips's daughter Rebecca married Isaiah Moses. Beginning with Isaiah Moses, the descent continues through the male line—from Isaiah Moses' son Levy to Levy's son Alfred, the father of Adeline Moses Loeb.

—⚮—

Descendants of
Jacob Phillips & Hannah Isaacks

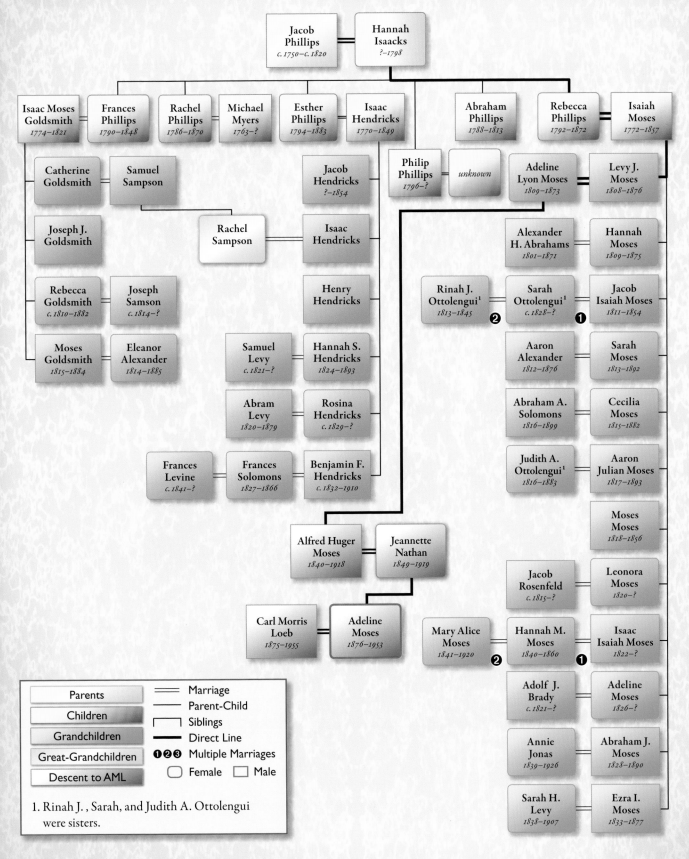

Jacob Phillips *c. 1750–c. 1820* — Hannah Isaacks *?–1798*

Isaac Moses Goldsmith *1774–1821* — Frances Phillips *1790–1848* — Rachel Phillips *1786–1870* — Michael Myers *1763–?* — Esther Phillips *1794–1883* — Isaac Hendricks *1770–1849* — Abraham Phillips *1788–1813* — Rebecca Phillips *1792–1872* — Isaiah Moses *1772–1857*

Catherine Goldsmith — Samuel Sampson

Jacob Hendricks *?–1854*

Philip Phillips *1796–?* — *unknown* — Adeline Lyon Moses *1809–1873* — Levy J. Moses *1808–1876*

Joseph J. Goldsmith

Rachel Sampson — Isaac Hendricks

Alexander H. Abrahams *1801–1871* — Hannah Moses *1809–1875*

Rebecca Goldsmith *c. 1810–1882* — Joseph Samson *c. 1814–?*

Henry Hendricks

Rinah J. Ottolengui[1] *1813–1845* ❷ — Sarah Ottolengui[1] *c. 1828–?* ❶ — Jacob Isaiah Moses *1811–1854*

Moses Goldsmith *1815–1884* — Eleanor Alexander *1814–1885*

Samuel Levy *c. 1821–?* — Hannah S. Hendricks *1824–1893*

Aaron Alexander *1812–1876* — Sarah Moses *1813–1892*

Abram Levy *1820–1879* — Rosina Hendricks *c. 1829–?*

Abraham A. Solomons *1816–1899* — Cecilia Moses *1815–1882*

Frances Levine *c. 1841–?* — Frances Solomons *1827–1866* — Benjamin F. Hendricks *c. 1832–1910*

Judith A. Ottolengui[1] *1816–1883* — Aaron Julian Moses *1817–1893*

Moses Moses *1818–1856*

Alfred Huger Moses *1840–1918* — Jeannette Nathan *1849–1919*

Jacob Rosenfeld *c. 1815–?* — Leonora Moses *1820–?*

Carl Morris Loeb *1875–1955* — Adeline Moses *1876–1953*

Mary Alice Moses *1841–1920* ❷ — Hannah M. Moses *1840–1860* ❶ — Isaac Isaiah Moses *1822–?*

Adolf J. Brady *c. 1821–?* — Adeline Moses *1826–?*

Annie Jonas *1839–1926* — Abraham J. Moses *1828–1890*

Sarah H. Levy *1838–1907* — Ezra I. Moses *1833–1877*

Legend:
Parents
Children
Grandchildren
Great-Grandchildren
Descent to AML

Marriage
Parent-Child
Siblings
Direct Line
❶❷❸ Multiple Marriages
◯ Female ▢ Male

1. Rinah J., Sarah, and Judith A. Ottolengui were sisters.

The Children of Jacob and Hannah Isaacks Phillips

1. **Rachel** (born October 5, 1786, Newport, Rhode Island; died October 5, 1870, Charleston, South Carolina). Married Michael Myers (born October 25, 1763, Brightkaleraston, England) in Charleston on October 10, 1802. They had no children.

2. **Abraham** (born March 24, 1788, New York; died April 15, 1813, off the coast of Norfolk, Virginia). A midshipman in the War of 1812, he drowned when his ship overturned near Norfolk, Virginia. He died unmarried.

3. **Frances (Fanny)** (born February 5, 1790; died March 4, 1848). Married Isaac Moses Goldsmith of Charleston (born 1774, Rotterdam, Holland; died September 26, 1821, Charleston, South Carolina). They had four children: Catherine, Moses, Joseph J., and Rebecca.

4. **Rebecca** (born March 19, 1792, at sea; died December 24, 1872, Savannah, Georgia). Married Isaiah Moses (born March 18, 1772, Bederkese, Hannover, Germany; died January 28, 1857, Charleston, South Carolina) on November 11, 1807. He was a widower with four children. Rebecca and Isaiah Moses had twelve children of their own: Levy J., Hannah, Jacob I., Sarah, Cecilia, Aaron J., Moses, Leonora, Isaac I., Adeline, Abraham J., and Ezra I. **Levy, their first-born, was the grandfather of Adeline Moses Loeb.**

5. **Esther** (born December 6, 1794, England; died January 21, 1883). Married Isaac Hendricks of Augusta, Georgia (born 1770, Poland; died March 13, 1849, Augusta, Georgia). Isaac and Esther Hendricks had six children: Jacob, Henry, Isaac, Hannah S., Benjamin Franklin, and Rosina.

6. **Philip** (born November 5, 1796). Married a Christian woman, name unknown.[8]

—⟋⟍—

1. Alexander, "Abraham Phillips," 126.
2. "Earliest Extant," 148–49.
3. Alexander, *Notes*, 89.
4. Emmanuel, *Netherland Antilles*, 1066.
5. Rosenswaike, "An Estimate," 42.
6. Alexander, *Notes*, 90; Rosengarten, *Portion of the People*, 100.
7. Alexander, *Notes*, 61.
8. Alexander, "Abraham Phillips," 125–27; Stern, *First American*, 84, 210, 247.

CHAPTER NINE

ISAIAH MOSES
(1772–1857)

and

REBECCA PHILLIPS MOSES
(1792–1872)

IN THE EARLY NINETEENTH CENTURY, Charleston, South Carolina, was a bustling commercial city, the second busiest export center in the United States after New York. King Street was Charleston's major commercial thoroughfare, the address of many of the city's retail establishments.

The city had a substantial Jewish population, although exact numbers are difficult to calculate. At the time of the first federal census of 1790, estimates of the Jewish population ranged from 200 to 250. The population of Charleston in 1790 was 16,359; the white population was 8,089. Jews constituted about 3 percent of the city's white population, making its Jewish population second only to New York's. Charleston Jews made up about 15 percent of the total American Jewish population of around 1,500, and by 1800 Charleston's Jewish community of about 600 was the largest in the country. Charleston retained that dominance until 1830, when both New York's and Philadelphia's Jewish populations (1,150 and 750, respectively) surpassed Charleston's 650–700 Jewish residents.[1]

The first settlers in Charleston were primarily Spanish and Portuguese Jews from London, although Ashkenazi Jews were included among the earliest families. Germany was the most common foreign birthplace of Charleston's antebellum Jewish community, followed by England. Over 27 percent of foreign-born Jews came from Germany; 24 percent came from England.[2]

One German Jewish immigrant who settled in Charleston in the late eighteenth century was Isaiah Moses, who was born in Bederkese near Bremerhaven,

Rebecca Phillips Moses
(1792–1872)

Rebecca was born at sea on a brigantine, a sailing ship captained by her father, Jacob Phillips, while her parents were en route from Columbia, South Carolina, to St. Eustatius, a Dutch West Indies island. It was a trip they made frequently. Married at the age of fifteen (almost sixteen), Rebecca was the mother of twelve children and four stepchildren. Her oldest daughter, Hannah, commissioned this portrait of her mother when Rebecca was fifty-one. This second wife of Isaiah Moses was a passionate supporter of the Confederacy, and according to family legend, suffered a stroke when she heard of General Robert E. Lee's surrender to the Union in April 1865. Her grandfather, Jacob Isaacks, was one of the founders of the Touro Synagogue in Newport, Rhode Island.

—Rebecca Phillips Moses was the great-grandmother of Adeline Moses Loeb
C. W. Uhl, oil on canvas, 1843; Cecil A. Alexander Jr. collection

Isaiah Moses
(1772–1857)

Isaiah was a Charleston King Street dry-goods merchant and shop owner who achieved the Southern businessman's ideal of success: owning a plantation. Unhappily, the 794 acres of The Oaks had been overcultivated and hence were unproductive by 1813, when Isaiah purchased the property. Though profit from his dry-goods business helped to maintain it, after a twenty-eight-year struggle and many loans taken to keep it going, he gave up after the house burned in 1840. In 1841 he sold the property and its slaves at a loss.

Always intensely religious, Isaiah Moses was a staunch traditionalist, known as a leader in the fight against reforms to the service of the Sephardic Beth Elohim.

—Portrait by Theodore Sidney Moïse, born 1808
Oil on canvas, undated but thought to be c. 1830–1835
Cecil A. Alexander Jr. collection

Family genes have shown up in at least one of the great-great-great-grandsons of Isaiah
Moses. The similarity in looks and demeanor is evident in this 1970 photo of Ambassador
John L. Loeb Jr. standing beside his ancestor's portrait.

—Ambassador John L. Loeb Jr. collection

Hannover, Germany, on March 18, 1772. Isaiah Moses migrated to America with
his brother Levy, and we know he was a resident of Charleston by 1800, because
his name appears in the earliest cashbooks of Congregation Beth Elohim of
Charleston, which date from 1800. He is also listed in the Charleston city directory of 1800 as the proprietor of a grocery on King Street.[3]

Isaiah Moses was married sometime in the 1790s, probably after settling in
America. His first child, Phineas, was born in 1798 and was followed by Morris,
Solomon, and Simeon. His wife then died and Isaiah Moses was left with the care
of four young sons, but not for long. On November 11, 1807, the thirty-five-
year-old widower married fifteen-year-old Rebecca Phillips, second daughter of
Jacob and Hannah Phillips. Isaiah and Rebecca Moses were Adeline Moses Loeb's
paternal great-grandparents.[4]

Eleven months after their marriage, their first child, Levy, was born on October 7, 1808. Eleven more children followed Levy. The last, Ezra, was born August 14, 1833. Remarkably, not only did all of these children survive their infancy and childhood and live to adulthood, but Rebecca herself survived twelve pregnancies and deliveries. It was rare to find a family that had not suffered the loss of an infant or a child—or the loss of the mother herself in childbirth. Rebecca's own mother died at a young age, probably in childbirth, and the first wife of Isaiah Moses probably shared a similar fate.

The first three Moses children were born in Columbia, South Carolina, in 1808, 1809, and 1811. It is not known whether the family was living in Columbia at the time or if Rebecca went there to have her babies, as the name of Isaiah Moses remained in the Charleston city directory during those years. Beginning with the fourth child, Sarah, in 1813, the remaining nine children were all born in Charleston.[5]

The Southern economy was predominantly agrarian, and the large plantation owners set the tone and style of life. The most prosperous urban dwellers—whether lawyers, physicians, or merchants—aspired to be plantation owners. This was as true for Jews as for non-Jews. Most Jewish planters first had successful careers as merchants or professionals. Many retained their city businesses, which they could always fall back on should their plantation debts accumulate.[6]

The white urban population in the South was small—fewer than 8 percent lived in towns with a population of over 4,000. However, most Southern Jews lived in towns and cities, earning their livings as shopkeepers and merchants. Isaiah Moses was one of a small group of Southern Jews who became plantation owners. (Charleston city directories and other records list a total of only twelve Jewish planters.) In 1813 he invested the profits from his King Street shop in 794 acres of land in St. James, Goose Creek, then a part of Charleston County. Moses paid $6,000 for the property known as "The Oaks." The socially prominent Middleton family had owned the plantation from 1678 to 1794. Although thirty-five slaves worked the plantation at the time, it was no longer profitable. By the time Moses bought the land, the soil was depleted and the sixty acres of rice land were not enough to support the expenses required for profitable cultivation. Moses used the

A Northwest by North View of Charles Town from on Board the Bristol, 1776
1776 etching by William Faden — courtesy of United States Library of Congress

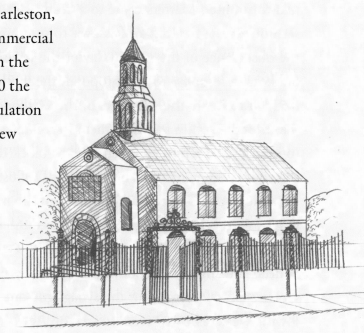

Kahal Kadosh Beth Elohim (dedicated 1794)

In the early nineteenth century Charleston, South Carolina was a bustling commercial city, the second busiest export center in the United States after New York. By 1790 the city had the second largest Jewish population in the country, again second only to New York; Charleston Jews made up about 15 percent of the total American Jewish population of around 1,500.

Kahal Kadosh Beth Elohim (dedicated 1841)

Ten years later, in 1800, Charleston's Jewish community of about 600 was the largest in the country. Many of Adeline Moses Loeb's ancestors and familial connections were among these early citizens.

Charleston, South Carolina

c. 1860–1870

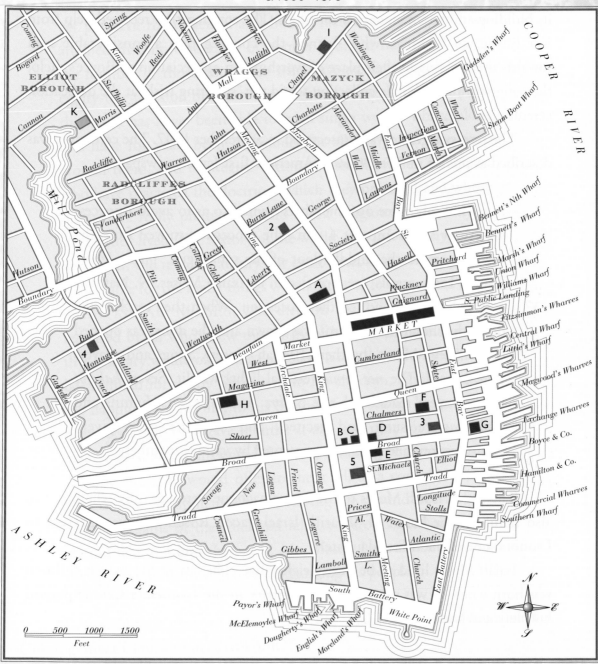

Buildings are not to scale. Placement is approximate.

0   500   1000   1500
Feet

Public Buildings
A. Kahal Kadosh Beth Elohim
B. Hebrew Orphan Society
C. City Hall
D. Courthouse
E. St. Michaels Church

F. Slave Mart
G. Exchange
H. County Jail

Parks & Cemeteries
K. Coming Street Cemetery (1762)

Private Homes & Businesses
1. Moses Family residence
2. Alfred Huger Moses home
3. Alfred Huger Moses business
4. Moses Isaacs home
5. Moses Cohen Mordecai home

Descendants of
Isaiah Moses & Rebecca Phillips

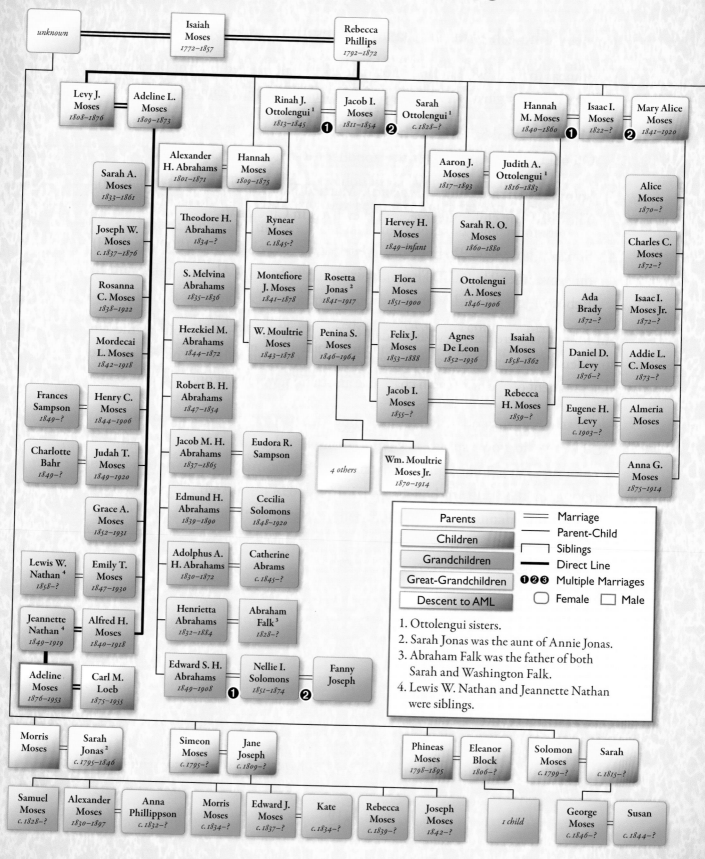

Isaiah Moses *1772–1857*
Rebecca Phillips *1792–1872*
unknown

Levy J. Moses *1808–1876*
Adeline L. Moses *1809–1873*
Rinah J. Ottolengui [1] *1813–1845* ❶
Jacob I. Moses *1811–1854* ❷
Sarah Ottolengui [1] *c.1828–?*
Hannah M. Moses *1840–1860* ❶
Isaac I. Moses *1822–?* ❷
Mary Alice Moses *1841–1920*

Sarah A. Moses *1833–1861*
Alexander H. Abrahams *1801–1871*
Hannah Moses *1809–1875*
Aaron J. Moses *1817–1893*
Judith A. Ottolengui [1] *1816–1883*
Alice Moses *1870–?*

Joseph W. Moses *c.1837–1876*
Theodore H. Abrahams *1834–?*
Rynear Moses *c.1845–?*
Hervey H. Moses *1849–infant*
Sarah R. O. Moses *1860–1880*
Charles C. Moses *1872–?*

Rosanna C. Moses *1838–1922*
S. Melvina Abrahams *1835–1836*
Montefiore J. Moses *1841–1878*
Rosetta Jonas [2] *1841–1917*
Flora Moses *1851–1900*
Ottolengui A. Moses *1846–1906*
Ada Brady *1872–?*
Isaac I. Moses Jr. *1872–?*

Mordecai L. Moses *1842–1918*
Hezekiel M. Abrahams *1844–1872*
W. Moultrie Moses *1843–1878*
Penina S. Moses *1846–1964*
Felix J. Moses *1853–1888*
Agnes De Leon *1852–1936*
Isaiah Moses *1858–1862*
Daniel D. Levy *1876–?*
Addie L. C. Moses *1873–?*

Frances Sampson *1849–?*
Henry C. Moses *1844–1906*
Robert B. H. Abrahams *1847–1854*
Jacob I. Moses *1855–?*
Rebecca H. Moses *1859–?*
Eugene H. Levy *c.1903–?*
Almeria Moses

Charlotte Bahr *1849–?*
Judah T. Moses *1849–1920*
Jacob M. H. Abrahams *1837–1865*
Eudora R. Sampson
4 others
Wm. Moultrie Moses Jr. *1870–1914*
Anna G. Moses *1875–1914*

Grace A. Moses *1852–1931*
Edmund H. Abrahams *1839–1890*
Cecilia Solomons *1848–1920*

Lewis W. Nathan [4] *1858–?*
Emily T. Moses *1847–1930*
Adolphus A. H. Abrahams *1830–1872*
Catherine Abrams *c.1845–?*

Jeannette Nathan [4] *1849–1919*
Alfred H. Moses *1840–1918*
Henrietta Abrahams *1832–1884*
Abraham Falk [3] *1828–?*

Adeline Moses *1876–1953*
Carl M. Loeb *1875–1955*
Edward S. H. Abrahams *1849–1908* ❶
Nellie I. Solomons *1851–1874* ❷
Fanny Joseph

Legend
Parents	═══ Marriage
Children	── Parent-Child
Grandchildren	⌐ Siblings
Great-Grandchildren	━━ Direct Line
Descent to AML	❶❷❸ Multiple Marriages
	◯ Female ▢ Male

1. Ottolengui sisters.
2. Sarah Jonas was the aunt of Annie Jonas.
3. Abraham Falk was the father of both Sarah and Washington Falk.
4. Lewis W. Nathan and Jeannette Nathan were siblings.

Morris Moses
Sarah Jonas [2] *c.1795–1846*
Simeon Moses *c.1795–?*
Jane Joseph *c.1809–?*
Phineas Moses *1798–1895*
Eleanor Block *1806–?*
Solomon Moses *c.1799–?*
Sarah *c.1815–?*

Samuel Moses *c.1828–?*
Alexander Moses *1830–1897*
Anna Phillippson *c.1832–?*
Morris Moses *c.1834–?*
Edward J. Moses *c.1837–?*
Kate *c.1834–?*
Rebecca Moses *c.1839–?*
Joseph Moses *1842–?*
1 child
George Moses *c.1846–?*
Susan *c.1844–?*

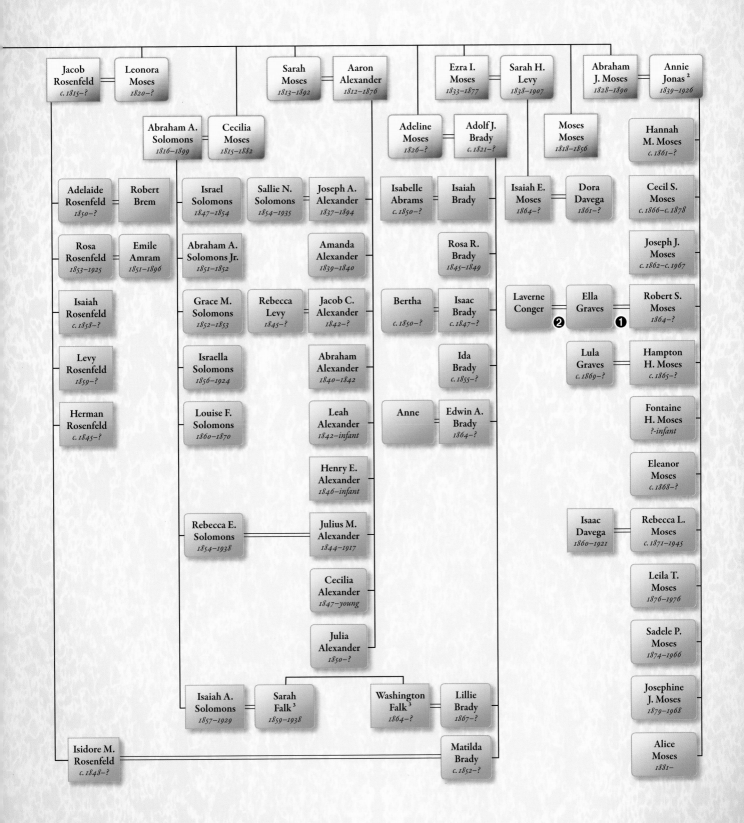

The Children of Isaiah and Rebecca Phillips Moses

1. **Levy J.** (born October 7, 1808, Columbia, South Carolina; died July 21, 1876, Montgomery, Alabama). Married Adeline Lyon Moses (born October 23, 1809, Charleston, South Carolina; died November 19, 1873, Montgomery, Alabama) on November 21, 1832, in Charleston, South Carolina, where he worked as a bookkeeper and notary public. Levy and Adeline had nine children: Sarah A., Joseph Winthrop, Rosanna Cecilia, Alfred Huger, Mordecai Lyon, Henry Clay, Emily Touro, Judah Touro, and Grace Aguilar. **Their fourth child, Alfred Huger Moses, was the father of Adeline Moses Loeb, who was named for her paternal grandmother.**

2. **Hannah** (born December 17, 1809, Columbia, South Carolina; died April 18, 1875, Charleston, South Carolina). Married Alexander Hezekiel Abrahams (born June 18, 1801, Berkhoff, near Bremen, Germany; died October 16, 1871, South Carolina) on April 8, 1829, in Charleston, South Carolina. They had nine children: Adolphus Alexander Hezekiel, Henrietta, Theodore H., Sarah Melvina, Jacob Melvin H., Edmund H., Hezekiel Moses, Robert Brown H., and Edward Sebring H.

3. **Jacob I.** (born March 31, 1811, Columbia, South Carolina; died December 10, 1854, Charleston, South Carolina). First married Rinah J. Ottolengui (born September 27, 1813, Charleston, South Carolina; died April 25, 1845) on December 7, 1839. Jacob and Rinah had three children: Montefiore Jacob, William Moultrie, and Rynear. William's son, W. Moultrie Moses Jr., married his cousin Anna Green Moses. After Rinah died, Jacob married her younger sister Sarah Ottolengui (born c. 1828, South Carolina) on May 24, 1848. Jacob and Sarah had four children: Hervey Hall, Flora (married her cousin Ottolengui Aaron Moses), Felix Jacob, and Jacob Isaiah (married his cousin Rebecca Hannah Moses).

4. **Sarah** (born May 25, 1813, Charleston, South Carolina; died July 10, 1892, Atlanta, Georgia). Married Aaron Alexander (born March 7, 1812, Charleston,

South Carolina; died June 1, 1876, Atlanta, Georgia) on October 5, 1836, in Charleston, South Carolina. They moved to Montgomery before the Civil War and their nephew Alfred Huger Moses lived with them while he was a law student. They had nine children: Joseph Albert, Amanda, Abraham, Jacob Clarence, Leah, Julius Mortimer (married his cousin Rebecca E. Solomons, below), Cecilia, Henry Eugene, and Julia.

5. **Cecilia** (born July 18, 1815, Charleston, South Carolina; died April 27, 1882, Charleston, South Carolina). Married Abraham Alexander Solomons (born May 2, 1816, Georgetown, South Carolina; died August 3, 1899, Savannah, Georgia) on December 6, 1843, in Charleston, South Carolina. They had seven children: Israel, Abraham A. Jr., Grace Moses, Rebecca Ella (married her cousin Julius M. Alexander), Israella, Isaiah Abraham, and Louise Freighley.

6. **Aaron Julian** (born January 5, 1817, Charleston, South Carolina; died April 14, 1893, New York). Married Judith A. Ottolengui (born May 1, 1816, Georgetown, South Carolina; died September 1, 1883, New York), on September 30, 1844. Judith was a sister of Rinah and Sarah Ottolengui, the two wives of Aaron's brother Jacob. Aaron and Judith Moses had two children: Dr. Ottolengui Aaron Moses, who married his first cousin, Flora, daughter of Jacob and Sarah Moses, and Sarah Rebecca.

7. **Moses** (born March 26, 1818, Charleston, South Carolina; died January 1856).

8. **Leonora** (born July 14, 1820, Charleston, South Carolina). Married Rabbi Jacob Rosenfeld, *hazan* of the traditionalist synagogue of Charleston, Shearith Israel (born 1815, Prussia). They had six children: Adelaide, Rosa, Isaiah, Herman, Levy, and Isidore (married his cousin Matilda Brady).

9. **Isaac Isaiah** (born July 19, 1822, Charleston, South Carolina). Married Hannah Maria Moses (born March 24, 1840, St. Joseph, Florida; died July 3, 1860) on June 24, 1856, in Columbus, Georgia. Hannah Maria was the daughter of Raphael J. and Eliza M. Moses. Isaac and Hannah Maria Moses

had two children: Isaiah and Rebecca Hannah (married her cousin Jacob Isaiah Moses). After Hannah Maria died in 1860, Isaac married Mary Alice Moses (born April 4, 1841, Oakland, South Carolina; died March 7, 1920, Girard, Alabama) on October 5, 1869, in Columbia, South Carolina. Mary Alice Moses was no relation either to Isaac or to Hannah Maria. Isaac and Mary Alice Moses had six children: Alice, Isaac Isaiah Jr., Charles Clifton, Addie L. C., Anna Green (married W. Moultrie Moses Jr., her cousin), and Almeria.

10. **Adeline** (born February 25, 1826, Charleston, South Carolina). Married Adolf J. Brady (born c. 1821, Hamburg, Germany). They had seven children: Matilda (married her cousin Isidore Rosenfeld), Isaiah, Lillie, Edwin, Ida, Isaac, and Rosa Rebecca.

11. **Abraham J.** (born October 25, 1828, Charleston, South Carolina; died December 29, 1890, Florence, Alabama). Married Annie Jonas (born September 4, 1839, Ohio; died April 17, 1926, New York). They had twelve children: Hannah Marie, Joseph Jonas, Robert S., Hampton H., Cecil S., Fontaine H., Eleanor, Rebecca Louise, Leila Tyndall, Sadele Pickett, Josephine Jonas, and Alice.

12. **Ezra I.** (born August 14, 1833, Charleston, South Carolina; died May 3, 1877, Philadelphia, Pennsylvania). Married Sarah Hannah Levy (born February 18, 1838, South Carolina; died July 17, 1907, Philadelphia, Pennsylvania). They had one son: Isaiah Ezra.[27]

1. Reznikoff, *Charleston*, 65–67; Hagy, *This Happy Land*, 14–17.
2. Hagy, *This Happy Land*, 11–12.
3. Elzas, *History of Congregation Beth Elohim*, 4; Charleston city directories, 1782–1801; Hagy, *This Happy Land*, 14.
4. An alternative narrative is offered in Rosengarten, *Portion of the People*, 102, which states that Isaiah Moses migrated to England in the 1790s, married there and had four sons. After his wife's death, sometime before 1800, he came to America with his brother Levi, initially leaving his sons in England. However, since the eldest child was born in 1798 and Isaiah appears in the Charleston city directory of 1800, this scenario seems unlikely.
5. Stern, *First American*, 210.
6. Rosengarten, *Portion of the People*, 100–102.
7. Morrison, *Oxford History*, 504; Korn, "Jews and Negro Slavery," 13; Breibart to Loeb; Gray to Shier.
8. Marcus, *Memoirs,* vol. 1, 146,161; Rosengarten, *Portion of the People,* 103.
9. Hagy, *This Happy Land*, 91–95; Rosengarten, *Portion of the People*, 103–105; Inventory of estate of Isaiah Moses; www.serve.com/rim.
10. Wade, *Slavery*, 38–39; Greene, *Slave Badges*, 4–10, 173.
11. The Web site www.serve.com/rim includes transcriptions from Rebecca's daybooks; Rosengarten, *Portion of the People*, 111.
12. Reznikoff, *Charleston*, 116–17.
13. Hagy, *This Happy Land*, 128–32, 144–45, 237.
14. Hagy, *This Happy Land*, 236–40; Tarshish, "Charleston Organ," 290.
15. Hagy, *This Happy Land*, 240–43; Tarshish, "Charleston Organ," 291–302.
16. Tarshish, "Charleston Organ," 299; Hagy, 249–53.
17. Tarshish, "Charleston Organ," 305–7; Hagy, 253–55.
18. *Occident*, August 1846, 260; April 1847, 49; September 1847, 311; September 1846, 357–58.
19. *Occident*, September 1847, 311.
20. Charleston *Courier*, February 2, 1857, p. 2; January 29, 1857, p. 2, Alexander, *Notes*, p. 51.
21. Inventory of estate of Isaiah Moses.
22. *List of Taxpayers for 1859*, 238; *List of Taxpayers for 1860*, 194; *Census for 1861*, 123; www.serve.com/rim.
23. Alexander, *Notes*, 67.
24. Ibid.
25. Probate file of Rebecca Moses.
26. "Cincinnati," *Jewish Encyclopedia*, 1910, 90–91.
27. Stern, *First American*, 5, 8, 9, 136, 164, 206, 210, 212, 234; U.S. Census for 1860 in www.Ancestry.com.

CHAPTER TEN

LEVY J. MOSES
(1808–1876)

and

ADELINE LYON MOSES
(1809–1873)

ON OCTOBER 7, 1808, ELEVEN MONTHS after the second marriage of Isaiah Moses, his sixteen-year-old wife Rebecca gave birth to Levy J. Moses, the first of twelve babies the young mother would bear. Levy was born in Columbia, South Carolina, and may have lived there briefly as an infant, but spent most of his life in Charleston. Levy Moses was Adeline Moses Loeb's grandfather, although she never knew him—he died a year before she was born.

The life of Levy Moses lacks the high drama and adventure that characterized the lives of many of his ancestors. He was not an immigrant but the son of an immigrant, and he remained in his hometown of Charleston until late in life. He did not make his living from the risky business of merchant shipping, nor did he attain the status of plantation owner, as his father had done. He worked as a bookkeeper and notary public for several Jewish auction and brokerage houses in Charleston, an unexciting but steady occupation. At the time of his marriage in 1832, Levy Moses was employed by S. Hart, Senior and Co., one of several Jewish-owned King Street auction houses. He later worked for the auction house of Israel Moses, a firm in which his father had a partial interest. A Georgia legislator and lawyer, Raphael J. Moses, whose daughter, Hannah Maria, married Levy's brother Isaac, described in his memoirs how he modeled his signature after that of his father's bookkeeper—Levy Moses:

> When I reached home, I went to my father's auction store. I think
> Mr. Isaiah Moses had some interest in the business. At all events, L. I.

Moses, the father of Moses Bros., of Montgomery, was bookkeeper and in imitating his signature I obtained my present signature.[1]

Slaveholding (though he owned no land) was apparently Levy's principal investment. In 1859 he had six slaves; a year later, in 1860, he had increased his holdings to fifteen slaves, whom he hired out annually. Levy helped his mother hire out her slaves as well.

Unlike his father, whose second wife (Levy's mother Rebecca) was twenty years his junior, Levy Moses married a woman his own age. Levy was twenty-four and Adeline Lyon Moses, also a native of Charleston, was twenty-three when they married on November 21, 1832. Adeline Lyon Moses, born on October 23, 1809, was one of six children of Joseph Moses (1772–1814) and Rachel Lyon Moses (1781–1860). Her parents were immigrants from Germany who settled in Charleston in the late eighteenth century. Adeline's father died when she was five; her mother never remarried.[2]

Levy and Adeline Moses first made their home on Chapel Street, where all of their nine children were born. By 1861 Levy had bought a home at 26 Montague Street, valued in the city census at $5,000. It was located near the residences of the Tobias and Ottolengui families. Two of Levy Moses' brothers married Ottolengui sisters. All three families provided leadership for Congregation Beth Elohim.

Levy distinguished himself with service to the Hebrew Orphan Society of Charleston, founded in 1801. He was secretary and treasurer for eighteen years, from 1848 to 1866. In 1866 the society presented him with a silver pitcher and testimonial as gratitude for safeguarding the financial assets of the society from General Sherman during the Civil War. He wrote very touchingly of that award in a letter to his mother on August 20, 1866:

> You will doubtless be pleased to hear that I have received a very
> handsome silver pitcher from the Hebrew Orphan Society . . . with
> a very flattering letter written upon parchment bound with ribbon

228

and which I shall have framed— . . . Now if you come here, I will use it in honor of yourself and you shall have a silver goblet to drink out of."[3]

All nine of Levy and Adeline Moses' children survived to adulthood, although only four married. In keeping with a popular custom of the time, the couple named several of their children after famous people—Alfred Huger, for a South Carolina senator; Henry Clay, for the great American statesman; Judah Touro, for the American Jewish philanthropist; and Grace Aguilar, for a popular Anglo-Jewish writer.

Levy Moses belonged to the generation that spanned the Civil War, and he endured the privations of the war with his fellow Charlestonians. Although too old to fight himself, three of his five sons served in the Confederate Army. The South's defeat brought devastation to Charleston. Beth Elohim was in a "state of dilapidation," with broken windows, fallen plaster, and damage from shells launched during the bombardment of the city. Levy Moses suffered personal financial losses as well: Levy's major investment was in slaves; the defeat of the South in April 1865 freed them all.[4]

Even before the war, the economy of Charleston was stagnating. In 1860 Levy and Adeline's two oldest sons, Joseph and Alfred, moved to Montgomery, Alabama, whose booming economy offered greater opportunities than Charleston. Two more sons, Mordecai and Henry, soon joined Joseph and Alfred. The rest of the family eventually followed. After the war, Levy and Adeline left their native city. They lived briefly in Brooklyn with their daughter Grace, before joining the rest of their children in Montgomery.[5]

Adeline Moses died in 1873 and was buried in the Moses lot of the Jewish section of the Oakwood Cemetery in Montgomery, where Levy was buried three years later. Their children Sarah, Mordecai, and Rosanna, along with Alfred, his wife Jeannette, and two of their children, are buried there as well.[6]

—m—

DESCENDANTS OF
MORRIS NATHAN & HANNAH DINKELSPIEL

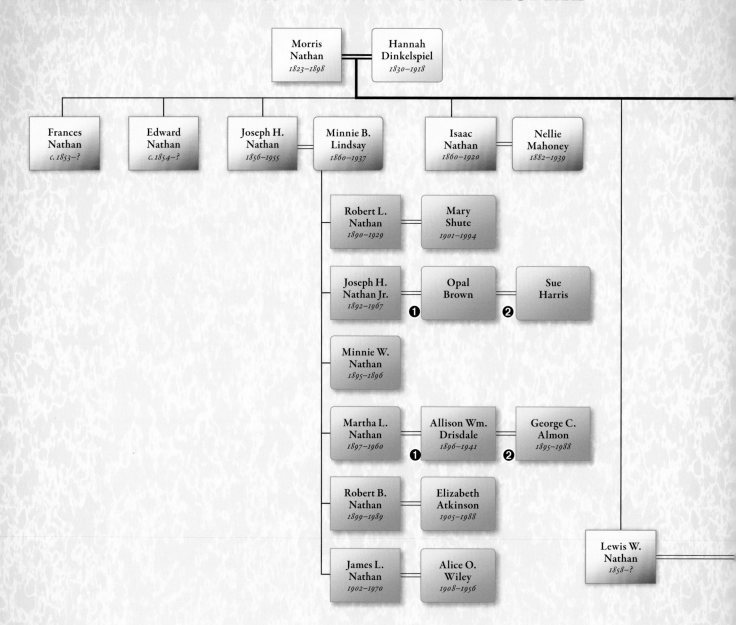

Morris Nathan *1823–1898* ═ **Hannah Dinkelspiel** *1830–1918*

Frances Nathan *c. 1853–?*

Edward Nathan *c. 1854–?*

Joseph H. Nathan *1856–1955* ═ **Minnie B. Lindsay** *1860–1937*

Isaac Nathan *1860–1920* ═ **Nellie Mahoney** *1882–1939*

Robert L. Nathan *1890–1929* ═ **Mary Shute** *1901–1994*

Joseph H. Nathan Jr. *1892–1967* ❶═ **Opal Brown** ❷═ **Sue Harris**

Minnie W. Nathan *1895–1896*

Martha L. Nathan *1897–1960* ❶═ **Allison Wm. Drisdale** *1896–1941* ❷═ **George C. Almon** *1895–1988*

Robert B. Nathan *1899–1989* ═ **Elizabeth Atkinson** *1905–1988*

James L. Nathan *1902–1970* ═ **Alice O. Wiley** *1908–1956*

Lewis W. Nathan *1858–?*

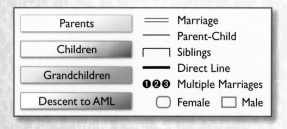

Parents	═══ Marriage
Children	── Parent-Child
Grandchildren	⌐ Siblings
Descent to AML	━━ Direct Line
	❶❷❸ Multiple Marriages
	◯ Female ▢ Male

DESCENDANTS OF
LEVY J. MOSES & ADELINE LYON MOSES

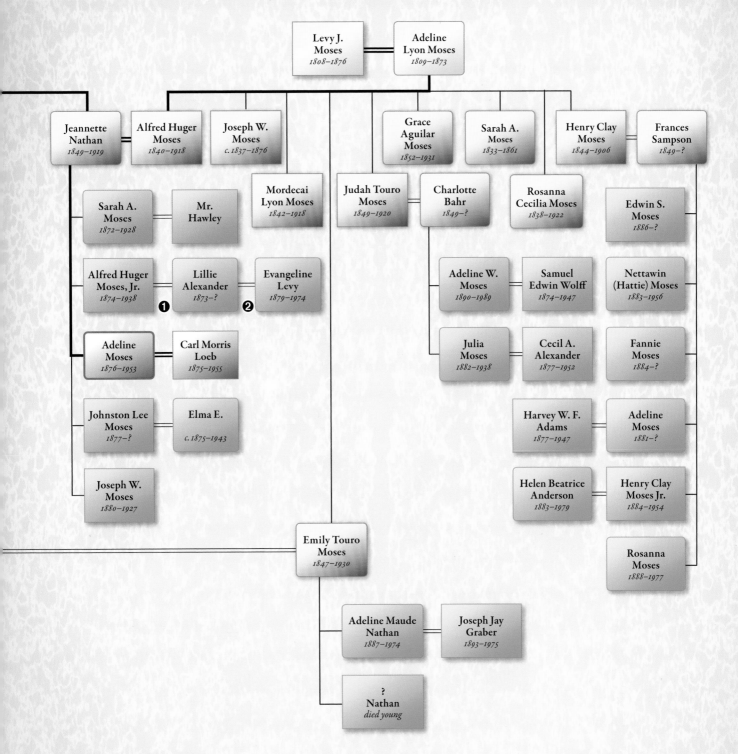

Levy J. Moses *1808–1876* ══ **Adeline Lyon Moses** *1809–1873*

Jeannette Nathan *1849–1919* ══ **Alfred Huger Moses** *1840–1918*

Joseph W. Moses *c. 1837–1876*

Grace Aguilar Moses *1852–1931*

Sarah A. Moses *1833–1861*

Henry Clay Moses *1844–1906* ══ **Frances Sampson** *1849–?*

Sarah A. Moses *1872–1928* ══ **Mr. Hawley**

Mordecai Lyon Moses *1842–1918*

Judah Touro Moses *1849–1920* ══ **Charlotte Bahr** *1849–?*

Rosanna Cecilia Moses *1838–1922*

Edwin S. Moses *1886–?*

Alfred Huger Moses, Jr. *1874–1938* ══ **Lillie Alexander** *1873–?* ❶ ══ **Evangeline Levy** *1879–1974* ❷

Adeline W. Moses *1890–1989* ══ **Samuel Edwin Wolff** *1874–1947*

Nettawin (Hattie) Moses *1883–1956*

Adeline Moses *1876–1953* ══ **Carl Morris Loeb** *1875–1955*

Julia Moses *1882–1938* ══ **Cecil A. Alexander** *1877–1952*

Fannie Moses *1884–?*

Johnston Lee Moses *1877–?* ══ **Elma E.** *c. 1875–1943*

Harvey W. F. Adams *1877–1947* ══ **Adeline Moses** *1881–?*

Joseph W. Moses *1880–1927*

Helen Beatrice Anderson *1883–1979* ══ **Henry Clay Moses Jr.** *1884–1954*

Emily Touro Moses *1847–1930*

Rosanna Moses *1888–1977*

Adeline Maude Nathan *1887–1974* ══ **Joseph Jay Graber** *1893–1975*

? Nathan *died young*

The Children of Levy J. and Adeline Lyon Moses

1. **Sarah A.** (born November 25, 1833, Charleston, South Carolina; died August 1, 1861, Charleston, South Carolina). She was the only member of the family who never left Charleston. Died unmarried.

2. **Joseph Winthrop** (born c. 1837, Charleston, South Carolina; died 1876, Montgomery, Alabama). Moved to Montgomery with his younger brother Alfred before the Civil War. He became an attorney and was head of the Montgomery public school system at the time of his death. Never married.

3. **Rosanna Cecilia** (born September 20, 1838, Charleston, South Carolina; died February 8, 1922, St. Louis, Missouri). Moved to Montgomery, Alabama after the Civil War with her sisters Grace and Emily, then moved to St. Louis, Missouri in the late nineteenth century. Never married.

4. **Alfred Huger** (born September 16, 1840, Charleston, South Carolina; died May 24, 1918, St. Louis, Missouri). Married Jeannette Nathan (born November 22, 1849, Louisville, Kentucky; died November 15, 1919, St. Louis, Missouri) on November 8, 1871, in Louisville, Kentucky. Alfred and Jeannette had five children: Sarah A., Alfred H. Jr., Adeline, Johnston Lee (aka Lee Johnson), and Joseph Winthrop. **Adeline married Carl Loeb on November 12, 1896.**

5. **Mordecai Lyon** (born August 20, 1842, Charleston, South Carolina; died June 6, 1918, St. Louis, Missouri). Followed his older brothers to Montgomery, Alabama, arriving in 1861. Served as mayor of Montgomery from 1875 to 1881. Never married.

6. **Henry Clay** (born October 22, 1844, Charleston, South Carolina; died December 11, 1906, New York City). Married Frances Sampson (born 1849, South Carolina). They had six children: Adeline, Nettawin (Hattie), Fannie, Edwin S., Rosanna, and Henry Clay Jr. The family lived in Montgomery,

Alabama, until about 1900 and then relocated to New York City, where Henry worked as an insurance agent.

7. **Emily Touro** (born September 16, 1847, Charleston, South Carolina; died July 11, 1930, St. Louis, Missouri). Married her mother's brother Lewis Winthrop Nathan (born October 1858, Kentucky), probably in 1884 in Montgomery, Alabama. They had a daughter, Adeline Maude, and a second child, name unknown, who died young. They moved to St. Louis, Missouri, in the late nineteenth century. Lewis was a wholesale liquor dealer.

8. **Judah Touro** (born January 1849, Charleston, South Carolina; died November 18, 1920, Montgomery, Alabama). Married Charlotte Bahr (born January 1849, Frankfurt am Main, Germany) on June 29, 1881, New York City. They had two children: Julia and Adeline Winthrop. Judah moved to Montgomery after the Civil War, and then moved to New York City, where he met and married Charlotte and worked as a cotton broker. In the late 1880s the family moved back to Montgomery, where Judah worked as a bookkeeper.

9. **Grace Aguilar** (born November 1852, Charleston, South Carolina; died October 1931, Montgomery, Alabama). Moved with her siblings to Montgomery after the Civil War and later to St. Louis, Missouri. Never married.[7]

—✸—

1. Elzas, *Jewish Marriage Notices,* 15; Marcus, *Memoirs,* v. 1, 146, 161.
2. Elzas, *Jewish Marriage Notices*, 15; Moses file.
3. www.serve.com/rim.
4. Elzas, *Jewish Marriage Notices*, 15; Moses file; Tobias, *Hebrew Orphan Society*, 20.
5. U.S. Census for 1860, 1870 in www.Ancestry.com.
6. Moses file.
7. New York City Marriage Record, 29 June 1881, Manhattan certificate #3714; U.S. Census for 1850, 1860, 1870, 1880, 1900, 1910, 1920 in www.Ancestry.com; Stern, *First American*, 211; Alexander, *Notes*, 19–21, 58–59.

Alfred Huger Moses
(1840–1918)

Adeline's adored father is shown here in both an 1886 or 1887 photograph (left) and a replication of that photo (oil on canvas, right). The photograph was taken around the peak of his success shortly after he established the city of Sheffield, Alabama. A commissioned artist in the 1980s shed several years from the Captain Moses visage in an idealized version of the photo, while also adding a glimpse in the background of the six-story Moses office building, once located on Montgomery's Court Square.

The painting hangs in what is known in Montgomery as The House of the Mayors. (Alfred's brother Mordecai served three terms as mayor of Montgomery after the Civil War, and was one of several mayors who lived in the house on South Perry Street, which is now home to the regional United Way.) The home of the Alfred Moses family, also on South Perry Street, was restored and became known as the Moses-Haardt house and is now the office of Sterne, Agee, and Leach.

—Photo, left: Ambassador John L. Loeb collection
Oil on canvas, right: River Region United Way, Montgomery, Alabama

Jeannette Nathan Moses
(1849–1919)

Adeline's mother, Mrs. Alfred Huger Moses, was thirty years old in 1879 when this photo is thought to have been taken. She was a "great belle, slim, nice looking rather than beautiful," according to her granddaughter Margaret Loeb Kempner. "She was very musical, played the piano beautifully, loved to sing and act in amateur theatricals, and generally played the female lead." Without doubt, the musically talented Adeline was given her first piano lessons by her mother.

—Thomas L. Kempner collection

growing antislavery movement all affected the city's fortunes. Charleston implemented improvements in its port, but the city never allowed the railroads to build all the way to the docks, making the cost of shipping to Charleston less competitive. Even agriculture was suffering, because the soil in the surrounding region was worn out and planters were moving westward. The city was not growing as rapidly as other Southern cities. Its native population was migrating to other states (primarily Georgia, Alabama, Mississippi, and Louisiana), and it was failing to attract newcomers to Charleston.[2]

Alfred Huger Moses, the father of Adeline Moses Loeb, was born in Charleston on September 16, 1840, the son of Levy J. and Adeline L. Moses. Alfred was the son of two native-born Charlestonians and the grandson of a plantation owner, but this could not compensate socially for the fact that the Moseses were German Jews. In addition, Alfred's father, Levy Moses, was a bookkeeper, an occupation offering little in the way of social status. The Jewish bookkeeper's ambitious young son probably saw little opportunity for success in his hometown. After graduating from the College of Charleston with first honors in 1860 at the age of twenty, Alfred, with his older brother Joseph, moved west to Montgomery, Alabama, to study law in the offices of Watts, Judge and Jackson. In Montgomery, they initially boarded with their aunt and uncle, Aaron and Sarah Moses Alexander.[3]

Montgomery, Alfred's new home, combined a cotton economy with business, commerce, and manufacturing. The leisurely planter's life of Charleston and the surrounding tidewater district was not the style of Montgomery and its Black Belt counties.* Unlike their South Carolina cousins, Alabama's planters did not frown on trade, and they eagerly engaged in real estate speculation, construction, and railroad and streetcar promotion. By 1830 the per capita wealth of free persons in Montgomery was already over $700, a figure never attained by the rest of

---

* "Black Belt" refers to the crescent-shaped region that stretches from Texas to Virginia. Although the term originally referred to the color of the soil, it was also the area of the South with the largest number of slaves.

the country during the antebellum period. In 1846, when Montgomery became Alabama's capital, its population was 3,800, 48 percent of whom were slaves. In 1861, when it became the "Cradle of the Confederacy," Montgomery's population was 9,000, with slaves forming a large minority.[4]

Montgomery had a special attraction for those in the legal profession, bringing the city a superabundance of attorneys. Montgomerians were not excessively litigious, however. It seems that the planter class wanted their sons to become professionals by reading law. In 1846 there was one licensed attorney for every sixty-seven adult white males in Montgomery County. (Doctors were not far behind. In the 1850 and 1860 censuses, Montgomery had five doctors to every seven lawyers.) By comparison, in the eight Tennessee Valley counties of northern Alabama, there was one lawyer for every 259 adult white males; in southeastern Alabama, the ratio was only one attorney for every 5,884 adult white males.[5]

Alfred was reading law in Montgomery for only a few months when his studies were interrupted by the dramatic events that followed the election of Abraham Lincoln to the presidency in November 1860. That election ignited the South's secessionist movement; in late 1860, 80 percent of Montgomery's eligible voters went to the polls and voted for secession by 94 percent. Within a few months, the first shots were fired at Fort Sumter in the Charleston harbor, embroiling the country in war for the next four years.[6]

Alfred Moses spent the war years in Montgomery serving as a clerk for the Circuit Court of the Middle District of Alabama. As clerk of the Confederate District Court, Alfred Moses was excused from active service because of the Enrollment Act passed by the Confederate Congress in the spring of 1862, exempting all Confederate and state officials from active duty. The law was revised in February 1864, limiting exemptions to members of Congress, state legislators, and other high officials. This may account for his active service toward the end of war, when he was "made captain of a company and saw some service in and around Pensacola and Mobile."[7]

On May 29, 1865, President Andrew Johnson began his attempts at restoration by proclaiming amnesty to all members of the Confederacy except for certain specified classes. The taking of the oath of allegiance to the United States granted a pardon and restored all rights of property, except for slaves. However, certain categories of Confederate, military, and state officials were excluded from the benefits of the general proclamation and had to apply for a pardon. Because of his position with the Confederate District Court, Alfred Moses was not covered by the general amnesty proclamation, and he had to make a special application to the president to receive a pardon.[8]

His granddaughter, Margaret Loeb Kempner (Adeline Moses Loeb's only daughter), offered a more colorful story about Alfred's need for a presidential pardon. Margaret may have heard the story from her mother, an enthusiastic raconteur, or perhaps directly from her grandfather, who lived until she was twenty. She wrote in her memoir, *Recollection:*

> He was almost hanged or shot because he was found burning official papers. When he knew the South had lost the war, he managed to get into the State House in Atlanta where records were stored, and he destroyed all the credentials of men who had been spies or engaged in wartime activities which would have led to their deaths. A real hero, he saved the lives of many of his friends. He was caught, court-martialed, and pardoned by President Johnson.[9]

Whatever the reason, Alfred's name appears in the "Final Report of the Names of Persons Engaged in Rebellion Who Have Been Pardoned by the President, December 4, 1867, Exemption Under Amnesty Proclamation of May 29, 1865." The Reconstructionist governor of Alabama, Lewis E. Parsons, and M. J. Saffold recommended "A. H. Moses, Clerk of the rebel district court" for pardon. Johnson granted the pardon on March 2, 1866.[10]

Alfred's younger brother Mordecai had followed him to Montgomery, arriving in May 1861, only a month after the first shots were fired at Fort Sumter in Charleston. Although Mordecai had read law in his brother Joseph's office in Charleston, in Montgomery he took a job as a clerk in the hardware store of Wyman,

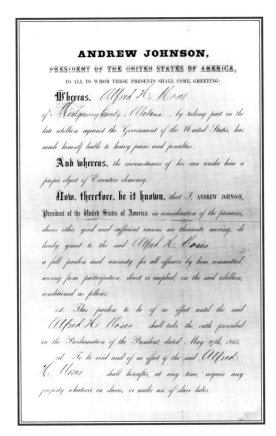
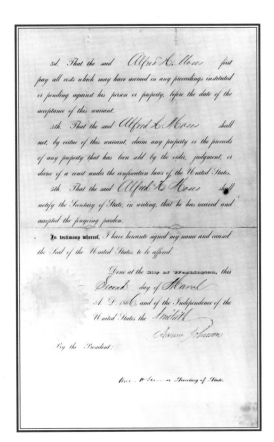

The pardon of Alfred Huger Moses for his participation as a Confederate official during the Civil War, signed by President Andrew Johnson on March 2, 1866, today hangs in the office of his great-grandson, Thomas L. Kempner.

Adeline's father had served as clerk of the Confederate District Court in Montgomery, Alabama, through most of the war, but was made captain of a company late in the conflict. Margaret Loeb Kempner's memoir recounts that he was "almost hanged or shot" after being court-martialed for burning Confederate papers in Atlanta, but no other records of this piece of history have come to light.

—Thomas L. Kempner collection

Moses and Co. When the 46th Alabama Regiment was organized, he enlisted as a private in Captain James W. Powell's company. Mordecai was later commissioned by the Confederate government for special work in Canada and the West Indies and was out of the country when Lee surrendered to Grant at Appomattox.[11]

Their brother Henry Clay moved to Montgomery from Charleston before the end of the war and served with the Alabama Rebels. After a brief residence in Brooklyn, New York, their parents, Levy and Adeline Moses, and their sister Grace moved to Montgomery. The whole family eventually made their way to Montgomery, except for the oldest child, Sarah, who died in Charleston in 1861.[12]

In *Civil War and Reconstruction in Alabama*, Walter Fleming points out that the heaviest losses after the war "fell upon the old wealthy families, who by the loss of wealth and by political proscription, were ruined. In middle life and in old age, they were unable to begin again." With most of the former leaders financially destroyed, a new group rose to power and influence—the lawyers, farmers, and merchants who had formerly been content to let the old ruling class direct public affairs.[13]

In 1865 the Moses brothers were in their twenties and unmarried. When the war started, they had just embarked on their careers and had no fortune to lose. After the war they became part of the new generation, who would eventually take the reins of leadership in Alabama and rescue the state from the excesses of Reconstruction.

Alfred, Mordecai, and Henry entered the real estate and insurance business in Montgomery, doing business as Roberts, Moses and Co. After Mr. Roberts retired, the name of the firm was changed to Moses Bros. and the brothers added banking to the firm's business. The war had depressed real estate values, and the Moses brothers began to buy up property at bargain prices. Their firm quickly became one of the leading real estate investment firms in the city. One of their many investments led to the construction of Montgomery's first skyscraper, at the corner of Court Square and Commerce Street. Called the Moses Building, it was demolished in 1907 and replaced by the First National Bank Building.[14]

As the firm prospered, the Moses brothers began looking beyond Montgomery for potential investments or development sites. Alfred Moses made periodic trips through the South for this purpose, and on one of these trips he

The six-story Moses office building at Montgomery's Court Square was erected in 1887 by the Moses brothers. Pictured here in 1901, Alabama's first "skyscraper" was considered something of a tourist attraction and drew admiring visitors from around the state. But fame is fleeting; the building was torn down in 1907, twenty years after it was built, to make way for a twelve-story building to house the First National Bank.

Just behind the Moses structure is the Lehman Durr building, which housed the Lehman Brothers' cotton business. Although the Moses family and the Lehmans knew each other in Montgomery, it was in New York City that the two families were merged in 1926 through the marriage of Mayer Lehman's granddaughter, Frances Lehman, to Alfred Moses' grandson, John L. Loeb.

—Ambassador John L. Loeb Jr. collection

passed through Louisville, Kentucky, where he met his future bride, Jeannette Nathan. In her memoir, *Recollection*, Margaret Loeb Kempner wrote of her grandmother Jeannette that she was "a great belle; she was slim, nice looking rather than beautiful. She was very musical—she played the piano beautifully, sang and loved to act in amateur theatricals. She was generally the female lead . . . my mother said my grandfather was tone deaf so it wasn't my grandmother's music that won him. She must have been very appealing."[15]

Jeannette Nathan was the American-born daughter of German Jews, one of many families who had migrated from Germany in the mid-nineteenth century and settled in the towns and cities of the South and Midwest. Her father, Morris, was born in 1823 in Hesse-Darmstadt, a region in southwestern Germany, east of the Rhine and north of the Main rivers. Her mother, Hannah (née Dinkelspiel), was born in 1830 in the city of Hamburg in northern Germany. Morris probably immigrated to America as a young man on his own and started out as a peddler before he acquired enough capital to settle down and open a store. Hannah probably came to America as a young woman with her parents sometime after 1840.[16]

It is not known exactly when Morris and Hannah married or when they first came to Louisville. Jeannette, their oldest daughter, was born in Kentucky in 1849, but by 1850 the family was living in Perrysville in southern Indiana's Vermillion County. Also resident in the house were fifteen-year-old Mina Dinkelspiel, possibly Hannah's younger sister, and eighteen-year-old Isidore Deitch, probably a boarder. Morris Nathan's name first appears in the Louisville city directory for 1855-1856 in which he is described as a "clothier," or clothing merchant, living on Water Street. By 1866 he had shifted from selling clothing to selling "china, glass and queensware" in partnership with his brother Henry. The city directory lists their business as "M & H Nathan" on 4th Street, but by 1872 Morris had returned to the wholesale and retail clothing business.[17]

Morris and Hannah Nathan had six children, all born in Kentucky: Jeannette (1849–1919), Frances (born c. 1853), Edward (born c. 1854), Joseph Harrington (1856–1955), Lewis Winthrop (born 1858), and Isaac (1860–1920). The Nathan family is listed in the 1860 and 1870 federal census returns for Louisville. In 1860

Alfred Huger
(1788–1872)

This South Carolina state senator after whom Alfred Huger Moses was named, was a Princeton graduate, a plantation owner, and an early Charleston postmaster. Though a genial man, and sympathetic to Confederate views, his respect for the federal position of postmaster was so great that he once stood alone with a ready rifle at the door of his post office, thwarting an angry mob determined to enter and destroy leaflets sent through the mail by Northern abolitionists. The group later succeeded, returning in the dead of night to burn the inflammatory articles before they could be delivered to the recipients.

—Ambassador John L. Loeb Jr. collection

Sarah Moses
(1872–1928)
This photo, taken around 1895, shows the elder (and only) sister of
Adeline Moses, as a young woman. Sarah "attracted men without trying,"
according to tales that Margaret Loeb Kempner heard from her mother.
Unfortunately, Sarah's brief marriage at the age of twenty-six, to a
widower recorded for posterity only as "Mr. Hawley," ended in divorce.
She died at the early age of fifty-five, causing Adeline to "lose her already
limited faith in God."

—Thomas L. Kempner collection

the Nathan household included one domestic, the Bavarian-born Henrietta
Bierman, and two German-born boarders, Isaac Levy and Morris Kramer. By the
time of the 1870 federal census, the family had prospered. They no longer took in
boarders, and they could afford two Kentucky-born domestics, Julia Kelly and Eliza
Bowman (Julia was white; Eliza, black). Hannah's mother Sarah (born 1802), and
brother Lee (born 1840 in Prussia), were also members of the household.[18]

The Louisville directory for 1875 is the last one in which any names of the
Nathan family appear. Sometime after that, the Nathan family relocated to
Austin, Mississippi, where Morris continued in retail trade. Joseph and Isaac
Nathan continued to live at home; both worked as store clerks.[19]

This home—once the residence of the Alfred Moses family—is located on South Perry Street in Montgomery, Alabama. Now part of a historic district and one of seven homes included in Montgomery's "Old Homes Revived Tour," it was restored in 2005 and is known as the Moses-Haardt house. Dating from the nineteenth century, it now houses local businesses.
—*Montgomery Advertiser*, April 23, 2005

Alfred Moses and Jeannette Nathan were married in Louisville in November 1871. After their marriage, Jeannette moved with her new husband to Montgomery, where all of their five children were born—Sarah, Alfred H. Jr., Adeline, Johnston Lee, and Joseph Winthrop.[20]

By the time Alfred married Jeannette, the Moses family was already prominent in Montgomery. Joseph Moses was an attorney in partnership with Colonel J. W. A. Sanford; at the time of his death in 1876, he was president of the school board. Mordecai Moses, a bachelor, was first elected as alderman of Montgomery in 1871, a position he held until 1875 when he was elected mayor, making him the first Democrat elected to that post after the Reconstruction period. The residence of Mordecai Moses in Montgomery was "an elegant antebellum mansion, built in the 1850s by Jack L. Thornington, one of Montgomery's first mayors.[21]

Mordecai served three two-year terms as mayor until 1881, when he retired from politics and for several years served as president of the Montgomery Gas and Electric Light Company. He was president of the State Fair Association, president of the North Alabama Land and Immigration Company, and president and director of several large land and development companies, as well as several railroad and furnace companies. The Moses brothers made many significant contributions to the city of Montgomery, but their most ambitious and ultimately calamitous venture was their promotion and development of the city of Sheffield on the Tennessee River in northern Alabama. An article in the Tuscumbia *North Alabamian* of January 14, 1887, observed:

> Never in the history of our country have we heard of such a great boom in real estate as is going on in North Alabama. Our lands . . . are being bought as fast as they are offered for sale, and capitalists are to be found on every street corner asking for more. Railroads are not only being built, but as we look out of our office window now we see great gangs of men laying ties for one of the street car lines to Sheffield, the great manufacturing town of the South.[22]

In the 1880s and early 1890s, such scenes of frenzied activity were commonplace, as a boom spirit spread throughout the country. Investors and speculators made systematic searches for areas that might be ripe for economic expansion. Land booms took place with increasing frequency in the South and West during the 1880s. The New Orleans Industrial & Cotton Exposition of 1884 further promoted the resources and economic potential of the New South. The town of Birmingham in northern Alabama fired the boom in the South, where boomtowns were tied to the development of the iron industry. Between 1885 and 1893, thirty-one new blast furnaces were erected in the state, and approximately twenty-four new towns were promoted with varying degrees of success.[23]

Birmingham was founded on June 1, 1871, by a group of real estate investors who had purchased 4,000 acres and began selling lots near the planned crossing of two major railroads. The investors, who called themselves the Elyton Land Company, envisioned the city as a great center of industry and consequently they named it for Birmingham, England. The significance of the site was its proximity to extensive deposits of iron ore, coal, and limestone, the three principal materials used in making steel. The company suffered several setbacks in its early years, but by 1880 the fortunes of the city began to revive, thanks to the opening of the nearby Pratt Coal Mines and the erection of two large blast furnaces. At this point the company began to show a profit, and from then on its profits steadily increased.[24]

The strength of Birmingham lay in its mineral resources and its railroad facilities, so each new town based its claim for future prosperity on the possession of these two features, usually claiming to be "the center of the universe and a spot where the cheapest iron on earth could be made." Birmingham's site was key to its success because it was one of the few places where all three of the natural resources used in the making of steel were found in close proximity. [25]

Alfred Moses was not immune to "boom fever." With the Birmingham success story fresh in his mind, on his way home from the Louisville Exposition in 1883, he passed through Florence, Alabama, and visited the iron ore deposits of Franklin County. He thought the gently rolling lands across the Tennessee River from Florence would be an ideal location for a great iron industry. After this visit, Moses and his traveling companion, Colonel Walter S. Gordon, purchased almost 3,000 acres, plus 30,000 acres of mineral land in the counties immediately to the south, all for approximately $100,000. The pair envisioned the acreage as a site for the projected city of Sheffield to be named for the famous industrial city of northern England.[26]

Following these purchases, the Sheffield Land, Iron and Coal Co. was organized, and the developers engaged in extensive advertising. The first meeting of stockholders was held in Atlanta, Georgia, on November 10, 1883, and officers

Downtown Montgomery, Alabama, c. 1870
postcard — courtesy of David M. Kleiman collection

Adeline Moses Loeb's grandparents, Levy and Adeline Moses, spent most of their lives bringing up nine offspring in Charleston, South Carolina. They belonged to the generation that spanned the Civil War and endured the devastating aftermath of the South's defeat. But even before the war the city's economy was stagnating, and it is not too surprising that their two oldest sons, Joseph Winthrop Moses and Alfred Huger Moses (Adeline's father), had already moved to Montgomery, Alabama, to seek their fortunes.

Kahl Montgomery (dedicated 1862)

There they found a booming economy and inviting business opportunities; they were soon followed by their parents and other siblings. In Montgomery they first met with major success, but in the end, painful failure.

Moses Brothers in the Liverpool & London & Globe Insurance Building, c. 1881

Montgomery, Alabama

c. 1880–1895

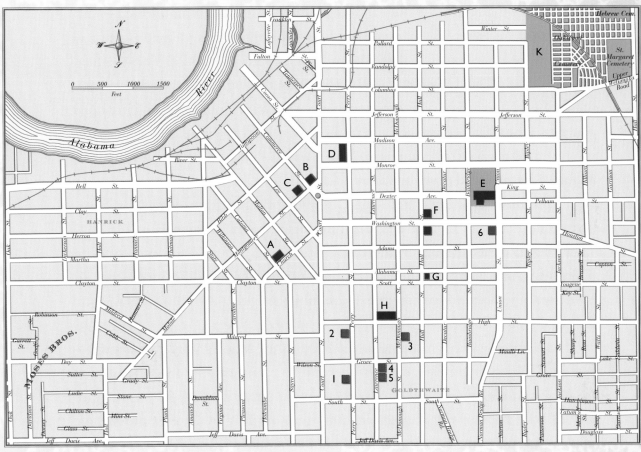

Buildings are not to scale. Placement is approximate.

Public Buildings & Businesses

A. Kahal Montgomery (1862)
B. Moses Bros. Insurance & Real Estate, Moses Building (1887)
C. Lewis W. Nathan (1891)
D. Montgomery City Hall
E. Alabama State Captiol
F. Alfred Huger Moses (1880/1881)
G. Henry Clay Moses (1880/1881)
H. Central High School

Parks & Cemeteries

K. Oakwood Cemetery

Family Homes

1. Alfred Huger & Jeannette Moses
2. Mayor Mordecai Moses [House of the Mayors]
3. Judah Touro Moses (1891)
4. Emily Touro Moses & Lewis Nathan
5. Judah Touro Moses (1910–1920)
6. First White House of the Confederacy

were elected. The twelve directors of the firm came from Montgomery, Atlanta, and Clarksville, Tennessee. Walter S. Gordon was elected president; Alfred H. Moses, vice president and general manager; and F. M. Coker, secretary and treasurer.[27]

The company issued a stock offering with specified amounts allotted to different Southern cities. The Moses Bros. firm, whose business included both real estate and banking, purchased the entire Montgomery allotment. The Sheffield Land, Iron and Coal Company began promoting the site to kick off the first sale of lots. At the same time, the company graded streets, laid out lots, and developed plans for a hotel, a waterworks, and an iron furnace. The company claimed that several railroads were planning tracks to connect Sheffield with Birmingham, Mobile, Chicago, and other important cities.[28]

Pamphlets, brochures, and maps described plans for the city and the "inexhaustible" quantities of iron ore, coal, and other natural resources in the area. They touted great advantages in transportation, either by railroad or Tennessee River boats, that Sheffield "the Iron Manufacturing Center of the South," would have over other locales, even though at the time there were no railroad lines going to the proposed site of the new city.[29]

The first sale of Sheffield lots was scheduled for May 8, 1884. It was important in a speculative venture such as Sheffield to create an atmosphere of excitement around the sale of lots in order to promote public buying. As was the case with all such boomtowns, the lots had almost no intrinsic value; their prospective value depended entirely upon the realization of promises made by the company. Land auctions for proposed new towns used all sorts of tricks and subterfuge to create enthusiasm and interest that would stimulate bidding and raise prices. For example, the railroad built a temporary track to Sheffield to bring in prospective buyers during the three-day sale, which prospective buyers probably assumed was a permanent line.[30]

A paragraph from *The Early Days of Sheffield,* a history published in 1934 and written by Judge Joseph H. Nathan (brother-in-law of Alfred Moses), conveys the contagious excitement generated by the fledgling town's boomtown fever:

On the morning of May 8 the nearby town of Tuscumbia awoke to an unusual bustle. Vehicles of every description were in demand and the road from Tuscumbia looked like a procession going to a festival. The next morning more than 500 well-dressed gentlemen from Alabama, Georgia, Tennessee, Mississippi and Kentucky gathered in a cotton field while nearby gangs of men with wagons, mules, scrapers, picks and shovels were grading streets and marking blocks and lots preparatory to the land sale. The attendance of bidders and onlookers increased from day to day and the prices increased likewise. The first lot was sold to Captain Moses's brother Mordecai. In three days, 75 acres (originally bought for $50,000) had been sold for $350,000.[31]

The auctioneer was George W. Adair of Atlanta, who later became one of the largest real estate operators in the South. Before he began the auction, Adair announced that the Sheffield Land, Iron and Coal Co. would devote all proceeds from the sale of lots to the establishment of a water system, the completion of a railroad to the Franklin County line, and the erection of a blast furnace producing at least one hundred tons of pig iron per day.[32]

The road to success was not easy for the Sheffield developers. A few days after the land sale, a number of large New York banks failed, including the Metropolitan Bank and Grant & Ward, financiers of the railroad being built from Sheffield to the Franklin County line. The panic of 1884 was partially caused by the draining of bank reserves into excessive railroad development as well as other speculative enterprises. With the loss of the Sheffield railroad's financial backing, work on the line halted, causing an immediate depreciation in value of the recently purchased Sheffield properties. Panic set in, and the new landowners began to dump their properties; the industrialists who had agreed to build smelters and furnaces in Sheffield withdrew their offers; the stock of the Sheffield Land, Iron and Coal Co. could find no purchasers. The entire enterprise appeared to be a failure.[33]

In 1886 Alfred Moses built an imposing home on Montgomery Avenue overlooking the Tennessee River in the boomtown of Sheffield. But the family had only a short time to enjoy the home before investment failures forced them to move to St. Louis, Missouri. The house was ultimately destroyed by fire.

—Sketch restored by Ardeth Abrams
From *Sheffield, City on the Bluff,* 1885–1985
Published by Friends of the Sheffield Library

However, the company had enough assets to survive the brief money panic, and by the end of 1884 when financial equilibrium had been reestablished, Sheffield was again showing signs of activity. As general manager, Alfred Moses went to work to build a city. He put up houses, graded streets, and laid out industrial sites. He encouraged industries to locate in Sheffield and successfully negotiated with various railroads to run their lines into Sheffield. In February 1885 the town was incorporated by the state legislature.[34]

By 1886 confidence had been restored and the establishment of an iron city began in earnest. In the summer of 1886 the first furnace company, the Sheffield Furnace Co., was organized with capital of $125,000. Work on a 125-ton blast furnace began in September. In February 1887, the management of Alabama and Tennessee Iron and Coal Co., with capital of $2,200,000, decided to make Sheffield the center of its operations. They agreed to build three blast furnaces in Sheffield, each with a capacity of 150 tons. Soon after this, The Lady Ensley Furnace Co. let a contract for a 125-ton furnace to be ready in 1888.[35]

Word about the construction of the five blast furnaces and the projected railroad lines to Sheffield brought a positive shift in Sheffield's fortunes and attracted a number of small industries to Sheffield. Stock in the Sheffield Land, Iron and Coal Co. rose, as did the price of real estate. Those who had bought lots on speculation were able to sell them at a profit because houses were being rapidly built for the growing population. Two banks were established—the First National (C. D. Woodson, president) and the Bank of Sheffield (Alfred H. Moses, president), each with a capital of $100,000.[36]

Alfred Moses played many important roles in the new city. He was mayor of Sheffield, president of the Bank of Sheffield, general manager of the Sheffield Land, Iron and Coal Co., director of the Sheffield Furnace Co., the Sheffield Pipe and Nail Works, and the Sheffield and Tuscumbia Street Railway Co.[37]

By January of 1888 the first blast furnace was operational. The Alfred Moses family lived in nearby Tuscumbia during the completion of their elegant new home in Sheffield at the head of Montgomery Avenue. In about 1888, Alfred Moses resigned as general manager of the Sheffield Land, Iron and Coal Co. His successor, William L. Chambers, began an aggressive campaign to market the city. Chambers opened sales offices in Philadelphia and Boston and created the position of Manager of Eastern Operations. He subsidized plants that relocated to Sheffield, including a hat factory, a shoe factory, a knitting mill, and a harness factory. However, none of these companies was able to survive once the Sheffield Land, Iron and Coal Co. no longer provided operating subsidies.[38]

In his memoir, Judge Nathan attributed the failure of the Sheffield Land, Iron and Coal Co. to the financial difficulties of Baring Brothers, the British merchant-banking firm. When Baring Brothers became overextended, the Bank of England stepped in to guarantee the firm's liabilities up to $75 million. The financial storm spread to the United States, causing a brief panic on Wall Street and considerable liquidation of American securities by European holders. During this period several banks failed, including the Moses Brothers bank in Montgomery. The companion failure of the Sheffield Land, Iron and Coal Co. occurred in 1890-1891.[39]

While one can point to many contributing causes, the major blame for the failure of Moses Bros. and the Sheffield Land, Iron and Coal Co. was neither the expansionist policies of William Chambers nor the troubles of Baring Brothers. The elemental cause of the Sheffield failure, "the great iron manufacturing center of the South," was the site itself.

Sheffield's reputed central location, access to transportation, and bounteous natural resources were not quite what Sheffield promoters claimed them to be. The promoters of Sheffield placed great faith in the Tennessee River to transport Sheffield's products throughout the Mississippi Valley and beyond. They envisioned a busy Tennessee River filled with ships carrying Sheffield products to market. The truth was that neither the Tennessee River nor the Ohio River supported year-round navigation. The Tennessee River was subject to seasonal low water, and winter ice periodically closed the Ohio River. Moreover, river transportation had been overshadowed by railway development for some twenty years. Railroads, not riverboats, were rapidly becoming the dominant means of transportation.[40]

Sheffield, however, was not on any railroad line. At the time of the first sale of lots in 1884, the closest line was a spur line of the Memphis and Charleston, which

The Sheffield Land, Iron and Coal Company was not shy about touting the economic advantages of the new boomtown in this nearly full-page ad in the *Daily Enterprise* on September 7, 1890.

—*Daily Enterprise,* Sheffield, Alabama

ran from Tuscumbia to Florence, two miles away. Sheffield's promoters first had to convince the Memphis and Charleston Railroad management to extend the spur line, then convince other railroads to provide full service to Sheffield. Sheffield's promoters hoped that a railroad such as the Louisville and Nashville (L&N), the major north-south line, would come forward to support the development with rail lines and favorable rates. The L&N had played a major role in the development of Birmingham with a new rail line and favorable rates, and investment in the city. Although the promoters of Sheffield claimed that the L&N had plans to build a line to Sheffield, only the Memphis and Charleston Railroad ever built one.[41]

The third element of Sheffield's future promise—its natural resources and mineral deposits—was also not quite up to its promoters' claims. The requisite engineer's report in the sales literature for most boomtowns always described the area's "extensive" mineral and ore deposits. These uniformly glowing reports were typically the product of a dishonest engineer, misrepresentation of the true facts by the promoters, or the suppression of an honest report and the substitution of a positive, but inaccurate one. Brown ore deposits for the city's iron furnaces were inadequate for large-scale operations. The area's resources could not actually support a significant iron and steel industry. The railroads' lack of interest in Sheffield may have reflected their knowledge of the true nature of the area's mineral raw materials.[42]

The lack of local coal, coupled with the lack of railroad connections to Alabama's coalfields, meant that coal to operate the Sheffield furnaces had to be shipped in from West Virginia. Due to the high cost of operations and the falling price of pig iron, the Sheffield operations lost $1.50 on each ton of iron they produced. Sheffield's situation was not helped by an oversupply of pig iron in the late 1880s, attributed to the increasing number of blast furnaces. In 1888, as reported in Joseph Nathan's memoir, the Sheffield furnace made pig iron for $15 per ton but sold it for $13.50 per ton. In 1893 the price had declined to $12.50 per ton. Marginal furnace operations such as Sheffield's could not sustain operations at such low prices.[43]

Sheffield failed in 1890-1891 because its investors were overextended, it was off the transportation grid, and its natural resources were lackluster. Sheffield was not alone. Its failure was part of a general decline in Alabama boomtowns beginning in 1890. These towns faced competition from other booming areas, such as West Virginia, and fell prey to the natural tendency of a bubble to burst. Between 1890 and 1893, ten Alabama boomtowns, including Sheffield, closed their blast furnaces.[44]

With the failure of the Sheffield Land, Iron and Coal Co., most of the town's industries went into receivership. The Moses family, who had invested heavily in the town, was ruined, and they were forced to close their Montgomery bank. Of the bank failure, Margaret Loeb Kempner wrote that her grandfather, "As an honorable Southern gentleman, permitted a run on the bank, and as a result, most of the money was withdrawn."[45]

Alfred and Jeannette moved to St. Louis, Missouri, with their children, Jeannette's widowed mother Hannah, Alfred's bachelor brother Mordecai, and their unmarried sisters, Rosanna and Grace Aguilar. The families set up two households in St. Louis, both on McPherson Avenue. Alfred and Jeannette, their children Sarah, Adeline, Lee, and Winthrop, and Jeannette's mother lived at one address. Mordecai, Rosanna, and Grace boarded down the street with Adeline Nathan (possibly Jeannette's niece). Their brother Henry, who had remained in Montgomery, moved to New York, where he prospered as an insurance broker. Of the extended family members who had settled in Sheffield, only Jeannette's brother, Joseph Nathan, a lawyer and judge, remained in the fledgling town and prospered there. At the time of the 1930 census, Joseph, his wife Minnie, their four sons (one of whom was also a lawyer), and one daughter were living on Park Boulevard in Sheffield, along with three live-in servants.[46]

Alfred Moses died in St. Louis on May 24, 1918, his only assets listed as "a claim against the United Railway Company and a deposit in the Mercantile Trust Company of St. Louis, of $412." He left no will, and the size of his estate was so small his widow Jeannette refused the Letters of Administration.[47]

Two weeks after Alfred's death, his brother Mordecai died on June 6, 1918. At the time of his death Mordecai was employed by the St. Louis Street Department, although earlier he had worked as an insurance agent. Two weeks after Mordecai's death, Jeannette wrote her will. She left her children Alfred H. Jr., Adeline (Loeb),

In 1992 the annual meeting of the Southern Jewish Historical Society was held in Montgomery, Alabama, and was highlighted by the dedication of the Alfred Huger Moses room at The House of the Mayors. Pictured here are attendees Rabbi Malcolm Stern (author of the genealogical breakthrough book, *First American Jewish Families, 1654–1988*), his wife Louise, and Ambassador John L. Loeb Jr. A portrait of Captain Moses is in the background.

—Ambassador John L. Loeb Jr. collection

Johnston Lee, and Joseph Winthrop a token dollar each. The remainder of her $400 estate she left to her eldest daughter, Sarah Hawley, who was divorced and employed as a secretary and notary public. At the time of Jeannette's death on November 15, 1919, the family was dispersed. Adeline, who had married Carl Loeb in 1896, lived in New York; Alfred H. Jr. lived in London; Johnston Lee lived in Dardanelle, Arkansas; Joseph Winthrop (called "Winthrop" in the records from the probate court); and Sarah lived in St. Louis. Possibly all three—Alfred, Mordecai, and Jeannette—were victims of the flu epidemic of 1918–1919.[48]

Although the Moses family lived in St. Louis for many years, Montgomery remained their spiritual home. The bodies of Alfred, Mordecai, and Jeannette were returned to Montgomery for burial in the Moses lot of the Jewish section of Oakwood Cemetery. When Sarah died in St. Louis on December 5, 1928, her body was also returned to Montgomery for burial.[49]

The town of Sheffield remained inactive for about nine years. In 1899 the Sloss Iron and Steel Co. purchased the two furnaces erected by Colonel Ensley at Sheffield—the Lady Ensley and the Hattie Ensley—and the Philadelphia furnace at Florence, as well as 20,000 acres of brown ore lands in Franklin and Colbert counties. The company then changed its name to the Sloss-Sheffield Steel and Iron Co. That same year the Tennessee, Coal, and Iron Co. (TCI) bought the furnaces of the Sheffield Coal, Iron, and Steel Co.[50]

In 1907 a Wall Street panic threatened TCI's expansions. To avoid further panic and destabilization of the market, a group of influential businessmen, including J. P. Morgan and Henry C. Frick, proposed a buyout of TCI by U.S. Steel. President Roosevelt consented to the merger, convinced that it was the only way to "prevent a panic and a general smashup." U.S. Steel paid $35,317,632 for the TCI assets, which became one of the company's most important subsidiaries.[51]

But even U.S. Steel was not able to maintain the Sheffield furnaces. In 1929 the last of the remnants of an active iron industry disappeared from the region when the last two furnaces in Sheffield were closed. In 1933 the creation of the Tennessee Valley Authority finally brought electricity, flood control, and economic development to the region.[52]

Although he never returned to his earlier financial success, according to his granddaughter Margaret, Alfred Huger Moses eventually paid off all his debtors, and he is remembered warmly in his adopted state of Alabama. The main conference room in The House of the Mayors in Montgomery is named in his memory, as well as a local history room in the Sheffield Public Library.[53]

Descendants of
Alfred Huger Moses & Jeannette Nathan

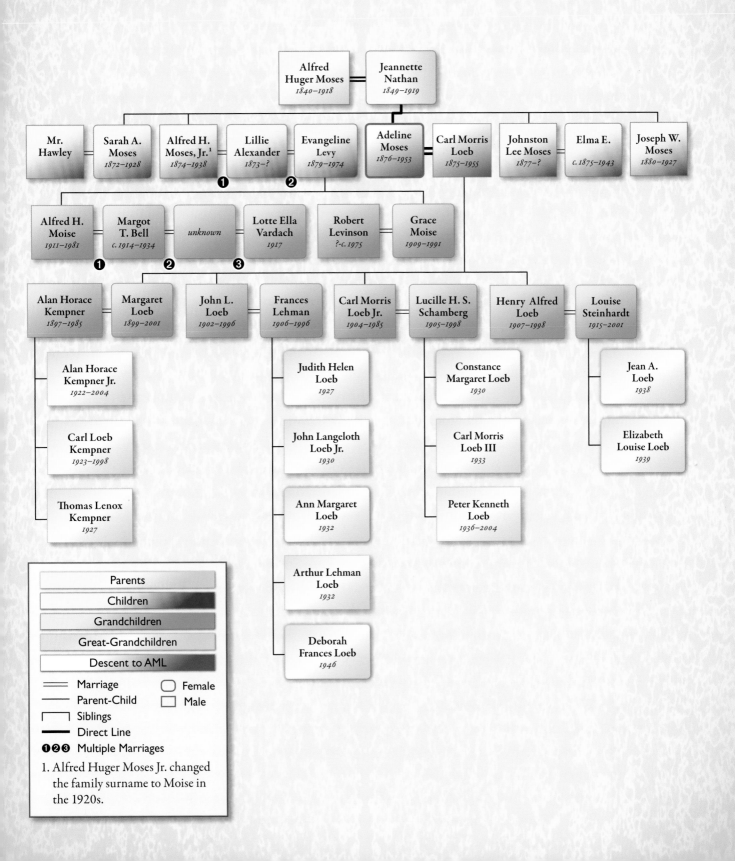

Alfred Huger Moses *1840–1918* ══ **Jeannette Nathan** *1849–1919*

- **Mr. Hawley**
- **Sarah A. Moses** *1872–1928*
- **Alfred H. Moses, Jr.** [1] *1874–1938* ❶ **Lillie Alexander** *1873–?* ❷ **Evangeline Levy** *1879–1974*
- **Adeline Moses** *1876–1953* ══ **Carl Morris Loeb** *1875–1955*
- **Johnston Lee Moses** *1877–?*
- **Elma E.** *c. 1875–1943*
- **Joseph W. Moses** *1880–1927*

- **Alfred H. Moise** *1911–1981* ❶ **Margot T. Bell** *c. 1914–1934* ❷ *unknown* ❸ **Lotte Ella Vardach** *1917*
- **Robert Levinson** *?–c. 1975* ══ **Grace Moise** *1909–1991*

- **Alan Horace Kempner** *1897–1985* ══ **Margaret Loeb** *1899–2001*
- **John L. Loeb** *1902–1996* ══ **Frances Lehman** *1906–1996*
- **Carl Morris Loeb Jr.** *1904–1985* ══ **Lucille H. S. Schamberg** *1905–1998*
- **Henry Alfred Loeb** *1907–1998* ══ **Louise Steinhardt** *1915–2001*

- **Alan Horace Kempner Jr.** *1922–2004*
- **Carl Loeb Kempner** *1923–1998*
- **Thomas Lenox Kempner** *1927*

- **Judith Helen Loeb** *1927*
- **John Langeloth Loeb Jr.** *1930*
- **Ann Margaret Loeb** *1932*
- **Arthur Lehman Loeb** *1932*
- **Deborah Frances Loeb** *1946*

- **Constance Margaret Loeb** *1930*
- **Carl Morris Loeb III** *1933*
- **Peter Kenneth Loeb** *1936–2004*

- **Jean A. Loeb** *1938*
- **Elizabeth Louise Loeb** *1939*

Legend:

- Parents
- Children
- Grandchildren
- Great-Grandchildren
- Descent to AML

- ══ Marriage
- │ Parent-Child
- └ Siblings
- ━ Direct Line
- ❶❷❸ Multiple Marriages
- ◯ Female
- ▢ Male

1. Alfred Huger Moses Jr. changed the family surname to Moise in the 1920s.

The Children of Alfred Huger and Jeannette Nathan Moses

1. **Sarah A.** (born September 3, 1872, Montgomery, Alabama; died December 5, 1928, St. Louis, Missouri). At twenty-six, Sarah married a Mr. Hawley, who had four children from a previous marriage. The couple was quickly divorced, but the 1910 federal census listed her as a "widow." She had no children. In 1910 we find her working as a secretary and notary public in St. Louis and living with her parents, brothers Johnston Lee and Winthrop, and grandmother Hannah Nathan. After her parents' death, she moved to the home of her aunts, Grace and Rosanna Moses. She died in St. Louis but was buried in Montgomery, Alabama, in the Moses lot in Oakwood Cemetery.

2. **Alfred Huger Jr.** (born June 18, 1874, Louisville, Kentucky; died October 14, 1938, Los Angeles, California). Alfred was born in Louisville, Kentucky, his mother's hometown, and graduated from Alabama Polytechnic Institute in 1891 and the Massachusetts Institute of Technology. With an aptitude for mechanics and a particular interest in cameras and projectors, he became a pioneer cinematographer and worked on at least thirty-seven films, including the first Lumière Cinematograph brought to this country (in 1892). In February 1898 he married Lillie Alexander (born May 1873), a native New Yorker and the daughter of German immigrants Isidor Alexander and Rosa Posner. The federal census of 1900 shows them living at 60 W. 11th Street in Manhattan, with Alfred working as an "electrical engineer." His grandchildren report that he helped wire both the Statue of Liberty and the battleship *Maine*. His time with Lillie was short (whether because of a divorce or a death is not known). On December 25, 1906, he married Evangeline Levy (born June 18, 1879, Fairoaks Plantation, Louisiana; died February 11, 1974, Mendoecino, California), daughter of Eugene Henry Levy and Almeria Emma Moses. Evangeline, a native of Fairoaks Plantation, Lafayette Parish, Louisiana, was his (and therefore Adeline's) sixth cousin.

    His cinematic career began in 1907 and he lived for a time in Hollywood. He worked for Peerless (*The Little Duchess*), George Backer Film Corporation (*The Sin Women*), Triangle-Fine Arts (*The Social Secretary*), six years with

Thanhouser (at least twenty-eight films between 1910 and 1916), Rolfe-Metro (*Life's Shadows*), Blaché (*Who So Taketh a Wife*) and with Norma Talmadge in 1917. But he didn't really like Hollywood, and a profile of Alfred in the *New Rochelle Pioneer*, June 12, 1915, reported that he lived in New Rochelle, New York, at 18 Pratt Street, with his "charming wife and two children." The 1918 edition of the Motion Picture Studio Directory listed his employment at the Norma Talmadge Film Corporation and his home address as 465 West 152d Street, New York City. He subsequently moved to England and worked for two years as chief cameraman for the British and Colonial Kinematograph Company. In 1921 he was chief cameraman for George Ridgwell Productions at the Stoll Picture Company in Cricklewood. The probate records filed at the time of his mother's death in 1919 gave his home as London. He later moved to France and changed his name to "Moise," ("Moe-eece") making it easier for the French to pronounce. However, filmmaking was not his favorite career. He ultimately returned to his original craft in electrical work and resettled in the Los Angeles area. Alfred and Evangeline had two children: a daughter, Grace, and a son, Alfred Huger Jr.

3. **Adeline** (born February 11, 1876, Montgomery, Alabama; died November 28, 1953, New York City). Adeline married Carl Morris Loeb (born September 28, 1875, Frankfurt am Main, Germany; died January 3, 1955, New York City) on November 12, 1896 in St. Louis, Missouri. In 1892 the Metallgesellschaft Company of Frankfurt sent the young German immigrant Carl M. Loeb (son of Adolph and Minna Cohn Loeb of Frankfurt) to St. Louis to work in the offices of their American branch, the American Metal Company. In St. Louis, Carl boarded at the home of Grace and Rosanna Moses, the unmarried sisters of Alfred Moses, where he met their niece, Adeline. Their children Margaret (1899–2001), John Langeloth (1902–1996), and Carl Morris Jr. (1904–1985), were all born in St. Louis. Son Henry Alfred (1907–1998) was born in New York City. In 1905 Carl Loeb was made a vice president of American Metal and the family relocated to New York City. He became president in 1915 and

"The Earliest Extant Minute Book of the Spanish and Portuguese Congregation Shearith Israel, 1728–1786," *PAJHS* 21 (1913): 1–171.

Elzas, Barnett. *A History of Congregation Beth Elohim of Charleston, South Carolina 1800–1810*. Charleston, SC: Daggett Print Company, 1902.

———. *Jewish Marriage Notices from the Newspaper Press of Charleston, S.C., 1775–1906*. New York: Bloch, 1917.

Emmanuel, Isaac S. *Precious Stones of the Jews of Curaçao: Curaçaon Jewry, 1656–1957*. New York: Bloch, 1957.

Emmanuel, Isaac S., and Suzanne A. *History of the Jews of the Netherland Antilles*. Cincinnati: American Jewish Archives, 1970.

Endelman, Todd M. *The Jews of Britain, 1656 to 2000*. Berkeley: University of California Press, 2002.

Faber, Eli. *A Time for Planting; The First Migration, 1654–1820*. Baltimore: Johns Hopkins University Press, 1992.

Fleming, H. S. "Causes of Failure in 'Boom' Towns," *The Engineering Magazine* 6 (December 1893): 276–84.

Fleming, Walter L. *Civil War and Reconstruction in Alabama*. New York: Columbia University Press, 1905.

Friedenwald, Herbert. "Jacob Isaacs and His Method of Converting Salt Water into Fresh Water," *PAJHS* 2 (1894): 111–18.

Friedman, Lee M. "Jacob Mears and Simon Valentine of Charleston, S.C.," *PAJHS* 41 (1951): 77–82.

———. "Wills of Early Jewish Settlers in New York," *PAJHS* 23 (1915): 147–62.

Fuller, Justin. "Boom Towns and Blast Furnaces: Town Promotion in Alabama, 1885–1893," *Alabama Review* 29 (January 1976): 37–48.

Gottesman, Rita Susswein. *The Arts and Crafts in New York, 1726–1776*. New York: New York Historical Society, 1938.

Greene, Harlan, and Harry S. Hutchins Jr. *Slave Badges and the Slave-Hire System in Charleston, South Carolina, 1783–1865*. Jefferson, NC: McFarland, 2004.

Gutstein, Morris A. *The Story of the Jews of Newport*. New York: Bloch, 1936.

Hagy, James William. *This Happy Land: The Jews of Colonial and Antebellum Charleston.* Tuscaloosa: University of Alabama Press, 1993.

Hamilton, Virginia Van der Veer. *Alabama: A Bicentennial History.* New York: Norton, 1977.

Hart, R. J. D'Arcy. "The Family of Mordecai Hamburger and Their Association with Madras," *MJHSE* 3 (1937): 57–75.

Hershkowitz, Leo. "Some Aspects of the New York Jewish Merchant and Community, 1654," *AJHQ* 66 (September 1976): 10–34.

———. *Wills of Early New York Jews (1704–1799).* New York: American Jewish Historical Society, 1967.

Hershkowitz, Leo, and Isidore S. Meyer, eds. *The Lee Max Friedman Collection of American Jewish Colonial Correspondence: Letters of the Franks Family (1733–1748).* Waltham, MA: American Jewish Historical Society, 1968.

Hudson, Charles. "Louisbourg Soldiers," *New England Historical and Genealogical Register* 25 (1871): 249–69.

Hühner, Leon. "The Jews of New England (Other than Rhode Island) Prior to 1800," *PAJHS* 11 (1903): 75–99.

"Items Relating to the Jews of Newport," *PAJHS* 27 (1920): 175–216.

Jacobson, Mark. "Jewish Merchants of Newport in Pre-Revolutionary Days," *RIJHN* 5 (1970): 332–381.

"Jeannette Moses" (death notice), *St. Louis Post Dispatch* (November 16, 1919): 11.

"Jewish Material in the Miscellaneous Champlin Papers, 1732–1784," *RIJHN* 5 (1970): 345.

Keith, Jean E. "The Role of the Louisville and Nashville Railroad in the Early Development of Alabama Coal and Iron," *Bulletin of the Business Historical Society* 25 (September, 1952): 165–174.

Kohler, Max J. "Civil Status of Jews in Colonial New York," *PAJHS* 6 (1897): 81–106.

Korn, Bertram W. "Jews and Negro Slavery in the Old South, 1789–1865," in *The Jewish Experience in America* (Waltham, MA: American Jewish Historical Society, 1969), 3: 177–219.

Leftwich, Nina. *Two Hundred Years at Muscle Shoals*. Tuscumbia, AL: privately printed, 1935.

Libo, Kenneth. "The Moseses of Montgomery: The Saga of a Jewish Family in the South," *Alabama Heritage* (Spring, 1995): 18–25.

Lightner, Otto C. *The History of Business Depressions*. 1922. Reprint, New York: Burt Franklin, 1970.

List of Taxpayers for the City of Charleston for 1859. Charleston: 1860.

List of Taxpayers for the City of Charleston for 1860. Charleston: 1861.

Loeb, John Langeloth, and Frances Lehman Loeb with Kenneth Libo. *All in a Lifetime: A Personal Memoir*. New York: John L. Loeb, 1996.

Louisville city directory, 1845/46–1881.

Louisville Courier-Journal (November 11, 1871).

Marcus, Jacob R. *American Jewry: Documents, Eighteenth Century*. Cincinnati: Hebrew Union College Press, 1959.

———. *The Colonial American Jew*. Detroit: Wayne State University, 1970.

———. "Light on Early Connecticut Jewry," *American Jewish Archives* 1 (January 1949): 3–52.

———. *Memoirs of American Jews*. Philadelphia: Jewish Publication Society, 1955.

———. *Studies in American Jewish History*. Cincinnati: Hebrew Union College Press, 1969.

"Miscellaneous Lopez Papers," *RIJHN* 5 (1970): 341–342.

Moore, Albert Burton. *History of Alabama and Her People*. Chicago: American Historical Society, 1927.

"Mordecai Lyon Moses" (obituary), *St. Louis Post-Dispatch* (June 8, 1918): 3.

Morrison, Samuel Eliot. *The Oxford History of the American People*. New York: Oxford University Press, 1965.

"Mrs. Carl M. Loeb" (obituary), *New York Times* (November 30, 1953): 2.

Nathan, Joseph H. "Early Days of Sheffield—Now Fifty Years Old—Retold Interestingly by Resident," *The Sheffield Standard* (December 21, 1934).

New Jersey Archives 12: 202.

Northern Alabama: Historical and Biographical. Birmingham: Smith & De Land, 1888.

Occident (newspaper).

Oppenheim, Samuel. "The Jews and Masonry in the United States before 1810," *PAJHS* 19 (1910): 1–94.

Otte, Herman Frederick. *Industrial Opportunity in the Tennessee Valley of Northwestern Alabama.* New York: Columbia University Press, 1940.

Phillips, N. Taylor. "Family History of the Reverend David Mendez Machado," *PAJHS* 2 (1894): 45–62.

———. "The Congregation Shearith Israel: An Historical Overview," *PAJHS* 6 (1897): 123–40.

———. "Items Relating to the History of the Jews of New York," *PAJHS* 11 (1903): 149–62.

Pool, David de Sola. *Portraits Etched in Stone.* New York: Columbia University Press, 1952.

Pool, David de Sola, and Tamar de Sola Pool. *An Old Faith in the New World.* New York: Columbia University Press, 1955.

Porto v. Michael et ux. (1707), Mayor's Court Minutes (New York), vol. 1704–1710: 302–304.

Rezneck, Samuel. *Unrecognized Patriots.* Westport, CT: Greenwood Press, 1976.

Reznikoff, Charles. *The Jews of Charleston.* Philadephia: Jewish Publication Society, 1950.

Rhodes, Irwin S. *References to Jews in the Newport Mercury, 1758–1786.* Cincinnati: American Jewish Archives, 1961.

Rosengarten, Theodore, and Dale Rosengarten, eds. *A Portion of the People: Three Hundred Years of Southern Jewish Life.* Columbia: University of South Carolina Press, 2002.

Rosenswaike, Ira. "An Estimate and Analysis of the Jewish Population of the United States in 1790," *PAJHS* 50 (September 1960): 23–67.

Ross, J. M. "Naturalisation of Jews in England," *TJHSE* 23 (1975): 59–72.

Roth, Cecil. *The Great Synagogue, London: 1690-1940*. London: Edward Goldston & Son, 1950.

Stern, Malcolm. *First American Jewish Families*. Cincinnati: American Jewish Archives, 1978.

Strauss, Leopold. "The Passing of Illustrious Family Living Here Over 40 Years Ago," *Montgomery Advertiser* (October 24, 1931).

Tarshish, Allan. "The Charleston Organ Case," in *The Jewish Experience in America* (Waltham, MA: American Jewish Historical Society, 1969), 2: 281–315.

Taylor, Rosser H. *Ante Bellum South Carolina: A Social and Cultural History*. Chapel Hill: University of North Carolina Press, 1942.

Tobias, Thomas J. *The Hebrew Orphan Society of Charleston, S.C.: An Historical Sketch*. Charleston, SC: Hebrew Orphan Society, 1957.

Wade, Richard C. *Slavery in the Cities: The South, 1820–1860*. New York: Oxford University Press, 1964.

Williams, Clanton W. "Conservatism in Old Montgomery, 1817–1861," *Alabama Review* 10 (April 1957): 96–110.

Willner, W. "Ezra Stiles and the Jews," *PAJHS* 8 (1900): 119–26.

Wolf, Simon. *The American Jew as Patriot, Soldier and Citizen*. Philadelphia: Levytype Company, 1895.

Archival and Manuscript Collections and Unpublished Material

Breibart, Solomon, to John L. Loeb Jr., June 12, 1980, personal correspondence.

Complaint of Jacob Mears against Aaron Hart, May 9, 1718, The Answer of Aaron Hart Defendant to the Bill of Complaint of Jacob Mears Complainant, May 19, 1718, C11/2652/33 399, PRO.

Complaint of John Vaughn against Jacob Mears, February 1717, The Answer of Jacob Mears Defendant to the Bill of Complaint of John Vaughn, Esq. Complainant, March 1717, A Schedule of the Severall Goods and the

Prices thereof and other things which the within Written Answer refers to and is therein Mentioned, January 5, 1717, C11/311/10 00400, PRO.

Complaint of Matthew Brandon…Moses Hart…and Joy Mears…against Moses Levy, November 1717, C11/2724/109 00397, PRO.

Complaint of Matthew Brandon…Moses Hart…and Joy Mears…against Moses Levy, November, 1717 C11/2724/109 00397, PRO.

Complaint of Thomas Wood against Sampson and Jacob Mears, January 2, 1708, C8/68/3426116, PRO.

Confederate States of America, Alabama Rebels muster rolls, National Archives, Washington, DC.

Gray, James W., Master in Equity, to Charles P. Shier, Conveyance of Plantation, St. James Goose Creek, Court of Equity for the District of Charleston, SC, July 1, 1841, copy in possession of John L. Loeb Jr.

Kempner, Margaret Loeb. *Recollection*. Unpublished memoir.

Libo, Kenneth. "In Quest of the Promised Land: The Moses Family and the Southern Jewish Experience, 1794–1918." Unpublished speech at the dedication of the Captain Alfred Huger Moses Conference Room, Montgomery, Alabama, October 1992.

Loeb, John L. Sr., Dedication of the Loeb Student Center at New York University, November 24, 1959, unpublished speech.

Moses, Alfred Huger, death certificate, Missouri State Board of Health, Bureau of Vital Statistics, Jefferson City, MO.

Moses, Alfred Huger, refusal of letters of administration, Probate Court, City of St. Louis, MO.

Moses, Isaiah, inventory of estate of December 17, 1857, South Carolina Department of Archives and History, Columbia, SC.

Moses, Jeannette Nathan, will, probate death certificate, Missouri State Board of Health, Bureau of Vital Statistics, Jefferson City, MO.

Moses, Rebecca, probate file of Probate Court of Chatham County, Savannah, GA.

Moses Brothers Savings Bank, records, 1881–1892, Alabama Department of
    Archives and History, Montgomery, AL.
Moses Vertical File, Alabama Department of Archives and History,
    Montgomery, includes the following:
    Memoranda for Biographical Sketch of Mordecai L. Moses;
    Moses Lot, Oakwood Cemetery, Montgomery County, New Division,
    Jewish Section.
U.S. Congress, House Exec. Document, 40th Congress, 2d Session, No. 16, vol. 7.

Web Sites
Ancestry.com. www.Ancestry.com. This Web site includes searchable full text of
    all available U.S. censuses, as well as additional genealogical data.
Civil War Soldiers and Sailor System. www.itd.nps.gov/cwss. This Web site
    includes indices to soldiers who served in the Union and Confederate armies.
Internet Movie Database. www.imdb.com. A Web site providing information
    on the movie industry.
Rebecca Isaiah Moses. www.serve.com/rim. This Web site incorporates a variety
    of materials relating to Rebecca Phillips Moses, including biographical
    notes, photographs of some personal materials, a transcription of
    references to slaves in her daybook, and other items.

Abbreviations
AJHQ—American Jewish Historical Quarterly.
MJHSE—Miscellanies of the Jewish Historical Society of England.
PAJHS—Publications of the American Jewish Historical Society.
PRO—Public Record Office, London.
RIJHN—Rhode Island Jewish Historical Notes.
TJHSE—Transactions of the Jewish Historical Society of England.

FAMILY CHARTS AND MAPS

Books

Alexander, Henry Aaron. *Notes on the Alexander Family of South Carolina and Georgia and Connections.* Privately published, 1954.

Arbell, Mordechai. *The Jewish Nation of the Caribbean: The Spanish-Portuguese Jewish Settlements in the Caribbean and the Guianas.* Jerusalem: Gefen Publishing House, 2002.

Barnes, Robert W. *Maryland Genealogies: A Consolidation of Articles from the Maryland Historical Magazine,* vol. 1. Baltimore: Genealogical Publishing Co., Inc., 1980.

Barnett, Richard D., and Philip Wright. *The Jews of Jamaica: Tombstone Inscriptions 1663–1880.* Jerusalem: Ben Zvi Institute, 1997.

Bingham, Emily. *Mordecai, An Early American Family.* New York: Hill and Wang, 2003.

Bockstruck, Lloyd deWitt. *Denizations and Naturalizations in the British Colonies in America, 1607–1775.* Baltimore: Genealogical Publishing Co., Inc., 2005.

Brilliant, Richard. *Facing the New World: Jewish Portraits in Colonial and Federal America.* Munich and New York: Prestel, 1997.

Buck, J. Orton and Beard, Timothy Field. *Pedigrees of Some of the Emperor Charlemagne's Descendants,* vol. III. Baltimore: Genealogical Publishing Company, 1999.

Collections of the New-York Historical Society for the Year 1894. New York: New York Historical Society, 1895.

Collections of the New York Historical Society for the year 1885. New York: New York Historical Society, 1886.

DePeyster, John Watts, compiler. *Collections of the New York Historical Society for the Year 1904.* New York: New York Historical Society, 1905.

Egle, William Henry. *Notes & Queries Historical and Genealogical/Chiefly Relating to the Interior of Pennsylvania*. Baltimore: Genealogical Publishing Company, 1970.

Elmaleh, Reverend L. H., et al. *The Jewish Cemetery: 9th & Spruce Streets, Philadelphia*. Philadelphia: Congregation Mikveh Israel, 1962.

Elzas, Barnett. A. *The Old Jewish Cemeteries At Charleston, South Carolina: a transcrpt of the inscriptions on their tombstones, 1762–1903*. Charleston, SC: The Daggett Print Company, 1903. Quinton Publications Collection, 1903.

Gelles, Edith B., ed. *The Letters of Abigaill Levy Franks, 1733–1748*. New Haven, CT: Yale University Press, 2004.

Godfrey, Sheldon J., and Judith C. Godfrey. *Search Out the Land: The Jews and the Growth of Equality in British Colonial America, 1740–1867*. Montreal: McGill-Queen's University Press, 1995.

Gradwohl, David. *Tablets of the Law Thrown Down: Colonial Burying Ground in Newport, Rhode Island*. Newport, RI: Touro Foundation, 2007.

Gutstein, Morris. *The Story of the Jews of Newport, Two and Half Centuries of Judaism, 1658–1908*. New York: Bloch Publishing, 1936.

Hershkowitz, Leo, and Isadore S. Meyer, eds. *The Lee Max Friedman Collection of American Jewish Colonial Correspondence: Letters of the Franks Family (1733–1748)*. Waltham, MA: American Jewish Historical Society, 1968.

Hershkowitz, Leo. *Wills of Early New York Jews (1704–1799)*. New York: American Jewish Historical Society, 1967.

Hirschfeld, Fritz. *George Washington and the Jews*. Newark: University of Delaware Press, 2005.

Hotchkin, Samuel Fitch. *Ancient and Modern Germantown, Mount Airy, and Chestnut Hill*. Philadelphia: P. W. Ziegler & Co., 1889.

Hühner, Leon. *The Life of Judah Touro (1775–1854)*. Philadelphia: Jewish Publication Society of America, 1947.

Loeb, John Langeloth, and Frances Lehman Loeb, with Kenneth Libo. *All in a Lifetime: A Personal Memoir*. New York: John Langeloth Loeb, 1996.

Morais, Henry Samuel. *The Jews of Philadelphia: Their History from the Earliest Settlements to the Present Time.* Philadelphia, PA: The Levytype Company, 1894.

Navy Department, Bureau of Naval Personnel. *Register of Commissioned and Warrant Officers of the United States Navy and Marine Corps to January 1, 1903.* Washington, DC: United States Government Printing Office, 1903.

Owen, Thomas McAdory, LL.D. *History of Alabama & Dictionary of Alabama Biography, in Four Volumes.* Chicago: The S. J. Clarke Publishing Company, 1921.

Pool, David de Sola, and Tamar de Sola Pool. *An Old Faith in the New World.* New York: Columbia University Press, 1955.

Pool, David De Sola. *Portraits Etched in Stone: Early Jewish Settlers, 1682–1831.* New York: Columbia University Press, 1952.

Regenstein, Lewis. "Raphael Moses 1829–1882," in *The New Georgia Encyclopedia: History & Archaeology,* 2004. http://www.georgiaencyclopedia.org/nge/Article.jsp?id=h-2908.

Reynolds, Cuyler, compiler. *Genealogical and Family History of Southern New York and the Hudson River Valley,* vol. III. New York: Lewis Historical Publishing Company, 1914.

Sabine, Lorenzo. *Biographical Sketches of Loyalists of the American Revolution.* Boston: Little, Brown, 1864.

Seymour, Mary Jane. *Lineage Book: National Society of the Daughters of the American Revolution.* Washington, DC: Daughters of the American Revolution, 1896.

Spencer, Richard Henry, ed. *Genealogical and Memorial Encyclopedia of the State of Maryland.* Baltimore, MD: Clearfield, 1919.

Stern, Malcolm H. *First American Jewish Families: 600 Genealogies, 1654–1988,* 3rd ed., updated and revised, Baltimore, MD: Ottenheimer Publishers, 1991.

Urofsky, Melvin I. *The Levy Family and Monticello, 1834–1923: Saving Thomas Jefferson's House.* Monticello Monograph Series. Charlottesville, VA: Thomas Jefferson Foundation, 2001.

Various authors, *Baltimore: Its History and Its People.* Charlottesville, Virginia: University of Virginia Press, 1912. Digital edition by Lewis Historical Publishing Co, 2007 [ANC].

Wolf, Edwin, II, and Maxwell Whiteman. *The History of the Jews of Philadelphia from Colonial Times to the Age of Jackson.* Philadelphia: The Jewish Publication Society of America, 1956.

Journals and Periodicals

American Jewish Historical Society. *Publications of the American Jewish Historical Society (1893–1978).* Baltimore, etc.: American Jewish Historical Society. 50v. 1893-1978.

Arizona Republic (Phoenix, AZ). http://www.azcentral.com.

Baltimore Sun. http://www.baltimoresun.com.

Columbus Daily Enquirer (Columbus, GA). http://www.genealogybank.com.

Daily Mail [on-line edition]. (London, England) http://www.dailymail.co.uk.

Florence Morning News (Florence, SC).

McCarthy, Kerry. "Nan Kempner—The Original It Girl." *Marie Claire*, 2008. http://nz.blogs.yahoo.com/marie-claire/360/nan-kempnerthe-original-it-girl.

Montgomery Advertiser [online edition] (Montgomery, Alabama). http://www.genealogybank.com.

New York Times. http://www.nytimes.com.

Newport Mercury and Weekly News (Newport, RI). http://www.genealogybank.com.

Pitz, Marylinne. "A Frick Family Feud." *Pittsburgh Post-Gazette* (May 27, 2001). http://www.post-gazette.com/ae/20010527frickfightkmag2.asp.

Princeton Alumni Weekly. http://paw.princeton.edu.

"Saga of an Abduction," *Time Magazine* (August 25, 1975). http://www.time.com/time/magazine/article/0,9171,913409-1,00.html.

"Still a Reasonable Doubt," *Time Magazine* (December 20, 1976). http://aolsvc.timeforkids.kol.aol.com/time/magazine/article/0,9171,911913-1,00.html.

St. Louis Post-Dispatch. http://www.stltoday.com.

The London Independent (London, England). http://www.independent.co.uk.

The Times Archive (London, England). http://archive.timesonline.co.uk.

Washington Post (Washington, DC). http://www.washingtonpost.com.

Government Record Collections

Census Returns of England and Wales, 1861. Kew, Surrey, England: The National Archives of the UK (TNA): Public Record Office (PRO), 1861.

Census Returns of England and Wales, 1871. Kew, Surrey, England: The National Archives of the UK (TNA): Public Record Office (PRO), 1871.

Census Returns of England and Wales, 1881. Kew, Surrey, England: The National Archives of the UK (TNA): Public Record Office (PRO), 1881.

Census Returns of England and Wales, 1901. Kew, Surrey, England: The National Archives of the UK (TNA): Public Record Office (PRO), 1901.

General Register Office. *England and Wales Civil Registration Indexes.* London, England: General Register Office.

Kentucky. *Kentucky Birth, Marriage and Death Records—Microfilm (1852–1910).* Microfilm rolls 994027–994058. Kentucky Department for Libraries and Archives, Frankfort, Kentucky.

New York City, Boroughs of. *Births Reported in the City of New York, 1847–1909.* New York: Municipal Archives.

New York City, Boroughs of. *Marriage Records 1847–1929.* New York: Municipal Archives.

New York City, Boroughs of. *Deaths Reported in the City of New York, 1888–1965.* New York: Municipal Archives.

Passenger and Crew Lists of Vessels Arriving at New York, New York, 1897–1957; (National Archives Microfilm Publication T715, 8892 rolls) Records of the Immigration and Naturalization Service; National Archives, Washington, DC.

South Carolina. *South Carolina Death Records 1921–1955.* Columbia: South Carolina Department of Archives and History.

U.S. Bureau of the Census. *First Census of the United States, 1790.* Washington, DC: National Archives and Records Administration, 1800. Microfilm series M637, RG 29.

———. *Second Census of the United States, 1800.* Washington, DC: National Archives and Records Administration, 1800. Microfilm series M32.

———. *Third Census of the United States, 1810.* Washington, DC: National Archives and Records Administration, 1810. Microfilm series M252.

———. *Sixth Census of the United States, 1840.* Washington, DC: National Archives and Records Administration, 1840. Microfilm series M704.

———. *Seventh Census of the United States, 1850.* Washington, DC: National Archives and Records Administration, 1850. Microfilm series M432.

———.*Eighth Census of the United States, 1860.* Washington, DC: National Archives and Records Administration, 1860. Microfilm series M653.

———. *Ninth Census of the United States, 1870.* Washington, DC National Archives and Records Administration. Microfilm series M593, RG29.

———. *Tenth Census of the United States, 1880.* Washington, DC: National Archives and Records Administration, 1880. Microfilm series T9.

———. *Twelfth Census of the United States, 1900.* Washington, DC: National Archives and Records Administration, 1900. Microfilm series T623.

———. *Thirteenth Census of the United States, 1910.* Washington, DC: National Archives and Records Administration, 1910. Microfilm series T624.

———. *Fourteenth Census of the United States, 1920.* Washington, DC: National Archives and Records Administration, 1920. Microfilm series T625.

———. *Fifteenth Census of the United States, 1930.* Washington, DC: National Archives and Records Administration, 1930. Microfilm series T626.

U.S. Selective Service System. *World War I Selective Service System Draft Registration Cards, 1917–1918.* Washington, DC: National Archives and Records Administration. Microfilm series M1509.

Archival and Manuscript Collections and Unpublished Material

American Jewish Archives. *Guide to the Papers of the Seixas Family, undated, 1746-1911, 1926, 1939.* http://findingaids.cjh.org/?fnm=SeixasFamily&pnm=AJHS.

Gudis, Lucille. *Research on the Loeb/Low Family, Conducted for Ambassador John L. Loeb, Jr.* Unpublished charts and manuscripts in the possession of Ambassador Loeb.

Kleiman, David M. Transcript of interviews with the descendents and relations of Adeline Moses Loeb, including Alfred Charles Bell, James Guggenheim, Thomas Lenox Kempner, Hadassah Savetsky Loeb, Ambassador John L. Loeb, Jr., David Mack Moise, and Karen Moise. Unpublished, 2008.

Nathan, Robert L., "Winston Cemetery, Alabama Gravestone Pictures. " Unpublished, privately held digital images of family gravestones.

Nathan, Robert Lindsay III. "RE: Morris Nathan & Hannah Dinkelspiel." E-mail to David Kleiman, July 29, 2008. Unpublished.

Plotkin, Kathy. "Plotkin Correspondence File." Unpublished, 2008.

Symington, Leslie P. Letter from Leslie P. Symington to John L. Loeb Jr., July 3, 2007.

Symington, Leslie P. "Symington Family Tree: Descendants of Sampson Mears." Unpublished.

Touro Synagogue. *Interments by Horizontal Rows in the Colonial Jewish Cemetery at Bellevue and Touro Street.* Unpublished. Touro Synagogue Foundation, July 23, 1996.

Web Sites

Ancestry.com. Extensive collection of databases, digitized images and indexes. Databases consulted include:

"United States Federal Census Collection, 1790–1930." Compiled index and digital images.

"Arkansas Death Index, 1914–1950."

"Border Crossings: From Canada to U.S., 1895–1956."

"California Birth Index, 1905–1995."

"California Death Index, 1940–1997."

"California Marriage Index, 1960–1985."

"Census Returns of England and Wales, 1861–1901."

"Connecticut Death Index, 1949–2001."

"England & Wales, FreeBMD Marriage Index: 1837–1983."

"Georgia Deaths, 1919–1998."

"Index of Vital Records for Alabama: Deaths, 1908–1959."

"Kentucky Birth Records, 1852–1910."

"Maryland Marriages 1801–1820."

"Missouri Birth Records, 1851–1910."

"Missouri Death Records, 1834–1931."

"Montgomery, Alabama Directories, 1880–95."

"New York City Births, 1891–1902."

"New York City Deaths, 1892–1902."

"North Carolina Census, 1790–1890."

"North Carolina Death Collection 1908–2004."

"North Carolina Marriage Collection, 1741–2004."

"Passenger and Crew Lists of Vessels Arriving at New York, New York, 1897–1957."

"Passenger and Immigration Lists Index, 1500s–1900s."

"Philadelphia County, Pennsylvania Wills, 1682–1819."

"Social Security Death Index."

"South Carolina Death Index, 1950–1952."

"South Carolina Death Records, 1821–1955."

"South Carolina Marriages, 1641–1965."

"Texas Marriage Collection, 1814–1909 and 1966–2002."

"U.S. Passport Applications, 1795–1925."

"U.S. Veterans Gravesites, ca. 1775–2006."

"United States Obituary Collection."

"Washington Births, 1891–1907."

"World War I Draft Registration Cards, 1917–1918."

Bright, David L. "Confederate Railroads."
http://www.csa-railroads.com/Confederate%20Railroads.htm.

Coleman, Erwin. "Temple B'nai Israel Cemetery (Sheffield, Colbert County, Alabama)." http://www.rootsweb.ancestry.com/~alcolber/cem-TempleBnaiIsrael.htm.

Dunn, Norris N. "Our Family Genealogy—Dunn/Kress Family Tree: Matthias Williamson Jr." http://wc.rootsweb.ancestry.com/cgi-bin/igm.cgi?op=GET&db=norris40&id=I09294, 2008.

Freer, Alan. "Descendants of William the Conqueror."
http://www.william1.co.uk, 2008.

Herbert, Mirana C. and Barbara McNeil, comp. "Biography and Genealogy Master Index."Detroit: Gale Research Co., 2003.
http://www.ancestry.com/search/rectype/biohist/bgmi/main.htm

Heritage Muse, Inc. "Americans of Jewish Descent."
http://www.heritagemuse.com.

Italian Genealogical Group. "NYC Death Index 1891–1948."
http://www.italiangen.org/NYCDEATH.STM.

Italian Genealogical Group. "NYC Grooms Index 1908–1936."
http://www.italiangen.org/NYCMarriage.stm.

"Jewish Women's Archive." http://jwa.org.

JewishGen, Inc. "JewishGen Online Worldwide Burial Registry (JOWBR)."
http://www.jewishgen.org/databases/cemetery.

Kestenbaum, Lawrence. "Political Graveyard." http://www.politicalgraveyard.com.

Lundy, Darryl. "Peerage.com: A genealogical survey of the peerage of Britain as well as the royal families of Europe." http://www.thepeerage.com.

Mikveh Israel Congregation. "Welcome to Mikveh Israel." http://www.mikvehisrael.org.

Office of the General Counsel, U.S. Department of the Navy. "Department of the Navy Legal Community—History." http://ogc.navy.mil/ogchistory.asp.

"The Raymond S. Troubh Page." http://www.smokershistory.com/Troubh.htm.

Redwood Library. "Jacob Rodriguez Rivera." http://www.redwoodlibrary.org/notables/rivera.htm.

Rooks, Gene. "Gene's Genes-Ballentine Ancestors." http://wc.rootsweb.ancestry.com/cgi-bin/igm.cgi?op=GET&db=grooks&id=I3477.

Salzman, Rob. "Family Tree of Rob Salzman." http://www.e-familytree.net/F76/F76582.htm.

Schipper, Martin P. *A Guide to the Microfilm Edition of Southern Women and Their Families in the 19th Century.* Series D, Holdings of the Virginia Historical Society. http://www.vahistorical.org/wguide/wguide_intro.htm.

Susser, Rabbi Bernard. "Susser Archive: Moses Hart's Shool, 1722." http://www.jewishgen.org/JCR-uk/susser/roth/chfive.htm.

Tomsett, Brian C. "Master Index to Royal Genealogical Data—ordered by forename." http://www3.dcs.hull.ac.uk/genealogy/royal/gedx.html.

Torbert, Robert. "Colbert County, Alabama Cemeteries." http://www.rootsweb.ancestry.com/~alcolber/cem.htm.

USGenweb Archives. "Cecil County, Maryland, Marriage Notice Index." http://files.usgwarchives.org/md/cecil/vitals/marriages.

UsGenWeb Archives. "Index to Will Abstracts 1685–1825, County of Philadelphia." http://usgwarchives.net/pa/philadelphia/willsabst.htm.

The Weston Park Foundation. "Weston Park: Its Owners and Their Relations." http://www.weston-park.com/%5Cuserfiles%5Cpdf%5CFamily%20Tree.pdf.

Wikipedia. "Philip Goodhart." http://en.wikipedia.org/wiki/Philip_Goodhart.

Williford, Theo, Sr. "Index of Deaths in the Florence Times: 4 July 1890–31 December 1930: Lauderdale County Obituaries." Submitted by Robert Ellington Torbert. http://www.rootsweb.ancestry.com/~allauder/obits-indexdeaths1890n.htm.

Manalo, Beverly, Karen Jackson, and Jamie Perez. "Some Baltimore County Obituaries—1893." http://www.geocities.com/pauledely/archives/1893.html.

Wolf Haldenstein Adler Freeman & Herz, LLC. "Edgar J. Nathan 3rd." http://www.whafh.com/modules/attorney/index.php?action=view&id=72.

Abbreviations

ANC—Ancestry (http://www.ancestry.com).

—◊—

APPENDICES

APPENDIX ONE
THE ANATOMY OF PATRIOTISM
Ambassador John L. Loeb Jr.

and

APPENDIX TWO
CONTRIBUTORS

THE ANATOMY OF PATRIOTISM
by
Ambassador John L. Loeb Jr.

—⚇—

Remarks delivered at the reopening of the Adeline
Moses Loeb Gallery in the Fraunces Tavern Museum
of the Sons of the Revolution in the State of New
York, November 15, 2001.

THROUGH DESCENT FROM AN ENGLISH-JEWISH FAMILY by the name of Phillips of
London and Charleston, South Carolina, I am a member of the Sons of the
Revolution in the State of New York (SRNY), a membership that means a great
deal to me. My four-times great-grandfather, Jacob Phillips, was a member of the
South Carolina Militia during the War of Independence.

I should add that a number of the Phillips family were Tories and returned
from Charleston to England before the American Revolution, but from 1776
until modern times, a member of my family has served in the United States
Armed Forces in every war. They held public office, they pioneered in business,
they nurtured talent in many fields, and they demonstrated and transmitted from
generation to generation a spirit which I consider part of my heritage.

In their love of this land, my family shared an emotion which has been
widely felt with particular intensity in this country since the time of the Founding
Fathers—patriotism.

American patriotism must be an almost instinctive response to a land so
blessed. Who could not be attached to and awed by a country so vast in its continental sweep, so endowed with natural wondrous beauty? Who could not be

"The Anatomy of Patriotism" was an address given by Ambassador John L. Loeb Jr. at the Fraunces Tavern Museum for the reopening of the Adeline Moses Loeb Gallery on November 15, 2001, when the country was still reeling from 9/11. The World Trade Center had been only blocks away from the museum.

—Photo by Lou Manna, New York, New York

devoted to and protective of a nation whose government was entrusted to its citizens? And where life, liberty, and even pursuit of happiness were their birthright?

Patriotism does not require daring physical deeds and sacrifice in the defense of the nation for services performed in the glare of public attention. You don't have to be Nathan Hale or Daniel Webster to be a patriot.

In the truest sense, patriotism, to me, is expressed in the daily lives of ordinary men and women whose conduct as citizens is governed by their belief in and practice of the ideals and traditions that are the glory of the American democracy—men and women who believe in freedom not only for themselves but for their neighbors, who seek opportunity without denying it to others, who understand that democracy requires tolerance.

Two cousins, Thomas L. Kempner and Ambassador John L. Loeb Jr., agreed at the reopening of the Adeline Moses Loeb Gallery in 2001 that their mutual grandparents, Carl and Adeline Moses Loeb, left no doubt about their passion for "these United States of America," as Carl always called his adopted country.

—Photo by Lou Manna, New York, New York

Unhappily, patriotism has sometimes been invoked to camouflage bigotry—by the Know-Nothings of the 1840s, by the Ku Klux Klan, by the apostles of McCarthyism after World War II, and by the extreme Religious Right today. Almost every minority in America has, at some period, been subjected to intolerance.

Yet, when compared to the rest of the world, when we look at the racial, religious, and ethnic conflicts tearing apart the Middle East, the former Soviet Union, and Africa—there are too many examples to list—America's experiment in diversity and tolerance has succeeded beyond anybody's wildest dreams.

The anatomy of patriotism is complex.

One would think that patriotism would be difficult to sustain in a people as diverse as we are. We are, after all, a nation of immigrants—and we have all been immigrants. Each of us has pride in our special heritage as well as a great love of America.

Even in the eighteenth century, the Founding Fathers knew that a spirit of tolerance and freedom was crucial—no, indispensable—to preserve the unity and purpose of the new nation. That is why, for example, they took the revolutionary and historic step of separating the church from the state.

President George Washington often gave voice to these same sentiments of tolerance and liberty. I would like to read to you a part of a letter he wrote to the Hebrew Congregation of Newport, Rhode Island, (now the Touro Synagogue) on August 17, 1790.

> The citizens of the United States of America have a right to applaud themselves for having given to mankind examples of an enlarged and liberal policy, a policy worthy of imitation. All possess alike liberty of conscience and immunities of citizenship. . . . Happily, the government of the United States, which gives to bigotry no sanction, to persecution no assistance, requires only that they who live under its protection should comport themselves as good citizens.

—ᴍ—

CONTRIBUTORS

AMBASSADOR JOHN L. LOEB JR.

Author of the Foreword, Part Two, and Appendix One: The Anatomy of Patriotism

Inspired at an early age by family stories told by his Southern-born paternal grandmother, Adeline Moses Loeb, Ambassador John L. Loeb Jr., New York financier and philanthropist, has had a special place in his heart for Jewish genealogy since his late twenties. A scion of two famous Wall Street families—Lehman Brothers, and Loeb, Rhoades—his is a lineage of no small public interest. (He has twelve ancestors included in the Jewish Museum's 1997 publication *Facing the New World: Jewish Portraits in Colonial and Federal America*.)

A former ambassador to Denmark and an amateur genealogist, he has demonstrated his passion for ancestral history for more than fifty years through his own research as well as through support and publication of the historical work of others. Some of these projects include a book by the German writer and editor Dr. Roland Flade, *The Lehmans: From Rimpar to the New World, A Family History*, as well as *Lots of Lehmans: The Family of Mayer Lehman, of Lehman Brothers, Remembered by His Descendants*, compiled by historian Dr. Kenneth Libo. John

Loeb Jr. is also responsible for the publication of *The Levy Family and Monticello, 1834–1923: Saving Thomas Jefferson's House,* by historian Dr. Melvin I. Urofsky.

In the late 1970s Loeb funded and helped to organize "The Jewish Community in Early New York, 1654–1800," an exhibit shown at the Fraunces Tavern in New York City in 1979-1980. The exhibit then traveled in 1980 to the Daughters of the American Revolution (DAR) museum in their national headquarters near Constitution Hall in Washington, D.C. A December 12, 1980, article in the *New York Times* quoted from John's remarks at the opening of the DAR exhibit: "Jews as well as Christians do not know about the contribution made by early Jews to the founding of this country and its fundamental philosophy and values." The article went on to note that John Loeb had created the exhibit in honor of his Alabama-born grandmother, who had been a member of the DAR. In 1975 he and his family established the Adeline Moses Loeb Gallery in the Fraunces Tavern Museum in New York City.

In 1998 he funded his idea of placing an Internet portrait database of early American Jews on the American Jewish Historical Society Web site (www.AJHS.org), which also appears on www.loebjewishportraits.com. In 2005 he led the sponsorship of "Tolerance and Identity: Jews in Early New York, 1654–1825," an exhibit at the Museum of the City of New York. More recently, in honor of his father, John L. Loeb, he spearheaded a new direction for the Loeb Fellows program at Harvard Business School. Scholastic awards will now also be made through the Harvard Divinity School to those graduate students who have undertaken the study of the relationship between commerce and religious tolerance.

John is currently committed to the building of a visitors center at the oldest synagogue in the nation. Touro Synagogue in Newport, Rhode Island was named after Judah Touro, a collateral ancestor of the family. One of the synagogue's long-standing traditions is the annual reading to the congregation of a letter from President George Washington dated August 21, 1790, in which he expresses support for religious tolerance and signals the beginning of his campaign for the enactment of the First Amendment. It is a document Ambassador Loeb considers to be on a par with this country's most sacred national documents, such as the

Declaration of Independence, Lincoln's Gettysburg Address, and Martin Luther King Jr.'s "I Have a Dream" speech.

John L. Loeb Jr. is a member of the New York Genealogical and Biographical Society, and in 1981 he received the Lee Max Friedman Award (now known as the Emma Lazarus Award) from the American Jewish Historical Society. He is a member of the Sons of the Revolution in the State of New York, which awarded him its Distinguished Patriot Award in 1993. He is also a member of the Sons of the American Revolution and the Society of Colonial Wars. He is chairman of Loeb, Rhoades & Co., a money management firm in New York City, and vice chairman of the Council of American Ambassadors.

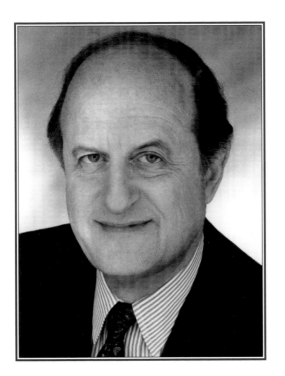

ELI N. EVANS
Author of the Introduction

Abba Eban, Israel's world renowned statesman, orator, and author, once said of the work of Eli Evans, "the Jews of the South have found their poet laureate." Critics and reviewers have labeled him a "master storyteller."

Not only because of his Jewish roots, but because of his historian's insights, author Eli Evans is uniquely and appropriately suited to weave the intricate strands of *An American Experience: Adeline Moses Loeb (1876–1953) and Her Early American Jewish Ancestors* into a colorful tapestry. In his introduction to this book, he has brought personal commentary and insights to a three-part history of one Jewish family, and at the same time demonstrated their story's relevance to understanding the depth of the difficult challenges that many Jewish families had to surmount in coming to America.

A native of Durham, North Carolina, Eli Evans has enjoyed a many-faceted career. Following graduation from the University of North Carolina in 1958 (Phi Beta Kappa), he spent two years in the U.S. Navy stationed in Japan, following which he graduated from Yale Law School in 1963. He served on the White House staff during 1964 and 1965 as a speech writer for President Lyndon Johnson. For the next decade he traveled extensively throughout the South as senior program officer for the Carnegie Corporation of New York, a national educational foundation. He became the first president of the Charles H. Revson Foundation in 1977, leading that organization until 2003. The foundation, under Eli's leadership, was a leading funder in a number of PBS series: *Heritage: Civilization and the Jews*, which has been broadcast in nineteen countries around the world; *Rechov Sumsum*, the Israeli *Sesame Street*, and *Shalom Sesame*, its American adaptation; and the Bill Moyers program, *Genesis: A Living Conversation*. Eli Evans is currently the Revson Foundation's president emeritus.

All through his career, he has found time to write: books, articles, and essays, and to lecture across the country. He is the author of *The Provincials: A Personal History of Jews in the South*, called by novelist Pat Conroy "one of a kind, a masterpiece," and two years ago was declared "an enduring classic" by former *Harper's Magazine* editor Willie Morris when the book celebrated its thirty-fifth year in print; *Judah P. Benjamin: The Jewish Confederate*, a Civil War biography of the South's attorney general and secretary of state known as the "brains of the Confederacy." Called "a very fine and moving book" by preeminent Yale historian C. Vann Woodward, the book and Eli were featured in the series *The Jewish Americans*. He is also the author of *The Lonely Days Were Sundays: Reflections of a Jewish Southerner*, a collection of essays concerned with the meaning of eighteenth- and twentieth-century Southern, American, and Jewish history, ranging from the Civil War, the abolition of slavery, and civil rights to U.S. presidential politics, the Holocaust, and Israeli history.

Among his many awards and recognitions are honorary degrees from the Jewish Theological Seminary in 2003 and Hebrew Union College in 2005. He also has the distinction of being inducted into the American Academy of Arts and Sciences in 2001 for "evoking the rhythms and heartbeat of Jewish life in the American South and capturing the interior landscape of what he has called 'a unique Southern Jewish consciousness.' The Academy honors him for his dual contribution to American letters and as a philanthropist of uncommon originality and leadership."

KATHY L. PLOTKIN

General editor and author of Part One:
Adeline Moses Loeb and Carl M. Loeb

A passion for words and the ability to type ninety words a minute launched Kathy Plotkin into professional writing by way of her first postgraduation job at a small weekly newspaper in the little college town of Salem, Virginia. There she served simultaneously as feature writer, society editor, circulation manager, columnist, ad salesman, and proofreader. "After helping to publish a paper every Thursday (wearing all those hats), no job thereafter has ever seemed daunting." It was for her humorous column, "Us Ladies," that she first received Virginia Press Association recognition. Later, she received similar recognition for her human interest features and photography.

For ten years following her newspaper stint, she produced and hosted *Panorama*, an interview-talk show at WDBJ-TV, the CBS affiliate in Roanoke, Virginia. During this period she was listed in *Foremost Women of Communications* and received one of the coveted Golden Mikes from the American Women of Radio and Television (AWRT), among other awards. While producing *Panorama*, she also wrote and performed a one-woman show throughout Virginia. Her videotaped production of *Emily of Amherst*, woven entirely from the letters and poetry of Emily Dickinson, has been acquired for the permanent collection of the Paley Center for Media (formerly the Museum of Television and Radio) in New York City.

The Pearson Girls: A Family Memoir of the Dakota Plains, the story of her North Dakota ancestors, was published by North Dakota University's Institute for Regional Studies in 1998. This preceded the formation of her company, Wordworks, which specializes in assisting clients in writing their memoirs and autobiographies. She is a member of the Association of Personal Historians and the Author's Guild.

MARGARET LOEB KEMPNER
Author of Part One:
Mother's Life with Father

In 1899, the eldest child and only daughter of Adeline and Carl M. Loeb, Margaret Loeb Kempner, was born in St. Louis Missouri, though she would spend most of her long and philanthropic life in New York City and Purchase, New York. As a girl she was a gifted athlete and a self-described tomboy, more than a match in the swimming pool and tennis court for the three brothers who followed her:

John Langeloth in 1902; Carl M. Jr. in 1904, and Henry in 1907, the year the family moved from St. Louis to New York City. She graduated in 1917 from the demanding Horace Mann School for Girls in New York, which she attended for eleven years, having skipped the first grade. "Horace Mann gave me a marvelous start—I loved that school," she later wrote. In her memoir *Recollection*, she says (over-modestly) that she was "an adequate" student but flunked a course in Latin because of an underestimation of study required for Caesar. She called it her "lucky failure" because the handsome, scholarly, and multitalented young tutor her parents hired as a result of this one lapse in scholarship was Alan Horace Kempner, who not too many years later would become her husband.

Though Margaret Loeb was accepted at Vassar College, she wanted to be a civilian participant in World War I and made plans to work instead as a secretary in the Navy Department in Washington, D.C. This, she thought, besides being patriotic, would be quite "exciting and glamorous." By the time she had learned to type and take dictation, however, the war was over. She studied for one year at Columbia Teachers College, and then married Alan Horace Kempner in June 1920. The couple spent sixty-five enviably happy years together until Alan's death at the age of eighty-eight in 1985. The Kempners had three sons: Alan Horace Kempner Jr., born in 1922, Carl Loeb Kempner born in 1923, and Thomas Lenox Kempner born in 1927.

When Margaret Kempner's favorite English teacher at Horace Mann met her prize student's fiancé, she commented that Alan was "very handsome, but I had hoped you would write." Margaret Kempner did indeed write—all of her life—but not for publication. She and Alan were inveterate travelers, and her long, insightful letters about their trips to such far-flung points as Tahiti, Pago Pago, New Zealand, Greece, Africa, and Leopoldville were so memorable that one son (Alan Jr.) compiled them all in a privately printed book, *Travels with Mum and Dad,* in 1994. At family gatherings she could always be counted on for sparkling and witty toasts, humorous skits, and warm encomiums to family members, filled with her hallmark warmth and affection. Perhaps the most important of her family legacies is her memoir,

Recollection, from which a portion of this book about her parents, Carl M. and Adeline Moses Loeb, has been drawn.

When she died on New Year's Eve, 2002, the headline in the *New York Times* read, "Margaret Loeb Kempner, 102, A Benefactor of Young and Old." The story went on to list her many philanthropic interests, with special emphasis on the money and time she and her husband gave to the Kempner Rare Book Library at Columbia University. She was also extremely active in fundraising for the Federation of Jewish Philanthropies of New York and was a lifetime trustee of its successor organization, the UJA-Federation of New York. She served for almost seven decades on the boards of the Blythedale Children's Hospital in Valhalla, New York, and the New York Eye and Ear Infirmary. The *Journal News* noted also that she was a "passionate member of the Daughters of the American Revolution."

JUDITH E. ENDELMAN
Author of Part Three: The Ancestors of Adeline Moses Loeb

Judith Endelman has been a writer, archivist, historian, and curator for nearly thirty-five years. She began her professional life at the American Jewish Historical Society. Little did she know that one day she would write about the Franks and Levy families whose stately portraits graced the society's walls. Her first publication was *A Guide to the Paintings, Daguerreotypes, and Artifacts of the*

American Jewish Historical Society in 1974. Her experience with American Jewish history inspired her to continue her education. In 1977 she received a Master of Arts in American Studies from Boston College.

In 1976 Endelman moved with her husband and infant son to New York City. She took a part-time position as archivist of the Jewish Theological Seminary and also conducted historical research for private clients. One of her clients was John L. Loeb Jr., who was passionately interested in finding out more about the fascinating ancestry of his grandmother, Adeline Moses Loeb. Endelman traced his family back to the mid-seventeenth century and found a wealth of information about the life and times of the Moses-Loeb ancestors in London, New York, Newport, and beyond.

In 1979 the Endelmans moved to Bloomington, Indiana, home of Indiana University. The Indiana Historical Society commissioned Endelman to write a history of the Jewish community of Indianapolis, which was published by Indiana University Press in 1984 as *The Jewish Community of Indianapolis, 1849 to the Present*. She also worked at Lilly Library, the rare book library of Indiana University, and coedited *Religion in Indiana: A Guide to Historical Resources*, which was funded by the Lilly Endowment and published by Indiana University Press.

In 1985 the Endelman family, which now included a daughter as well as a son, moved to Ann Arbor, Michigan. After a one-year fellowship at the Bentley Historical Library at the University of Michigan, Judith Endelman joined the staff of The Henry Ford Museum in Dearborn, Michigan, in 1986. In her twenty years there, she has held a variety of leadership positions in the collections, curatorial, and research areas. She has spearheaded many initiatives, including the construction of the Benson Ford Research Center, which opened in 2002, and where she currently serves as director. She has participated in the development of numerous exhibits, such as "Americans on Vacation" (and was coauthor of the exhibit catalog), and "Your Place in Time," as well as many other public programs and partnerships. She is the author of numerous articles, speaks frequently at conferences, serves as a museum consultant and grant reviewer, and sits on a variety of professional boards.

DAVID M. KLEIMAN
Genealogical Consultant and
Family Chart Designer

Of biographical credits, it has been said that after an individual's name, it's what's between the commas that counts. David M. Kleiman—genealogist, historian, publisher, museum educator, fund-raiser, systems consultant and software developer, lecturer, researcher, and musician—certainly fills the space after his name more extensively than many.

Kleiman's many talents reflect a lifetime of exploration and curiosity. His work includes tenure as assistant director of education for the South Street Museum; fund-raising for B'nai B'rith Youth Services, the Union of American Hebrew Congregations, and St. Jude's Children's Hospital; software and systems developer and trainer to Fortune 500 companies; a professional genealogist and lecturer; and president and founder of Heritage Muse, Inc. and ESPB Publishing, LLP, companies specializing in digital and print publishing for the Humanities. Heritage Muse's flagship product is an interactive, multimedia, digital edition (2005) of *The English and Scottish Popular Ballads*, by Professor Francis James Child.

Kleiman's genealogical credits are extensive. As a partner in Up-a-Tree Software, David developed and distributed family history computer utilities such as The Family Attic and CENDEX. He built the database application used for Eastern European records in Miriam Weiner's *Jewish Roots in Poland* (1997) and *Jewish Roots in Ukraine and Moldova* (1999) published by the Routes to Roots Foundation. He continues that work with oversight of the searchable online web version hosted by the foundation. David served as the coeditor of *Dorot*, the newsletter of the Jewish Genealogical Society and currently serves on the society's executive council. He is co-founder and chair of the twenty-four-year-old New York Computers and Genealogy Special Interest Group. Through Heritage Muse, David published the 2006 and 2008 syllabi for the International Association of Genealogical Societies (IAJGS). His popular lectures and workshops keep him traveling and his professional memberships include both the Association of Professional Genealogists and the Genealogical Speakers Guild.

David has been the genealogical consultant for both this book and for *Lots of Lehmans* (published by the Center for Jewish History, 2007). With his partner, Kate Myslinski, Heritage Muse designed, wrote, and is building the Web site (www.loeb-tourovisitorscenter.org) for the new Ambassador John L. Loeb Jr. Visitors Center at the Touro Synagogue in Newport, Rhode Island, scheduled to open in 2010. His work on these projects led him to further research on early American Jews, and the company's latest project is an online database expanding Rabbi Malcolm Stern's extraordinary work, *First American Jewish Families: 600 Genealogies 1654-1988*. The new research both extends and amends the scope of the original work.

As president of the New York PC Users Group in the early days of the personal computer revolution, David helped to bring emerging technologies and tools to the market. He has appeared in public technology forums with industry luminaries such as Bill Gates, Peter Norton, and Andy Groves. Kleiman and the leadership team he gathered turned NYPC into a 3,000-member volunteer organization that significantly affected the development of today's personal computing.

In his spare time David's musical activities include performing internationally in various ensembles, particularly folk music. He is one of the founders of the Traditional Music of the Sea Festival at Mystic Seaport Museum; served fifteen years as the program chair of the Folk Music Society of New York; and he is the producer of award-winning CD recordings for several vocal folk ensembles.

NAME INDEX

Married women are entered under both their maiden name and their married surname(s). The principal listing is under the maiden name with a cross-reference to the husband's surname in brackets [ ]. These entries are formatted as follows:

maiden surname, given name(s) [married surname][2nd married surname], page reference

A cross-reference from the married name directs the reader to the maiden name entry. (In the case of multiple marriages, there is a cross-reference under each surname.) These entries are formatted as follows:

married surname, given name(s). See maiden surname, given name(s)

Page numbers in *italics* indicate that the named individual is the subject of a photograph. Page numbers in **boldface** refer to graphics pages, map pages, or genealogical charts.

GENERAL INDEX

Page numbers in *italics* indicate that the indexed item is the subject of an illustration or photograph. Page numbers in **boldface** refer to graphic pages, map pages, or genealogical charts.

SELECTED RELATIVES AND CONNECTIONS OF ADELINE MOSES LOEB

ADELINE MOSES LOEB WAS ALWAYS AWARE of her early Jewish ancestry. The accompanying family tree (enclosed in the rear-cover pocket) reflects both her direct family lines, in which she took such great pride, and their connections to the broader American community. It illuminates the relationships between these Jewish individuals from early America and their colonial neighbors, regardless of faith. Their unions have produced some of the most influential and generous families on both sides of the Atlantic.

Though extensive (366 individuals), the lines presented on this family tree are not comprehensive. Not all offspring are shown for each couple and multiple interconnections through all marital lines have not been indicated. The editors regret that the limitations of space have precluded a complete listing of all of Adeline's family.

Relationship Key

ancestor—parents, grandparents, great-grandparents

descendant—children, grandchildren

descendant spouse—husband or wife of a descendant

collateral—sibling, aunt, uncle, cousin

collateral by marriage—husband or wife of a sibling, aunt, uncle, or cousin

connection—no direct blood or spousal relation to Adeline Moses Loeb.

These individuals are threaded to her family through parentage or marriage to a collateral or descendant spouse.

Married women can be found under both their maiden and married surnames.

maiden names [married surname] [second marriage]

married names (see maiden surname)

Surname, Given Names [married to] (see maiden name)	Relationship
Adolphus, Hetty [Hays]	connection
Alexander, Lillie [Moses]	collateral by marriage
Anderson, Helen Beatrice [Moses]	collateral by marriage
Asher, Michael	connection
Asher, Rachel [Myers-Cohen]	connection
Asher, Richea [Levy]	connection
Bahr, Charlotte [Moses]	collateral by marriage
Beaty, Judith Helen (see Loeb, Judith Helen)	*descendant*
Beaty, Richard N.	descendant spouse
Beckett, Constance Mary [Bruce]	connection
Beckett, Hamilton	connection
Beckett, Henry	connection
Beckett, Mary (see Lyle, Mary)	*connection*
Beckett, Sophia Clarence (see Copley, Sophia Clarence)	*connection*
Benenson, Dorothy F. [Cullman]	collateral by marriage
Bernhard, Ann [Kempner]	descendant spouse
Bloch, Sara Phila [Franks]	connection
Bloomingdale, Louise [Cullman]	collateral by marriage
Blumenthal, Louise Mayer [Sulzberger]	collateral by marriage
Brice, Deborah Frances (see Loeb, Deborah Frances)	*descendant*
Brice, John James	descendant spouse
Bridgeman, Anne Pamela [Pearson]	connection
Bridgeman, Gerald Michael Orlando	connection
Bridgeman, Joanne Elizabeth (see Miller, Joanne Elizabeth)	*connection*
Bridgeman, Margaret Cecilia (see Bruce, Margaret Cecilia)	*connection*
Bridgeman, Mary Willoughby (see Montgomery, Mary Willoughby)	connection
Bridgeman, Orlando	connection
Bridgeman, Richard Thomas Orlando	connection
Bronfman, Ann Margaret (see Loeb, Ann Margaret)	*descendant*
Bronfman, Edgar Miles	descendant spouse

Surname, Given Names [married to] (see maiden name)	Relationship
Bruce, Constance Mary (see Beckett, Constance Mary)	*connection*
Bruce, Constance Pamela Alice [Digby]	connection
Bruce, Eva Isabel Marion [Primrose] [Strutt]	connection
Bruce, Henry Campbell	connection
Bruce, Margaret Cecilia [Bridgeman]	connection
Burden, Margaret L. (see Partridge, Margaret L.)	*collateral*
Burden, William A. M., Jr.	collateral by marriage
Bush, Ann (see Marshall, Ann)	*collateral by marriage*
Bush, Mathias	collateral by marriage
Bush, Rebecca (see Myers-Cohen, Rebecca)	*connection*
Bush, Solomon	collateral
Bush, Tabitha (see Mears, Tabitha)	*collateral*
Cardozo, Albert Jacob	collateral by marriage
Cardozo, Benjamin Nathan	collateral
Cardozo, Rebecca W. (see Nathan, Rebecca W.)	*collateral*
Cecil, Elizabeth [Franks]	connection
Chace, Helen Clay (see Symington, Helen Clay)	*collateral*
Chace, Minturn Verdi	collateral by marriage
Chiara, Judith Helen (see Loeb, Judith Helen)	*descendant*
Chiara, Marco	descendant spouse
Churchill, Luce (see Danielson, Luce)	*connection*
Churchill, Mary Caroline (see d'Erlanger, Mary Caroline)	*connection*
Churchill, Pamela Beryl (see Digby, Pamela Beryl)	*connection*
Churchill, Randolph Frederick Edward	connection
Churchill, Winston Leonard Spencer	connection
Coates, Sarah [Levy]	collateral by marriage
Cohn, Constance Margaret (see Loeb, Constance Margaret)	*descendant*
Cohn, George Louis	descendant spouse
Coleman, Doris C. [Kempner]	descendant spouse
Conrad, Barnaby	collateral by marriage

Surname, Given Names [married to] (see maiden name)	Relationship
Conrad, Barnaby, Jr.	collateral
Conrad, Dale (see Cowgill, Dale)	*collateral by marriage*
Conrad, Helen Upshur (see Hunt, Helen Upshur)	*collateral*
Conrad, Mary (see Nobles, Mary)	*collateral by marriage*
Copley, Sophia Clarence [Beckett]	connection
Cordle, Marina Rose [Pearson]	connection
Cowgill, Dale [Conrad]	collateral by marriage
Crawford, Anna Brooks [Hambleton]	collateral by marriage
Cullman, Dorothy F. (see Benenson, Dorothy Freedman)	*collateral by marriage*
Cullman, Edgar M.	collateral
Cullman, Frances Nathan (see Wolff, Frances Nathan)	*collateral*
Cullman, Joseph F. III	collateral
Cullman, Joseph F., Jr.	collateral by marriage
Cullman, Lewis B.	collateral
Cullman, Louise (see Bloomingdale, Louise)	*collateral by marriage*
Cullman, Susan (see Lehman, Susan)	*collateral by marriage*
Daglish, Caroline [Primrose]	connection
Danielson, Luce [Churchill]	connection
Davidson, Mary [Franks]	connection
Davies, David John	descendant spouse
Davies, Deborah Frances (see Loeb, Deborah Frances)	*descendant*
d'Erlanger, Mary Caroline [Churchill]	connection
de Paul (see Michaels de Paul)	
de Rivera (see Rodrigues de Rivera)	
de Rothschild (see Rothschild)	
Digby, Constance Pamela Alice (see Bruce, Constance Pamela Alice)	*connection*
Digby, Edward Kenelm	connection
Digby, Pamela Beryl [Churchill] [Hayward] [Harriman]	connection
Dinkelspiel, Abraham	ancestor
Dinkelspiel, Hannah [Nathan]	ancestor

Surname, Given Names [married to] (see maiden name)	Relationship
Dinkelspiel, Sarah (see Dinkelspiel, Sarah)	*ancestor*
Dinkelspiel, Sarah [Dinkelspiel]	ancestor
Dunham, A. [Levy]	collateral by marriage
Evans, Margaret [Franks]	connection
First, Nancy Carol [Loeb]	descendant spouse
Fitzalan-Howard, Bernard M.	connection
Fitzalan-Howard, Lavinia Mary (see Strutt, Lavinia Mary)	*connection*
Franks, Aaron	connection
Franks, Abigail [Hamilton]	connection
Franks, Abraham (?–1748)	connection
Franks, Abraham (1713–?)	connection
Franks, Benjamin (1649–1716)	connection
Franks, Benjamin (dates unknown)	connection
Franks, Bilhah Abigaill (see Levy, Bilhah Abigaill)	*connection*
Franks, Catherine (see Who, Catherine)	*connection*
Franks, David	connection
Franks, David Salisbury	connection
Franks, Elizabeth (see Cecil, Elizabeth)	connection
Franks, Isaac	connection
Franks, Jacob	connection
Franks, Joy [Mears]	ancestor
Franks, Margaret (see Evans, Margaret)	*connection*
Franks, Mary (see Davidson, Mary)	*connection*
Franks, Moses B.	connection
Franks, Naphtaly Harte	connection
Franks, Rachel [Salomon][Heilbron]	connection
Franks, Rachel (see unknown, Rachel)	*connection*
Franks, Sara Phila (see Bloch, Sara Phila)	*connection*
Franks, Sarah (see Franks, Sarah) (?–1767)	*connection*
Franks, Sarah (see Franks, Sarah) (1755–1809)	*connection*

Surname, Given Names [married to] (see maiden name)	Relationship
Franks, Sarah [Franks] (?–1767)	connection
Franks, Sarah [Franks] (1755–1809)	connection
Frick, Martha Howard [Symington]	collateral by marriage
Frost, Barbara [Moses]	collateral by marriage
Fuhrman, Carol Fox [Sulzberger]	*collateral by marriage*
Giles, Anne Augusta [Myers]	collateral by marriage
Gomez, Aaron Lopez	connection
Gomez, Esther (see Lopez, Esther)	*connection*
Gomez, Hetty (see Hendricks, Hetty)	*connection*
Gomez, Moses Mordicia	connection
Gomez, Rosalie [Nathan]	collateral by marriage
Goodwin, Abigail (see Levy, Abigail)	*collateral*
Goodwin, Charles Ridgely (see Ridgely, Charles Goodwin)	collateral
Goodwin, Doctor Lyde	collateral by marriage
Goodyear, Wendy [Griswold]	collateral by marriage
Gottesman, Ruth [Nathan]	collateral by marriage
Grant, Barbara W. [Sulzberger]	*collateral by marriage*
Gratz, Michael	connection
Gratz, Miriam (see Simon, Miriam)	*connection*
Gratz, Rebecca	connection
Gratz, Richea [Hays]	connection
Gregg, Gail [Sulzberger]	collateral by marriage
Griswold, Arabella Leith (see Symington, Arabella Leith)	*collateral*
Griswold, Benjamin H. III	collateral by marriage
Griswold, Benjamin H. IV	collateral
Griswold, Carol A. (see Irwin, Carol A.)	*collateral by marriage*
Griswold, Jack S.	collateral
Griswold, Mac Johnston (see Keith, Mac Johnston)	*collateral by marriage*
Griswold, Wendy (see Goodyear, Wendy)	*collateral by marriage*
Hachar, Catherine [Michaels]	ancestor

Surname, Given Names [married to] (see maiden name)	Relationship
Hambleton, Anna Brooks (see Crawford, Anna Brooks)	*collateral by marriage*
Hambleton, Arabella (1829–1893) (see Stansbury, Arabella)	*collateral*
Hambleton, Arabella (1885–1963)[Symington]	collateral
Hambleton, Frank S.	collateral
Hambleton, Thomas Edward	collateral by marriage
Hamilton, Abigail (see Franks, Abigail)	*connection*
Hamilton, Andrew III	connection
Hamilton, Ann [Lyle]	connection
Harriman, Pamela Beryl (see Digby, Pamela Beryl)	*connection*
Harriman, William Averell	connection
Harrsen, Meta M. [Loeb]	descendant spouse
Hawley, Mr.	collateral by marriage
Hawley, Sarah A. (see Moses, Sarah A.)	*collateral*
Hays, David	collateral by marriage
Hays, David Solis	collateral by marriage
Hays, Grace (see Mears, Grace)	*collateral*
Hays, Hetty (see Adolphus, Hetty)	*connection*
Hays, Isaac	connection
Hays, Jacob	connection
Hays, Judah	collateral by marriage
Hays, Judith [Myers]	collateral
Hays, Judith Salzedo (see Peixotto, Judith Salzedo)	*collateral*
Hays, Michael	connection
Hays, Moses Michael	collateral
Hays, Rachel (see Myers, Rachel)	*collateral by marriage*
Hays, Rachel Peixotto [Sulzberger]	*collateral*
Hays, Rebecca (see Judah, Rebecca)	*connection*
Hays, Rebecca (see Michaels, Rebecca)	*collateral*
Hays, Reyna [Touro]	collateral
Hays, Richea (see Gratz, Richea)	*connection*

Surname, Given Names [married to] (see maiden name)	Relationship
Hays, Samuel	connection
Hays, Sara Ann [Mordecai]	collateral by marriage
Hays, Solomon	connection
Hayward, Leland	connection
Hayward, Pamela Beryl (see Digby, Pamela Beryl)	*connection*
Helbert, Sarah [Judah]	connection
Heilbron, David	connection
Heilbron, Rachel (see Franks, Rachel)	*connection*
Hendricks, Emily G. [Nathan]	collateral by marriage
Hendricks, Hetty [Gomez]	connection
Holland, Mary Sarah [Moses]	collateral by marriage
Hunt, Catherine H. (see Hunt, Catherine H.)	*collateral by marriage*
Hunt, Catherine H. [Hunt]	collateral by marriage
Hunt, Elizabeth Augusta (see Ridgely, Elizabeth Augusta)	*collateral*
Hunt, Gertrude (see Upshur, Gertrude)	*collateral by marriage*
Hunt, Helen Upshur [Conrad]	collateral
Hunt, Livingston	collateral
Hunt, William Henry	collateral by marriage
Hunt, William Henry, Jr.	collateral
Irwin, Carol A. [Griswold]	collateral by marriage
Isaacks, Hannah (see Mears, Hannah)	*ancestor*
Isaacks, Hannah [Phillips]	ancestor
Isaacks, Isaac	ancestor
Isaacks, Jacob	ancestor
Isaacks, Moses	collateral
Isaacks, Abraham	ancestor
Isaacks, Rachel (see Mears, Rachel)	*collateral*
Isaacks, Rebecca (see Mears, Rebecca)	*ancestor*
Judah, Abigail (see Seixas, Abigail)	*collateral*
Judah, Baruch	connection

Surname, Given Names [married to] (see maiden name)	Relationship
Judah, Hillel	collateral by marriage
Judah, Rebecca [Hays]	connection
Judah, Sarah (see Helbert, Sarah)	*connection*
Judah, Sarah [Myers]	collateral by marriage
Keith, Mac Johnston [Griswold]	collateral by marriage
Kempner, Alan Horace	descendant spouse
Kempner, Alan Horace, Jr.	descendant
Kempner, Ann (see Bernhard, Ann)	*descendant spouse*
Kempner, Carl Loeb	descendant
Kempner, Doris C. (see Coleman, Doris C.)	*descendant spouse*
Kempner, Margaret (see Loeb, Margaret)	*descendant*
Kempner, Nan Field (see Schlesinger, Nan Field)	*descendant spouse*
Kempner, Rosemary (see Smith, Rosemary)	*descendant spouse*
Kempner, Sandra (see Stark, Sandra)	*descendant spouse*
Kempner, Thomas L.	descendant
Lampley, Martha [Levy]	collateral by marriage
Lazarus, Emma	collateral
Lazarus, Esther (see Nathan, Esther)	*collateral*
Lazarus, Moses	collateral by marriage
Lehman, Frances [Loeb]	descendant spouse
Lehman, Susan [Cullman]	collateral by marriage
Levin, Elizabeth Louise (see Loeb, Elizabeth Louise)	*descendant*
Levin, John A.	descendant spouse
Levy, A. (see Dunham, A.)	*collateral by marriage*
Levy, Abigail [Goodwin] [Worthington]	collateral
Levy, Asser (also van Schwelm)	connection
Levy, Benjamin	collateral
Levy, Bilhah Abigaill [Franks]	connection
Levy, Evangeline [Moses]	collateral by marriage
Levy, Grace (see Mears, Grace)	*collateral*

Surname, Given Names [married to] (see maiden name)	Relationship
Levy, Jacob	collateral by marriage
Levy, Jochabed [Seixas]	collateral by marriage
Levy, Martha (see Lampley, Martha)	*collateral by marriage*
Levy, Mary (see Pearce, Mary)	*collateral by marriage*
Levy, Michal (see Unknown, Michal)	*connection*
Levy, Miriam (see Levy van Schwelm, Miriam)	*connection*
Levy, Moses	collateral
Levy, Moses Raphael	collateral by marriage
Levy, Nathan	connection
Levy, Rachel (see Levy, Rachel)	*collateral by marriage*
Levy, Rachel (see Michaels, Rachel)	*collateral*
Levy, Rachel (1739–1794) [Levy]	collateral by marriage
Levy, Rachel (1719–1797) [Seixas]	collateral
Levy, Rachel (dates unknown) [Valck van der Wilden]	connection
Levy, Richea (see Asher, Richea)	connection
Levy, Samuel Zanvil	connection
Levy, Samson	collateral
Levy, Samson, Jr.	collateral
Levy, Sarah (see Coates, Sarah)	*collateral by marriage*
Levy, Sophia [Stansbury]	collateral
Levy, Zipporah [Seixas]	collateral by marriage
Levy van Schwelm, Asser	connection
Levy van Schwelm, Miriam (see Unknown, Miriam)	*connection*
Lindsay, Minnie Burns [Nathan]	collateral by marriage
Livingston, Cornelia Louisiana [Ridgely]	collateral by marriage
Loeb, Adeline (see Moses, Adeline)	*Self*
Loeb, Ann Margaret [Bronfman]	descendant
Loeb, Arthur L.	descendant
Loeb, Carl Morris	Husband
Loeb, Carl Morris III	descendant

Surname, Given Names [married to] (see maiden name)	Relationship
Loeb, Carl Morris, Jr.	descendant
Loeb, Constance M. [Cohn]	descendant
Loeb, Deborah Frances [Davies] [Brice]	descendant
Loeb, Elizabeth Louise [Levin]	descendant
Loeb, Frances (see Lehman, Frances)	*descendant spouse*
Loeb, Hadassah (see Savetsky, Hadassah)	*descendant spouse*
Loeb, Henry Alfred	descendant
Loeb, Jean A. [Polikoff] [Troubh]	descendant
Loeb, Jeanette (see Winter, Jeanette)	*descendant spouse*
Loeb, John Langeloth, Jr.	descendant
Loeb, John Langeloth, Sr.	descendant
Loeb, Judith Helen [Beaty] [Chiara]	descendant
Loeb, Louise (see Steinhardt, Louise)	*descendant spouse*
Loeb, Lucille H. S. (see Schamberg, Lucille H. S.)	*descendant spouse*
Loeb, Margaret [Kempner]	descendant
Loeb, Meta M. (see Harrsen, Meta M.)	*descendant spouse*
Loeb, Nancy Carol (see First, Nancy Carol)	*descendant spouse*
Loeb, Nina (see Sundby, Nina)	*descendant spouse*
Loeb, Peter K.	descendant
Lopez, Aaron	connection
Lopez, Abigail [Lopez]	connection
Lopez, Abigail (see Lopez, Abigail)	*connection*
Lopez, Esther	connection
Lopez, Joshua	collateral by marriage
Lopez, Rebecca (see Touro, Rebecca Hays)	*collateral*
Lopez, Sarah (see Rodrigues de Rivera, Sarah)	*connection*
Louzada, Aaron	collateral by marriage
Louzada, Blume (see Michaels, Blume)	*collateral*
Lyle, Ann (see Hamilton, Ann)	*connection*
Lyle, James	connection

Surname, Given Names [married to] (see maiden name)	Relationship
Lyle, Mary [Beckett]	connection
Lyon, Rachel [Moses]	ancestor
Mahoney, Nellie [Nathan]	collateral by marriage
Manuel, Hannah [Seixas]	collateral by marriage
Marshall, Ann [Bush]	collateral by marriage
Maynadier, Sally Sandford	collateral by marriage
Mears (patriarch)	*ancestor*
Mears, Elkaleh (Joyce) [Myers]	collateral
Mears, Grace [Levy] [Hays]	collateral
Mears, Hannah [Isaacks]	ancestor
Mears, Jacob	collateral by marriage
Mears, Jochabed (see Michaels, Jochabed)	*ancestor*
Mears, Joy (see Franks, Joy)	*ancestor*
Mears, Judah	ancestor
Mears, Rachel [Isaacks]	collateral
Mears, Rebecca [Isaacks]	ancestor
Mears, Sampson	ancestor
Mears, Tabitha [Bush]	collateral
Michaels de Paul, Asher	connection
Michaels de Paul, Rebecca (see Valentine, Rebecca)	*connection*
Michaels, Blume [Louzada]	collateral
Michaels, Catherine (see Hachar, Catherine)	*ancestor*
Michaels, Jechiel of Herzfeld Germany	ancestor
Michaels, Jochabed [Mears]	ancestor
Michaels, Michael	collateral by marriage
Michaels, Moses	ancestor
Michaels, Rachel [Myers-Cohen] [Levy]	collateral
Michaels, Rebecca [Hays]	collateral
Miller, Joanne Elizabeth [Bridgeman]	connection
Montgomery, Mary Willoughby [Bridgeman]	connection

Surname, Given Names [married to] (see maiden name)	Relationship
Mordecai, Alfred	collateral
Mordecai, Alfred, Jr.	collateral
Mordecai, Dora (see Varney, Dora)	*collateral by marriage*
Mordecai, Jacob	collateral by marriage
Mordecai, Judith (see Myers, Judith)	*collateral*
Mordecai, Rebecca Mears (see Myers, Rebecca Mears)	*collateral*
Mordecai, Sally (see Maynadier, Sally Sandford)	*collateral by marriage*
Mordecai, Sara Ann (see Hays, Sara Ann)	*collateral by marriage*
Morgan, John Hill	collateral by marriage
Morgan, Lelia Augusta (see Myers, Lelia Augusta)	*collateral*
Morgan, Lelia Pegram [Wardwell]	collateral
Moses, Adeline [Loeb]	Self
Moses, Adeline Lyon (see Moses, Adeline Lyon)	*ancestor*
Moses, Adeline Lyon [Moses]	ancestor
Moses, Alfred Huger	ancestor
Moses, Alfred Huger, Jr.	collateral
Moses, Barbara (see Frost, Barbara)	*collateral by marriage*
Moses, Charlotte (see Bahr, Charlotte)	*collateral by marriage*
Moses, Elma E. (see Unknown, Elma E.)	*collateral by marriage*
Moses, Emily Touro [Nathan]	collateral
Moses, Evangeline (see Levy, Evangeline)	*collateral by marriage*
Moses, Frances (see Sampson, Frances)	*collateral by marriage*
Moses, Helen Beatrice (see Anderson, Helen Beatrice)	*collateral by marriage*
Moses, Henry Clay (1844–1906)	collateral
Moses, Henry Clay (1884–1954)	collateral
Moses, Henry Clay (1918)	collateral
Moses, Henry Clay (1941–2008)	collateral
Moses, Isaiah	ancestor
Moses, Jean Teresa (see Smith, Jean Teresa	*collateral by marriage*
Moses, Jeanette (see Nathan, Jeanette)	*ancestor*

Surname, Given Names [married to] (see maiden name)	Relationship
Moses, Johnston Lee	collateral
Moses, Joseph	ancestor
Moses, Joseph W. (1880–1927)	collateral
Moses, Joseph W. (1837–1876)	collateral
Moses, Judah Touro	collateral
Moses, Levy J.	ancestor
Moses, Lillie (see Alexander, Lillie)	*collateral by marriage*
Moses, Mordecai Lyon	collateral
Moses, Mary Sarah (see Holland, Mary Sarah)	*collateral by marriage*
Moses, Rachel (see Lyon, Rachel)	*ancestor*
Moses, Rebecca I. (see Phillips, Rebecca)	*ancestor*
Moses, Sarah A. [Hawley]	collateral
Myers, Anne Augusta (see Giles, Anne Augusta)	*collateral by marriage*
Myers, Elkaleh (?–1765) (see Mears, Elkaleh (Joyce))	*collateral*
Myers, Elkaleh (1737–1824) (see Myers-Cohen, Elkaleh)	*collateral*
Myers, Gustavus Adolphus	collateral
Myers, Judith (1696–1773) (see unknown, Judith)	*collateral*
Myers, Judith (1767–1844) (see Hays, Judith)	*connection*
Myers, Judith (1762–1796) [Mordecai]	collateral
Myers, Lelia Augusta [Morgan]	collateral
Myers, Martha West Pegram (see Paul, Martha West Pegram)	*collateral by marriage*
Myers, Myer	collateral by marriage
Myers, Rachel [Hays]	collateral by marriage
Myers, Rebecca Mears [Mordecai]	collateral
Myers, Samuel	collateral
Myers, Sarah (see Judah, Sarah)	*collateral by marriage*
Myers, Solomon	connection
Myers, William Barksdale	collateral
Myers-Cohen, Elkaleh (?–1765) [Myers]	collateral
Myers-Cohen, Elkaleh (1749–1785) [Seixas]	collateral by marriage

Surname, Given Names [married to] (see maiden name)	Relationship
Myers-Cohen, Rachel (1691–1732) (see Asher, Rachel)	*connection*
Myers-Cohen, Rachel (1707–1749) (see Michaels, Rachel)	*collateral*
Myers-Cohen, Rebecca [Bush]	connection
Myers-Cohen, Samuel	collateral by marriage
Nathan, Benjamin S.	collateral
Nathan, Edgar Joshua	collateral
Nathan, Edgar Joshua, Jr.	collateral
Nathan, Edgar Joshua III	collateral
Nathan, Edward	collateral
Nathan, Elvira [Solis]	collateral
Nathan, Emily G. (see Hendricks, Emily G.)	*collateral by marriage*
Nathan, Emily Touro (see Moses, Emily Touro)	*collateral*
Nathan, Esther [Lazarus]	collateral
Nathan, Frances	collateral
Nathan, Frances Louisa [Wolff]	collateral
Nathan, Gershom Seixas	collateral
Nathan, Grace Mendes (see Seixas, Grace Mendes)	*collateral*
Nathan, Hannah (see Dinkelspiel, Hannah)	*ancestor*
Nathan, Isaac	collateral
Nathan, Isaac Mendes Seixas	collateral
Nathan, Jeanette [Moses]	ancestor
Nathan, Joseph H.	collateral
Nathan, Lewis Winthrop	collateral
Nathan, Mabel (see Unterberg, Mabel)	*collateral by marriage*
Nathan, Minnie Burns (see Lindsay, Minnie Burns)	*collateral by marriage*
Nathan, Morris	ancestor
Nathan, Nellie (see Mahoney, Nellie)	*collateral by marriage*
Nathan, Rebecca W. [Cardozo]	collateral
Nathan, Rosalie (see Gomez, Rosalie)	*collateral by marriage*
Nathan, Ruth (see Gottesman, Ruth)	*collateral by marriage*

Surname, Given Names [married to] (see maiden name)	Relationship
Nathan, Sarah (see Seixas, Sarah)	*collateral*
Nathan, Sarah Nathan (see Solis, Sarah Nathan)	*collateral*
Nathan, Simon	collateral by marriage
Nobles, Mary [Conrad]	collateral by marriage
Ochs, Iphigene Bertha [Sulzberger]	*collateral by marriage*
Partridge, Margaret L. [Burden]	collateral
Partridge, Margaret Ridgley (see Schott, Margaret Ridgley)	*collateral*
Partridge, William Ordway	collateral by marriage
Paul (see Michaels de Paul)	
Paul, Martha West Pegram [Myers]	collateral by marriage
Pearce, Mary [Levy]	collateral by marriage
Pearson, Anne Pamela (see Bridgeman, Anne Pamela)	*connection*
Pearson, Marina Rose (see Cordle, Marina Rose)	*connection*
Pearson, Michael Orlando Weetman	connection
Pearson, Weetman John Churchill	connection
Peixotto, Daniel Levy Maduro	collateral by marriage
Peixotto, Judith Salzedo [Hays]	collateral
Peixotto, Rachel (see Seixas, Rachel)	*collateral*
Phillips, Esther B. (see Seixas, Esther B.)	*collateral*
Phillips, Hannah (see Isaacks, Hannah)	*ancestor*
Phillips, Jacob	ancestor
Phillips, Naphtali	collateral
Phillips, Rachel Mendes (see Seixas, Rachel Mendes)	*collateral*
Phillips, Rebecca I. [Moses]	ancestor
Pimentel, Hannah [Rodrigues de Rivera]	connection
Polikoff, Benet, Jr.	descendant spouse
Polikoff, Jean A. (see Loeb, Jean A.)	*descendant*
Primrose, Albert Edward Harry Mayer Archibald	connection
Primrose, Archibald Philip	connection
Primrose, Hannah (see Rothschild, Hannah)	*connection*

Surname, Given Names [married to] (see maiden name)	**Relationship**
Primrose, Alison Mary Deirdre (see Reid, Alison Mary Deirdre)	*connection*
Primrose, Caroline (see Daglish, Caroline)	*connection*
Primrose, Eva Isabel Marion (see Bruce, Eva Isabel Marion)	*connection*
Primrose, Harry Ronald Neil	connection
Primrose, Neil Archibald	connection
Reid, Alison Mary Deirdre [Primrose]	connection
Ridgely, Charles Goodwin	collateral
Ridgely, Cornelia Louisiana (see Livingston, Cornelia Louisiana)	*collateral by marriage*
Ridgely, Elizabeth Augusta [Hunt]	collateral
Ridgely, Margaret Maria [Schott]	collateral
Rivera (see Rodrigues de Rivera)	
Rodrigues de Rivera, Hannah (see Pimentel, Hannah)	*connection*
Rodrigues de Rivera, Jacob	connection
Rodrigues de Rivera, Sarah [Lopez]	connection
de Rothschild, Hannah [Primrose]	connection
Salomon, Haym	connection
Salomon, Rachel (see Franks, Rachel)	*connection*
Sampson, Frances [Moses]	collateral by marriage
Savetsky, Hadassah [Loeb]	descendant spouse
Schamberg, Lucille H. S. [Loeb]	descendant spouse
Schlesinger, Nan Field [Kempner]	descendant spouse
Schott, James	collateral by marriage
Schott, Margaret Maria (see Ridgely, Margaret Maria)	*collateral*
Schott, Margaret Ridgley [Partridge]	collateral
Schott, Rebecca Cornelia (see Schott, Rebecca Cornelia)	*collateral*
Schott, Rebecca Cornelia [Schott]	collateral
Schott, William Enges	collateral by marriage
Seixas, Abigail [Judah]	collateral
Seixas, Benjamin Mendes	collateral
Seixas, David G.	collateral

Surname, Given Names [married to] (see maiden name)	Relationship
Seixas, Elkaleh (see Myers-Cohen, Elkaleh)	*collateral by marriage*
Seixas, Esther B. [Phillips]	collateral
Seixas, Gershom Mendes	collateral
Seixas, Grace Mendes [Nathan]	collateral
Seixas, Hannah (see Manuel, Hannah)	*collateral by marriage*
Seixas, Isaac Mendes	collateral by marriage
Seixas, Jochabed (see Levy, Jochabed)	*collateral by marriage*
Seixas, Moses Mendes	collateral
Seixas, Rachel (see Levy, Rachel)	*collateral*
Seixas, Rachel [Peixotto]	collateral
Seixas, Rachel Mendes [Phillips]	collateral
Seixas, Sarah [Nathan]	collateral
Seixas, Zipporah (see Levy, Zipporah)	*collateral by marriage*
Simon, Miriam [Gratz]	connection
Smith, Jean Teresa [Moses]	collateral by marriage
Smith, Rosemary [Kempner]	descendant spouse
Solis, David Hays	collateral by marriage
Solis, Elvira (see Nathan, Elvira)	*collateral*
Solis, Sarah Nathan [Nathan]	collateral
Stacey, Allison [Sulzberger]	collateral by marriage
Stansbury, Arabella *(1829–1893)* [Hambleton]	collateral
Stansbury, Dixon	collateral by marriage
Stansbury, Sophia (see Levy, Sophia)	*collateral*
Stark, Sandra [Kempner]	descendant spouse
Steinhardt, Louise [Loeb]	descendant spouse
Straus, Ellen Louise (see Sulzberger, Ellen Louise)	*collateral*
Straus, R. Peter	collateral by marriage
Strutt, Algernon Henry	connection
Strutt, Eva Isabel Marion (see Bruce, Eva Isabel Marion)	*connection*
Strutt, Lavinia Mary [Fitzalan-Howard]	connection

Surname, Given Names [married to] (see maiden name)	Relationship
Sulzberger, Allison (see Stacey, Allison)	*collateral by marriage*
Sulzberger, Arthur Hays	collateral
Sulzberger, Arthur Ochs	collateral
Sulzberger, Arthur Ochs, Jr.	collateral
Sulzberger, Barbara W. (see Grant, Barbara W.)	*collateral by marriage*
Sulzberger, Carol Fox (see Fuhrman, Carol Fox)	*collateral by marriage*
Sulzberger, Cyrus L.	collateral by marriage
Sulzberger, David Hays	collateral
Sulzberger, Ellen Louise [Straus]	collateral
Sulzberger, Gail (see Gregg, Gail)	*collateral by marriage*
Sulzberger, Iphigene Bertha (see Ochs, Iphigene Bertha)	*collateral by marriage*
Sulzberger, Louise Mayer (see Blumenthal, Louise Mayer)	*collateral by marriage*
Sulzberger, Rachel Peixotto (see Hays, Rachel Peixotto)	*collateral*
Sundby, Nina [Loeb]	descendant spouse
Symington, Arabella (1885–1963) (see Hambleton, Arabella)	*collateral*
Symington, Arabella Leith [Griswold]	collateral
Symington, Helen Clay [Chase]	collateral
Symington, John Fife	collateral by marriage
Symington, John F. III	collateral
Symington, John F., Jr.	collateral
Symington, Martha Howard (see Frick, Martha Howard)	*collateral by marriage*
Tilghman, Sarah Williams	collateral by marriage
Touro, Abraham	collateral
Touro, Isaac	collateral by marriage
Touro, Judah	collateral
Touro, Rebecca Hays [Lopez]	collateral
Touro, Reyna (see Hays, Reyna)	*collateral*
Troubh, Jean A. (see Loeb, Jean A.)	*descendant*
Troubh, Raymond S.	descendant spouse
unknown, Elma E. [Moses]	collateral by marriage

Surname, Given Names [married to] (see maiden name)	Relationship
unknown, Judith [Myers]	connection
unknown, Michal [Levy]	connection
unknown, Miriam [Levy van Schwelm]	connection
unknown, Rachel (?–1744) [Franks]	connection
Unterberg, Mabel [Nathan]	collateral by marriage
Upshur, Gertrude [Hunt]	collateral by marriage
Valentine, Rebecca [Michaels de Paul]	connection
Valck van der Wilden, Rachel (see Levy, Rachel)	*connection*
Valck van der Wilden, Valentijn	connection
van der Wilden (see Valck van der Wilden)	
van Schwelm (see Levy van Schwelm)	
Varney, Dora [Mordecai]	collateral by marriage
Wardwell, Allen II	collateral
Wardwell, Edward Rogers	collateral by marriage
Wardwell, Lelia Pegram (see Morgan, Lelia Pegram)	*collateral*
Wardwell, Sarah Williams (see Tilghman, Sarah Williams)	*collateral by marriage*
Who, Catherine [Franks]	connection
Winter, Jeanette [Loeb]	descendant spouse
Wolff, Frances Louisa (see Nathan, Frances Louisa)	*collateral*
Wolff, Frances Nathan [Cullman]	collateral
Wolff, Julius Ruben	collateral by marriage
Worthington, Abigail (see Levy, Abigail)	*collateral*
Worthington, John	collateral by marriage

—ɰ—